D1460577

CHASING GHOSTS
not just
AN ADOPTION MEMOIR

Kamila Zahno

Rona Books

This book is a work of non-fiction based on the life, experiences and recollections of Kamila Zahno. In some cases names of people, places, dates or the detail of events have been changed to protect the privacy of others. The author states that, except in such minor respects not affecting the substantial accuracy of the work, the contents of this book are true.

Published by Rona Books, 2016
Copyright © Kamila Zahno 2016
The right of Kamila Zahno to be identified as the author of this work has been asserted by her in accordance with the Copyright Designs and Patent Act 1988

An extract of this work, an earlier version of chapter 3 was published by Tangled Roots (http://www.tangledroots.org.uk)

British Library Cataloguing-in-Publication Data
A catalogue record for this book is available on request from the British Library

ISBN 978-1-5272-0116-3

Cover illustration: Seema Manchanda
Edit, design and layout by Rahila Gupta
Printed by Russell Press, Nottingham NG6 0BT

Visit kamilazahno.com for more information about this book

To my family

Contents

ACKNOWLEDGEMENTS

I would like to thank:

All the characters in this book - you know who you are.

My cousins, aunt and uncle who listened as my story unfolded.

Rahila Gupta, my editor, who went beyond the call of duty; The Literary Consultancy for giving me feedback; Damian Barr my memoir writing tutor; Peter Forbes, creative non-fiction tutor at City University; Rukhsana Ahmad, Liz Morrison and Sibani Raychaudhuri of my memoir writing group; and members of my Book Group.

Naomi Paul who not only read drafts of chapters as they appeared but who also followed my cancer journey and kept me sane.

Dr Rebecca Kristeleit and her team at University College London Hospital who kept me alive; Dr Sue Gessler, my gentle counsellor who encouraged me to write this book; research nurses Nivea Douglas and Egla Atkins who took a special interest in my writing; the Macmillan Cancer Centre nurses who pricked and prodded my tiny, tiny veins, eventually to great success.

PREFACE

A few years ago I was enjoying mint tea and a semolina cake at a busy Turkish café with my friend Ulrich. The syrup from the cake was dripping all over my fingers and as I licked them Ulrich said, 'What happened about that book you were going to write about your life and times – the one where you'd describe your family's mixed heritage and your adoption?'

'I'd forgotten all about that. It could be a retirement project.'

I vowed that I would write the book as soon as I retired. But life had other plans for me.

In July 2013, just as I retired from my work as a management consultant, I was diagnosed with stage 4 ovarian cancer, a relapse of the cancer I thought I'd got rid of thirteen years previously. To say it was a huge shock is an understatement. Two operations and five months of chemotherapy held the cancer at bay for a while but it was always going to return. During treatment I couldn't concentrate on anything. I was offered counselling and I started talking about my family to my therapist. I mentioned my book project.

'This book must be written,' she said. 'Tell me, when you're interviewed on the Today programme what will you say to John Humphries?'

I laughed. But she was right. It's an important subject and I've got a lot to say. At the beginning of 2015, I got ill again and seriously started thinking of my end-of-life plan.

Writing this book was part of that plan. But while writing I didn't know how much time I had left and whether it was possible to finish the book. I was searching for my birth parents at the same time as writing. The quest was exciting and the words flowed. In true consultant's style I set myself a deadline. I would finish by the end of the year 2015. I joked with my oncologist that she had to keep me alive until I finished the book. She agreed to do what she could.

We all feel the need to know where we have come from, how we belong and where we are located in this world – the explosion of interest in tracing family histories in recent years is proof of that. For someone who is adopted, the curiosity is intense but also sharpened by the dread of what we might find.

To find your place in the world just before you lose it might seem like a pointless exercise but, paradoxically, locating yourself before you die brings a closure that makes death more bearable.

PROLOGUE

Feet first and clad only in my knickers underneath the faded hospital gown, I slide smoothly into the white doughnut-shaped tunnel.

'Breathe in. Hold your breath,' the disembodied computerised female voice orders me. Inside the CT scanner it's as quiet as a mountainside in the dark. I slide out again.

'Breathe normally,' the imperious woman instructs.

Charlie comes into the CT room to fit a tube into the cannula on my right arm and then exits hurriedly to avoid being zapped by rays from the scanner. The tube is fixed to a computer connected by a cable to the next room enabling Charlie to give me my injection of contrast dye remotely. I lie still with my arms raised above my head. I gaze at the figures on a small monitor which is fixed on top of the machine: 114, 445, 0. Who knows what these mean?

Charlie's voice comes over the intercom. 'OK, I'm going to give you your injection now.'

First I taste metal and, as the warm liquid courses through my body, I feel like I'm peeing, but I know I'm not – I'm used to these scans now. I enter the tunnel once more, this time full of dye which is lighting up my body tissues.

'Breathe in,' says the automaton. The computer silently takes images of slices of my pelvic area. 'Breathe normally,' she says. I start breathing again and slide out of the doughnut.

Charlie re-enters the CT room. 'That's it,' he says. 'Well done.'

I sit up and he leans over to take the cannula out. His hands are gentle and I notice that his nails are clean and short, with evenly pressed cuticles and absolutely no hangnails.

'Hold this,' he says, indicating the cotton wool ball he's using to stop my blood dripping, while he places surgical tape over it. 'Now keep this on for at least an hour.'

'I'm used to this, Charlie. I've been prodded and pricked every week for the past eighteen months.'

Charlie raises his head and looks at me properly now. He smiles and says, 'Of course, we've met before. Well, you wouldn't believe what some people get up to. Ripping the tape off before they leave the hospital, or dropping it on the pavement outside, or even on the Tube.'

How does he know? Does Transport for London ring up the hospital to complain of little balls of blood-stained cotton wool being left on the trains?

I walk slowly upstairs from the basement to the foyer of the Macmillan Cancer Centre, raising my eyes to the giant chandelier suspended in the atrium: lime-green flip-flops, a disposable lighter, a yellow plastic bottle, a broken plastic grill, a four-fingered rubber glove, half of a red spade, a manky toothbrush of indeterminate colour, the blue and white striped head of a broom, a pink plastic drinking straw in the shape of a penis, a comb missing half its teeth – assorted detritus collected by the artist Stuart Haygarth on a 500-mile coastal walk from Gravesend in Kent to Land's End in Cornwall. I see from the label description on a panel on the wall of the foyer that, according to the artist, *Strand* represents 'the mental and physical journey into the unknown taken by people diagnosed with cancer'. A rubbish journey. Suitably edified, I exit the Cancer Centre through the swing doors and I'm back on Huntley Street, just round the corner from Tottenham Court Road.

Crowds! All these people going about their business unaware that round the corner other people are being sliced into body parts by X-rays and scanners. It's a week-day lunchtime just before Christmas 2014 and people are dodging each other on the pavement, jamming themselves into coffee shops, queuing at fast food outlets, popping into the express supermarket for a sandwich. I decide that it's business as usual and join them.

1. THE FUNERAL

'Y ou'll want to see her now,' he said abruptly. 'Laura laid her out beautifully in the clothes she liked.' She's a nurse and would know how to do these things. I'd never seen a dead body, never mind touched one.

He took me to the bedroom. When he opened the door, I could feel a rush of cold air. I wondered whether it was her soul leaving her body but it was only because the window was ajar. If I believed in such things her soul would have already left through the open window. Mum lay there, uncovered, on one of the single beds in the room. Dad's idea of her favourite clothes was some old-fashioned M&S slacks and a plain white blouse. No sari for my mum. That was my first thought. My second thought was that she looked tranquil and there was no trace of furrows on her brow. My first glimpse of death wasn't terrifying but it was only then I realised it would create a void in my own life, despite her not being much in it of late. Still, I didn't shed a tear.

How are you supposed to feel when your mum dies? When Dad called to tell me earlier that day, I didn't feel a thing. Only practical thoughts came into my head.

Dad had waited for two hours to call my cousin Laura, three hours to call me and God knows if he'd even rung my sister, Ellen, who lives just round the corner from him.

'I woke up at six and it was silent. No snoring. I knew she must be dead.' There was a short silence before Dad started sobbing. I didn't know what to say. All I could think of was that Mum, whose snore had always been prodigious, would snore no more. I waited in an awkward silence for a few moments and he continued, 'I called Laura at eight. She came round immediately and called the doctor.'

'This is awful. I'll come up. Now. I'll let you know what train I'm on.'

I flung off my duvet, leaped into the shower and dressed hurriedly. I rang the station to book an open return to Edinburgh and asked the next-door neighbour to look after Appin, my cat. Ever since I moved to London in 1982, eight years ago, I very rarely visited my parents, I thought with a pang of guilt. In a daze I shoved some clothes into a small suitcase. After an interminable Sunday journey on my local train and the Tube, I managed to catch the noon train from King's Cross.

I arrived at the ground floor flat in Marchmont at around 6 pm. Ellen opened the door. She gave me a wry look as if to say 'Family, eh' and stood aside to let me in. So Dad *had* called Ellen after all. I dumped my bag, hung up my coat in the hall and went into the living room. Dad was sitting there with Laura.

In the mid-80s Mum had what Dad described as 'a fall', had been ill ever since and unable to walk much. I never really knew what her illness was but I think she'd had a stroke. The last time I visited, Mum was sitting in her green leather chair, dressed in old corduroy trousers and a cardigan. Her fine black hair was chopped short in a pudding bowl cut, most often seen on people in residential homes where it looks as if a bowl has been upended on their heads to make it easier for the scissors to snip round it. I suspected my dad cut it for her. Dad made me a cup of tea and chatted about day-to-day matters while Mum remained silent. I asked Mum how she was and what she'd been doing that week but all my questions were answered by my dad. Of course she could speak but seemed totally in awe of my dad, even after forty-five years of marriage. When he was in the kitchen I asked her directly how she was but all she said was, 'Frank's very good.' That was typical of my infrequent visits since 'the fall'. I loved Mum during my early childhood but it was hard to love the shadow she became during my teenage years. She wasn't a cold or unemotional woman but perhaps it was easier to be a shadow than to assert her personality over my dad.

If she couldn't do it in life, she certainly couldn't assert her personality in death. I think she would have preferred to wear a sari. Purple and green were the colours of my mother's favourite sari. Decluttering my flat when I retired in 2013, I discovered a torn piece of silk at the bottom of a green storage box – a deep purple fragment edged in green and gold. Memories of my mother's clothes came flooding back. When I was growing up in the '50s she often wore saris to go out in the evening and sometimes at home, but not usually for work. She wore this one for comfort around the house. My mother would pleat the skirt to perfection but when she forgot to pin the *pallu* to her bodice it would fall off so she would sweep it up and fling it over her shoulder with a majestic swoosh.

Purple and green are suffragette colours. My mother was too young to be a suffragette but she was a feminist in her own quiet way. In her early days as a doctor in the 1930s she worked in villages in rural Bengal, delivering babies and checking on the health of the mothers. She never told us much about those days but she did say she loved that period in her life. The new mothers would offer her roti and dal with buttermilk to drink on the side. Not to have eaten would have caused offence but she told us she was never sick from that simple home-cooked food.

Working as a doctor in 1960s Birmingham she wore dresses. I remember two in particular – a striped cotton dress with a belt and a shift dress patterned with psychedelic yellow and lime green flowers. At home she shoved on casual shirts and stretchy nylon stirruped slacks. When I left home in 1970 Mum retired and her clothes seemed to get drabber and drabber. I don't recollect her wearing saris again.

The days after arriving in Edinburgh for Mum's funeral passed by in a vacuum. The undertaker was contacted, funeral arrangements were made, my brothers arrived: Patrick from Nottingham and Tim from Stuttgart. Mum's body was taken away to the funeral parlour.

Laura's husband, Mike, a rector in the Scottish Episcopal Church, agreed to take the service.

On the day of the funeral the hearse arrived at ten, together with a large black car. Dad, my siblings and I got into that black car which drove immediately behind the hearse. Laura, Mike and Ellen's best school-friend followed in Mike's car. We drove at a snail's pace through the Grange with its substantial grey stone villas and onto the main Liberton Road, still creeping along with all other cars overtaking us. It seemed strange to be following a hearse down a main road. We reached Mortonhall Crematorium, set in a pretty woodland. The sun shone through the golden leaves of the oak trees and a breeze shook the branches, loosening the leaves which gently drifted down to join the others in a light rustle. That was the only part of the day Mum would have liked.

Mum's funeral was in the smaller of the two chapels, the Pentland chapel: an austere fortress built of white concrete bricks with a black portcullis of an entrance. A roof light above the coffin stand flooded the chapel in harshness. It's supposed to be non-denominational but to my mind the rows of pine pews and the gold cross in front of the curtains made the interior look like a conventional Christian church. We were rattling around the space that could have held fifty mourners. There were seven of us, not including Mike. My siblings were all present although they didn't feel present. Instead the chapel felt like a hollow space waiting to be filled with their emotions. Suddenly I felt cold.

I have no idea what the rest of my family wore, but I know Dad would have dressed in his grey three-piece suit with the waistcoat that he couldn't fasten. Would I have remembered to pack a black skirt or dress when I just shoved some clothes in my suitcase? Probably not. But I'm sure we all wore sober colours, certainly not green or purple.

We sat through the conventional Christian service, the one which begins with Jesus saying he is the resurrection and the life and everyone who believes in him will never die. But Mum didn't believe in Jesus. I think she would have liked the bit about *we are dust and to dust shall return*. It would have appealed to her scientific mind. Surprisingly, I'd agreed to read the epistle from the Corinthians about faith, hope and charity, removing mountains (as if I would want to) and seeing through a glass darkly. And, even more surprisingly, considering I'd spent the week in a state of nothingness, I started to choke with emotion when I came to the bit about charity not being puffed up. Perhaps it was my background working with the charity sector that set me off. Regaining my composure I managed to finish the piece. There were prayers, psalms and a sermon of sorts. I think this might have taken the form of a eulogy to Mum as I don't remember anyone from the family reading one. There must have been music but the only sound I could remember was Dad sobbing.

At the end of the service, blue velvet curtains opened at the front of the chapel. There was a slight whirr as the coffin slid on its electronic rails through the curtains into the dark tunnel beyond.

There was nothing about my mother's Indian self inside that coffin, dressed as she was in her pale slacks and blouse, being sent off to the accompaniment of a Christian ceremony.

2. INDIA

There's nothing of you that's Indian,' Mum said. Which I thought odd because I am partly Indian. 'Why do you want to go to India? I'm not going to give you any addresses for my relatives.' So they were her relatives, not mine.

I'd just come back from Canada, aged twenty-five. I'd thought of travelling in India with my friend Alison and asked Mum if I could visit her sister, Aunty Alice, and Uncle Sameer in Kasauli and also visit her distant relatives,Sanjay and Nandita in Calcutta. I didn't know what to do if she wasn't going to give me any contacts. There was no *Lonely Planet* guide to India then and I didn't really know how to sit down and plan an independent trip. I was utterly dismayed by Mum's attitude but there was not a lot I could do about it.

'When you're older, we can help you find a good tour of India,' said Dad.

How much older? Would I be going to India for the first time with a crowd of old fogies? Would *I* be an old fogy?

I wrote to Alison, who was travelling in the Highlands, telling her the bad news.

'Oh no,' she wrote back, 'I've just had all my injections, stopping off at doctors' surgeries as I've been travelling.' She suggested Crete instead. So that summer we went off to Crete, renting places to sleep on roofs and surviving on a diet of Greek salad, yogurt and honey.

I now realise that Mum's relationship with India was complex. She herself was mixed race. The story of how her mum and dad met was romantic. Mum's father, Gopal Roy, was a young solicitor working in Calcutta at the turn of the 20th century. He'd gone to sort out the affairs of a British indigo plantation owner from Wiltshire, who had been living in Mymensing, a town east of Calcutta. Gopal fell in love with his daughter April, and they married not long afterwards. The Roys were from the Calcutta upper classes: Gopal was educated at New College, Oxford. I knew, even with his background, it was unusual for a Bengali man to marry a white woman.

April became pregnant in spring 1910. To avoid the stifling heat of Calcutta she retreated to Darjeeling that summer, giving birth to Sita, my mum, in November. I don't know much about Mum's childhood as she rarely spoke of it. It appeared that she spent much of it in England and, although she told me she adored her father, he was hardly ever there for her. She was educated in English boarding schools and I remember her saying she went to no fewer than seventeen of them – who knew there were so many! Why exactly she was shifted around, I don't know, but I do know why she was asked to leave one of her schools. She told me about the time when, as a teenager, she'd stripped off her clothes to wash herself at the hand basin rather than taking a bath – the closest she could get to the shower she would have preferred. Showing your breasts was simply not done at an English girls' boarding school so she was asked to leave.

I got the impression that the period in her life she loved best was when, after graduating from Edinburgh's medical school, she worked in Calcutta and in rural Bengal as a paediatrician. Here, she felt Indian. But when she met and married my dad during the Second World War she returned to England forever. I think this is when she decided it would be easier to be English, and easier for her four mixed race children to be English too. The part of her that was Indian was hidden to all of us, except for the odd sari and infrequent visits from Indian relatives. We were an English family.

But I never bought into that Englishness. I, out of all my siblings, was desperate to reclaim my Indian heritage which I felt had been denied to me. Travelling to India would help me to understand

Mum a little better, but most of all it would help me understand myself.

In 1991, the year after Mum died, Dad scattered her ashes in Edinburgh's Botanic Gardens. He didn't ask me or my siblings to help him. He might have known I would have kicked up a fuss at changing the soil ecology so instead he asked a member of Cruse, the bereavement organisation, to accompany him. He told us that he had gone to one of the rhododendron shrubberies and asked the woman from Cruse to keep a look out while he surreptitiously scattered Mum's ashes in a pile at their roots.

Mum's death sharpened my need to discover more about her family, and perhaps myself. Now she couldn't stop me! Since Mum had died Dad understood that I wanted to visit India to find a part of myself so he was willing to give me Raadhika's address in Calcutta. Raadhika was a distant relative of Mum's and was very friendly with her when Mum worked in Calcutta in the '30s. And then of course I wanted to visit Darjeeling, where Mum was born.

This time I'd really prepared. Not only had I gone on an evening class at City University on 'Preparing a trip to India' (about which I now remember nothing), I'd spent the previous year doing a weekly evening course in Hindi and was proud of the fact that I could say basic touristy things. I knew I was going to Calcutta but surely people there would speak Hindi, the national language. Little did I realise that although Bengalis are taught Hindi at school, it's very much a second language – or actually a third language among the middle classes who were usually educated in English. After all, Bengali is the language of intellectuals, writers and poets from Calcutta and being made to speak Hindi is anathema. I wrote to Raadhika and found out that she lived with her daughter, son-in-law and grandson.

In late October 1991, one year after Mum's death, I set off alone on my Indian *yatra*. This would be a life-changing journey for me and I didn't want to share the experience with anyone else. The plane was full of Bengali families dressed in *salwar kameez* or saris. The one thing I hadn't thought of was buying a *salwar kameez* in

England. Would this have made me fit in better? I was sitting beside some of the few white tourists – some Italians off to trek in Sikkim. They were talking amongst themselves and the journey passed quietly. I had a mixture of feelings – excitement on the one hand and trepidation on the other – which were quite overwhelming so I didn't sleep much at all.

In a dishevelled state I arrived in the late afternoon at Calcutta's Dum Dum Airport, after breaking my journey for a short while in Dhaka. It was the first time I'd ever been met by someone holding up a card with my name on it. It was Arjun, Raadhika's son-in-law, who gave me a quick hug and took me to his car. He was driving his own car, unusual in Calcutta at that time as the middle classes generally hired drivers. We were soon passing Salt Lake City, built as a satellite town in the late 1950s. After about an hour's drive in slow-moving traffic we reached Broad Street, which was, in fact, a narrow street in the Ballygunge district. Negotiating the car through crowds of people and hand-pulled rickshaws we came to a high white wall with an iron gate manned by a security guard. The gate opened and we drove into an oasis of calm. The house in Broad Street was a rambling stone building set in a large lawned garden full of mature trees which cast mysterious shadows in the twilight. We were greeted by a contingent of servants who were very excited to meet me.

'*Namaste*,' I said, '*Mera naam* Kamila *hai*.' But my Hindi, such as it was, wasn't going to be useful here as everyone was speaking Bengali.

I was taken immediately to my room on the second floor which had the advantage of its own simple bathroom and toilet. But I was too excited to shower as I wanted to meet everyone so I dumped my rucksack and made my way to the large living room, lit by open windows running along its whole length. Raadhika, Mum's distant cousin and the matriarch of the house, was sitting on the sofa. Fifteen years my mother's junior she must have been in her mid-sixties at that time. She had long greying hair, worn in a bun, and was wearing a cream-coloured sari decorated with a pink and grey striped border.

'Sita's child,' she exclaimed, getting up to greet me. 'You're here at last. And where is Frank? Why didn't he come with you?' Raadhika chuckled as she said this, her brown glasses bobbing on her nose. She pushed them back with her index finger.

'He's still grieving about Mum and in any case I'm not sure he will ever come to India again.' And I added, 'In fact, he's never been to Calcutta.'

'That's right,' replied Raadhika. 'Your parents never visited India once they left after the War. I came once or twice to London and visited them but it was before you were born. Sit down beside me and tell me about yourself.'

'*Chai*!' she yelled at a young woman who was lurking in the corner.

I sat down on the sofa and the woman, whose name I discovered was Padma, brought us tea. I wasn't used to this servant stuff and found it quite uncomfortable.

'I really loved Frank,' Raadhika said. 'He was just right for Sita who was quite Europeanised. They were so in love and wrapped up in themselves. You'll find us quite different. A large family with people coming and going. Especially now it's the puja season.'

'Yes I'm hoping to see all the festivities while I'm here.' I had arrived in Calcutta in the middle of the four-day Durga Puja festival, a celebration of the Goddess Durga, and one which kicks off the month-long puja season culminating in Kali Puja in early November.

A large big-busted woman in a striking pink sari printed with crimson flowers entered the room, along with a boy who looked to be about seven.

'This is Soma, my daughter, and her son Anwit just home from school.'

I got up. Soma and I hugged each other. 'Wait a minute,' I said. 'I've got something for you, Anwit.' I went back into my room, hurriedly opened my rucksack and delved inside until I found a tee

shirt wrapped in a plastic bag. Returning to the living room, I gave
it to Anwit. It wasn't very original, just a tee shirt with *I love London*
on it. I wasn't sure whether it was exciting enough for a little boy,
but he seemed pleased and immediately rushed away to put it on.
Presents for the rest of the family could wait.

That evening passed by in a whirl. I showered and put on my all-
purpose uncrushable long black skirt and a green printed top and
returned to the living room. By this time two friends of Soma and
Arjun's had arrived to meet me.

'I hope you're not too jet-lagged,' Arjun said. 'Because we'd like
to take you out to the Bengal Club for dinner.'

I was feeling very keyed up and excited. 'I'm game for anything.'

Off we went, the five of us, packed into Arjun's Honda, to the
Bengal Club in the heart of Calcutta. Outside it seemed to still be
rush hour. Although it was 8 pm, we had to weave through the white
Ambassador cars, yellow taxis, bicycles and rickshaws, honking all
the way. The Bengal Club was a haven of peace, a magnificent old
colonial building dating from the days of the Raj. But it somehow
seemed odd to be using that Club where Indians were once
barred. The white stone shone in the evening darkness and I could
distinguish the arched windows and balconies of its façade. Inside
was luxurious and it seemed very formal. I was glad I was wearing
my skirt. However, we just sat on the terrace which was less formal
than some of the other dining areas, and ordered snacks.

Everyone was chattering at once and after a while another friend
came and joined our party. I was introduced and Moliya claimed to
be a cousin of mine on the Roy side. I was going to have to sort out
our family tree soon.

After a couple of hours Arjun said, 'Let's take you on a drive
to see Calcutta's sights at night.' It was quite a drive: the Maidan
which is the central park of Calcutta; the Indian Museum, another
imposing colonial building; Chowringhee Road, the main street;
the about-to-be completed Hooghly Bridge with its delicate steel
cables fanning out across the river. We ended up at the Taj Bengal
hotel, seated inside the atrium which rose for five storeys to the top

of the building. It was another of these oases in the midst of bustling Calcutta that was designed for tourists and the burgeoning Indian middle classes. We ordered coffee, sitting amongst palm trees, with ferns and ivy cascading from the balconies. Would I sleep drinking coffee so late at night?

In the event, I was so tired when we finally returned home that I fell asleep instantly and slept through the night. I woke early and went out into the living room where Padma, one of the servants, was carefully polishing the red oxide stone floor with a wet rag. The metal fan was whirring overhead, drying the wet floor.

'Hello,' she said. '*Chai*?'

'*Hanh*,' I replied, hoping that meant yes in Bengali.

A few minutes later, Raadhika emerged from her bedroom and we had breakfast together of eggs and toast. The house was quiet so Raadhika and I sat on the sofa together. I sat close to her, closer than I would have with Mum. I asked her to fill me in on my mother's family tree. I couldn't figure out how Raadhika fitted in.

I knew nothing much about Mum beyond her immediate nuclear family. Her mum and dad had died a long time before I was born, but we did know my aunts, Mum's sisters. A few other relatives came to visit too but I didn't understand how they were all related. Mum was always reluctant to talk about the family tree.

'I know about my second cousin, Sangam,' I said. 'He died from cancer about ten years ago. I did meet Sangam occasionally in London, but that was in the early '80s before I moved there, so we didn't see each other often. How is Sangam related to me?'

'Oh, Sangam,' Raadhika said. 'So sad. He died of lung cancer. But his brother Jagdeep lives right here in Calcutta. He's lovely and you must meet him. They're both your second cousins. Their father was your mum's cousin. You do know, don't you, that to us Indians cousins and second cousins are as close as brothers and sisters – that's why we sometimes refer to them as cousin-brothers and sisters. Such a shame your mum never brought you to India.'

'I know,' I said, resentment building up. 'I would love to have visited you all but I felt I didn't really know you.'

'Here why don't you get a piece of paper and write down all your relatives?' Raadhika seemed genuinely interested in imparting her knowledge of the family and not at all surprised at why I wanted to know.

I got out my red hard-backed notebook, bought specially to record this journey, and prepared to draw out my family tree.

'The trunk of the tree starts with your great grandfather, Bhaskar Roy. He had four children: your grandfather, Gopal, your great-aunt and two great-uncles.' As she named them I drew them in.

'Going down a branch you've got your mum and her sisters, Eva and Alice. Then you have your mother's cousins. And I think you know one of them, Tuk-Tuk.' Raadhika laughed and said, 'You know that's the name for an auto rickshaw, don't you? It makes the sound tuk-tuk as it putters along. We Bengalis are always giving nicknames to our children. She must have made that noise as a small child.'

'Those Bengali pet names. How embarrassing,' I said. 'You know Polly isn't my real name – it's Camilla. Mum said they called me Polly because I didn't talk till I was two and then I wouldn't shut up. Polly, the parrot. I hate it.'

'Polly's lovely. So homely and comfortable. Camilla's a bit exotic for you,' said Raadhika. A backhanded compliment.

'I've never met Tuk-Tuk or her daughter, Sanchita, who must be another second cousin,' I said. 'But I know Dad always writes to them at Christmas.'

'Frank's Christmas letters. I look forward to them every year. They tell me everything about you so I think I know all you children really well.' I groaned inwardly. I could imagine what those letters were like. Dad writes about a hundred gushing letters every Christmas to all and sundry. And he goes on and on about how marvellous we all are, sounding totally boastful. But it sounded like Raadhika loved them.

I scribbled down Mum's, my aunts' and Tuk-Tuk's names underneath my grandfather and his three siblings.

This was beginning to look like the book of Genesis: B N Roy begat Soumya who begat Tuk-Tuk who begat Sanchita. I scrawled down all the names but ran out of room as I got further to the right edge of the paper. I drew arrows further down the page but that confused the different levels. I would have to re-draw this tree so that the generations made sense. I was getting excited.

'When Mum's relatives came to visit us in Birmingham it was a real high point, but we were never encouraged to write to them and certainly it seemed out of the question that we should visit India.'

'I know. I think it's because your mum only actually lived in India continuously as an adult for ten years. April, her own mother, who was English passed that feeling of Englishness on to her perhaps. And then she passed that onto you. Such a shame. We would have loved to have had you for holidays when you were younger.' Raadhika chuckled affectionately. 'You could have learned Bengali and read Tagore. What an education for you that would have been.'

'Oh, I so wish that had happened. I think you're right about Mum. But I also think it was partly Dad. He thought our own nuclear family of Mum, Dad and four children was enough to be going on with. He might have kept up with people with his Christmas letters, but they were still outside our lives.'

'But his letters are so sweet. I'm sure that's not true,' she said. I suddenly realised that I might have hurt Raadhika with that comment.

'I don't mean he didn't want to write but I felt that we were very isolated as a family. Did you know there were only seven people at Mum's funeral?' I said, tears starting to well up. 'Not even Aunt Eva or my cousins on that side came to her funeral.'

'You poor thing. That would never happen here,' Raadhika said, putting her arm round me. I started to sniffle so she drew me even closer. Her talcum powder smelled of lily of the valley which really set me off, remembering that it was a favourite scent of Mum's. I burst into gulping sobs so loud they drowned out the fan. Raadhika just held me, not saying a word. After what seemed like an age I stopped sobbing. I was calm enough to go on with the family saga. In fact, now more than ever I wanted to know how this warm and loving woman fitted in with my family.

'Thanks so much. I'm OK now. It was just the thought of that awful funeral. I still want to know how you're related to me.'

'Oh Polly, my heart goes out to you. I'm so glad you're here. We must make up for lost time. Well, how are we related? We're not really, but we do count as family. Your great-grandfather Bhaskar Roy's first wife died and he married Kamini Roy. Kamini was a famous Bengali poet so you may have heard of her.'

To my shame I knew nothing about Bengali literature beyond a few novels by Tagore so had never heard of Kamini Roy in her own right. She would have been Mum's step-grandmother. Is there such a relative category? I guessed that was a step too far for my mum.

'My father was Kamini's brother so that's how we're related. She was my aunt. And you know my brothers, Amit and Sanjay as they go to the UK quite often.'

'Ah, so that's how you all fit in. I had no idea. I only knew Mum was really fond of you all.'

'Of course. She loved our family and was always visiting. It must seem quite a loose connection to you with your concentration on the immediate family, but for us Indians, it's normal.'

I was finding the whole tree thing really complicated but I was excited that it was coming together. Still, I was feeling quite resentful that my illustrious relatives had been denied me for so long. Raadhika in particular made me feel included and accepted as – if not exactly an Indian woman – definitely part of the family. I had done the right thing in making this *yatra*.

Raadhika continued. 'You'll meet everyone as it's the holidays. We love visiting and get very fat with all the sweets everyone brings.'

'I'm looking forward to trying fresh *rasgullas*,' I said, secretly dreading this experience. 'When we were young I remember Sanjay sending us Christmas parcels and tasting tinned *rasgullas*. They weren't very nice.' I remembered the texture most of all – spongy and rubbery, like eating sweet rubber foam.

'Oh my goodness. Who ever heard of such a thing?'

The house began to wake up. Arjun and Anwit went off to work and school. Soma, Raadhika's daughter, arose just before noon, coming into the room still dressed in her long kaftan which she obviously wore for sleeping, and looking dishevelled with her hair trailing down her back.

'Let's have another cup of tea,' she said. 'Then I'll get dressed, we'll have some lunch and I'll take you on a little sightseeing tour.'

Emerging into Broad Street after lunch we picked our way through the rubbish and puddles on our way to a taxi stand.

'You must see some of the *pandals* dedicated to Durga,' Soma said, gathering the bottom of her sari in her left hand. 'The closest one is round the corner.'

She led the way to a bamboo structure where a crowd of people had gathered. It was simply constructed with canes lying horizontally to form a gateway beyond which stood the *pandal* itself. Peering in, we saw the image of the Goddess Durga with eight of her ten hands holding different weapons: trident, conch shell, bow, arrow, thunderbolt, sword, lotus blossom. She spun a gold disc around one of her index fingers. Ma Durga, the all-powerful, was sitting on a golden lion with black stripes looking much more like a Bengal tiger. Her face looked human – red lips, kohl-lined eyes and eyebrows shaped like a comma. Chunky earrings adorned her ears and on her head she wore an elaborate gold crown. Beside her were her two daughters, Lakshmi and Saraswati. I wasn't sure which was which but one was holding lotus flowers while the other was playing what looked to be a lute to my western eyes.

Soma didn't seem very interested in explaining the symbolism and was almost dismissive.

'You know we're not Hindus. We're Brahmos like Tagore so really these *pandals* are just pretty structures for us. I'm almost as much a tourist as you are.'

Now, that I did know. I knew Mum was a Brahmo, or at least her father was. She was always a bit vague as to what the Brahmos were but I gathered they had re-invented Hinduism in the 19th century as a monotheistic religion blending elements of spiritual Hinduism with Christianity. Debendranath Tagore, the father of the poet Rabindranath, was one of its founders.

We walked down to a junction of several major streets, clambered into a yellow Ambassador taxi and took off on our tour.

'Victoria Memorial,' instructed Soma.

I wasn't very keen on museums, especially ones that specialise in history. I felt I should be interested in Indian history, but not having any background, events can be difficult to grasp. I was much more interested in modern Calcutta. It's true though that the Victoria Memorial is of architectural interest. It's an imposing early 20th century building, constructed entirely of marble in a European neo-classical style with a central dome looking like St Paul's Cathedral. In the corners are four domes, a passing reference to Moghul architecture. I found the displays inside boring, a throwback to being dragged round too many museums when I was a kid, but Soma took me to see a portrait of Kamini Roy. The black and white portrait showed Kamini in her later years, wearing small round glasses, with her sari covering her hair. I learned that my great-grandfather's wife was the first woman in India to get a degree and in 1921 fought for women's suffrage. I was glad that a woman like Kamini was sort of related to me: even such a remote connection made me feel proud. But Mum was very modest and not given to name-dropping, and her philosophy was that you made yourself who you were rather than hanging on anyone else's coat-tails. I think that's why I had never heard about the Kamini Roy connection. Years later, when my aunt Eva died and I was looking through her photo albums, I came across a picture of Kamini in her graduation gown worn over her sari, her mortar board and its tassel complementing her small neat face.

That was the first and last time Soma showed me round Calcutta since she was busy managing her block printing business, making patterns for fabric for saris and *salwar kameez*. The ground floor and outhouses were taken up with the block making, dying and printing, and the roof for drying the fabric. But she did take Raadhika and me visiting and we had lots of people coming to the house so that I got to meet some of my distant relatives. And at last I got to taste fresh *rasgullas* which turned out not to be rubbery at all. My favourite sweet, though, was *mishti doi*, a fermented sweet yogurt which came in an earthenware pot. Every visitor had a preferred sweet maker and the *doi* always tasted different. My favourite taste was one where the *doi* had a hint of lemons and tartness could be detected underneath its sweetness. When I got tired of the crowds of people visiting I used to escape to the flat roof and sit amongst the saris, freshly printed and waiting to dry. From the roof I could see palm trees in other gardens but blocks of gleaming white flats, six stories high, which were rapidly replacing these old Calcutta stone houses, mostly obscured the views.

I stayed in Calcutta for ten days before setting off on my pilgrimage to Darjeeling. What would I feel there? Would I feel my mum's spirit? Or would I just feel the nothingness I felt at her funeral? I was about to find out.

On the evening I left, Ahmed, who worked for Soma's print business, took me to Howrah Station to make sure I caught the right train. I'd booked a sleeping compartment in an overnight train and, if you knew the system, it was easy to find your place. Here in Calcutta you couldn't do anything alone and I was always taken around which was helpful but didn't teach me how things worked. Even at 10 pm Howrah Station was bustling. By then, I'd got used to busy Calcutta and, to be honest, apart from whole families sitting on the floor eating from their tiffin carriers, it wasn't so very different from Victoria Station in the rush hour. Ahmed found my name on the passenger list pasted up on the compartment and saw me onto the train.

'Have a great time, and you be careful, travelling alone,' he said.

I was in a women's compartment with five other women and a six-year-old girl. My companions were intrigued by me travelling alone, but accepted this was what English female tourists did. The seats converted into benches for sleeping and we were given a blanket to cover us. We all slept well and arrived at Siliguri at nine the following morning. The seven of us, now friends, piled into a taxi to take us to Kurseong, a Himalayan hill station about thirty-five kilometres from Darjeeling. Siliguri was even more bustling that Calcutta if that was possible – cycle rickshaws, goods carriers and taxis all vying for a spot on the narrow bridge. I'd wanted to take the toy train from Siliguri to Darjeeling but had been told in Calcutta that it wasn't running. So I was annoyed to see the train winding its way up the hill beside us. The journey was novel for me as it was the first time I'd seen Indian trucks decked out in all their glory. Each driver seemed to customise the body of the truck with multi-coloured decorations: slogans, symbols, tassels and pictures of deities, birds and animals. Garlands, photos and more tassels hung inside the cabin. On the back of each truck the instruction to *Sound Horn* was taken literally by other drivers. Arriving in Kurseong at around midday we had a bite to eat before making the last leg of our journey to Darjeeling. The truck-watching novelty rapidly wore off as the road to Darjeeling was much narrower and the sheer drops into the valley below took my breath away. We kept stopping to allow oncoming lorries to pass. After a tiring couple of hours we reached Darjeeling.

My first impression of Darjeeling was disappointing. Firstly it was misty and secondly the taxi dumped us unceremoniously at the bottom of a steep hill. My companions went their separate ways, leaving me to negotiate with another taxi to get up the hill. I was unsure how to negotiate a decent rate without them so I decided to climb to the top of the town, my rucksack on my back. Walking up a winding lane surrounded by ramshackle corrugated iron houses with roofs coloured in blue, yellow or green I arrived at the Moray Hotel in the twilight. Despite it being one of the top Darjeeling hotels, it appeared rundown. I was placed in an annex in the grounds. The room was large with a balcony. It was cold. I had arrived during a power cut and there was no heating or hot water in the shower. The staff mustered up a bucket of hot water, heated on their gas or coal stove, so I was able to warm up by having a bucket bath. Refreshed, I took a stroll around the mall. The mist shrouded most of the valley so there were no views.

I spent a depressing few days in Darjeeling. Despite Mum's ambivalence towards India I had thought that somehow I would feel her presence here in her birthplace. I'd hoped to come to some understanding about her origins. The trouble was, I didn't have a point of contact for Mum. I had no idea where in Darjeeling she was born and somehow this rundown town was far from the peaceful hill station I had imagined. How could I really find the spirit of a 1910 baby in this town? And what would it really mean for me – finding the spirit of a mother who'd been a shadow for much of my life?

So I settled instead on being the tourist. One of the things I wanted to do before I died was to see Kanchenjunga at dawn. You can get up before sunrise and go out to Tiger Point, a viewpoint looking across the valley to the third highest mountain in the world. But the mist swirled around the valley for the whole time I was in Darjeeling and I never caught a glimpse of the sun, never mind Kanchenjunga. I mooched around town visiting all the tourist spots but everything seemed desolate. I tried to visit a Snow Leopard's breeding centre but only found four men playing cards at the entrance.

'Sorry, Madam, Centre closed due to rain. What is your good name, please?'

'Camilla,' I said.

'And your native place, please?'

'My mother was born here, but I was born in London.'

They ignored the bit about my mum, only choosing to latch on to the London bit.

'Proper London?'

'Yes, proper London.' Although I did wonder whether Brockley, which is south of the Thames, would count as Proper London.

Our conversation exhausted, I set off for the Botanical Gardens. Mum would have liked them, so would I get a feel for her spirit there? It continued to rain; the gardens were overgrown and the mist was so thick I couldn't find the hothouses. Not a bit of Mum's spirit in these gardens. I began to abandon thoughts of laying Mum to rest here. After all, Dad had already scattered her ashes so perhaps there was no need for me to do anything. I'd brought a photo of her as a young woman meaning to burn it and scatter the ashes here with me but I'd left it in Calcutta. On reflection I wasn't sure I wanted to burn that lovely photo of Mum, dressed in a sari and looking really glamorous. What could I do instead?

The next day I made a connection of sorts when visiting the Tibetan Refugee Centre which provided work for Nepali migrants. I watched women at work weaving and knitting, but didn't like the voyeuristic feel. Visiting a secluded corner of the Centre I met two young women knitting on the doorstep of the room where the wool was dyed. Showing me the dyes, they pointed out the natural ones – indigo and dock leaves. I thought of April's father – my maternal great grandfather – and his indigo plantation. Not really anything to be proud of, as I believe the British owners exploited their workers quite badly.

In the afternoon I visited Tenzing Rock, named after the famous Sherpa, Tenzing Norgay, who had actually climbed it in front of India's first prime minister, Nehru. Located some way out of town, it was a pleasant walk on a quiet road. Certainly worth visiting, the sheer rock rose high above the road, but I didn't fancy having a go at climbing it. Nearby, at North Point, was the start of the Ropeway, the cable car which travels over tea gardens down to the bottom of the valley. I was finishing a cup of *chai* at North Point when the Ropeway started up. I clambered in and soon I was completely alone soaring high over the Ranjit Tea Gardens for five kilometres. An eerily silent experience. There were no views of the mountains beyond but being swathed in mist was surely more atmospheric. I thought of Mum then and, if I had burned that photo, this would have been the time to scatter the fragments of paper on the valley below.

Just before reaching the valley the sun burst through the swirls of mist, creating a moment of clarity for me. Dad was right. Mum did love Edinburgh Botanics and her true spirit remained there, not in Darjeeling. Perhaps I had an overly romantic view of my mum being Indian and an unrealistic expectation that I would find that part of her – and of me – here in Darjeeling. Back in Calcutta I had discovered her family background but Raadhika's kindness and patience only fuelled my anger at being left out of this warm and loving family for so long. Pieces of my Indian heritage had been put in place by this trip, and I was thrilled, but it didn't make me any more Indian.

And was it really my heritage? Who was I kidding? Just because I was Indian – partly Indian – didn't mean this was my heritage. I had to face up to the truth that I had been running away from – Mum wasn't my real mum. That's why she felt that I didn't belong to her Indian family. I needed to find my own family.

3. MY GOOD NAME

S trangely Patrick didn't feel the need to find out who he really were or at least he didn't think that the answer lay with his birth parents.

'So what did you know about being adopted as a child?' I asked him once.

'We all knew we were adopted very early on – four or five I think. Mum told me that my mother was young and had wanted to keep me but couldn't.'

'Weren't you curious? Didn't you want to find your mother?' It was a rhetorical question. Because I myself started searching quite late and then only half-heartedly.

'Yes,' he said. 'I became curious as an adult. I thought it would have been good if I could find out what happened to my parents and observe them from a distance. But I certainly didn't feel that I wanted to go and find them. There was a voice in the back of my head saying it would be nice for my birth mother to know how I was getting on. I suppose I had some interest in whether I inherited certain traits from my mother or father, but really the feeling was vague.'

I began my own search because I wanted to affirm my ethnic origin – I guess I was obsessed about that.

So on a bright Wednesday morning in October 1992, I walked from Brockley to Lewisham town centre, where I took the bus down the High Street, getting off at the Broadway opposite the Catford Cat. The Cat is an evil-looking black and white fibreglass monster fixed to the top of the metal Catford Centre sign above a rundown shopping mall. Absent-mindedly I crossed the busy Catford Road to reach Laurence House, the 1960s Brutalist glass and concrete building that everybody but me loves to hate. It was cold and the stairwell smelled of smoke but the stairs were clean. I climbed to the first floor. I felt very nervous, almost sick.

I was on my quest to track down my adoption papers but before I could even get access to my original birth certificate I had to undergo a counselling session where a social worker would talk me through the implications of what I might find.

I perched on the edge of a red, suitably institutional, chair in the reception area of Lewisham Adoption and Fostering Services. I was waiting for a Ms Coffey. She entered promptly and was unexpectedly beautiful: tall, with black shoulder-length hair braided into cornrows which showed off her gold-hooped earrings. She was wearing a thick blue and brown gingham dress with a brown belt accentuating her narrow waist, and a long beaded necklace. My eyes travelled down her legs to highly polished black kitten heels.

'Good morning, Miss Wray,' she smiled. 'I'm Jenny Coffey – Jenny. Please come with me.'

She ushered me through to a small windowless interview room just big enough for a wooden table and two upright chairs. We sat opposite one another. I looked for a ring on her left finger – I didn't see one. Suddenly I felt under-dressed in my black trousers, baggy grey sweater and Doc Martens.

'So let's start with you. Where do you live and work?'

'I'm Camilla.'

'I guessed that,' she laughed. I would have liked to have made her laugh more.

'I work for Southwark Council. In my spare time I help run the women's bar at the Lewisham Labour Club on a Wednesday – Women at Reds. Have you been?' I gushed.

Jenny shook her head.

'So tell me what you already know about your adoption.'

I gave Jenny the usual potted version of my story: I'd always known I was adopted; I'd got two brothers and a sister, also adopted and also mixed race; our adoptive mother was Indian and our father was English. Apart from my mum, who died last year, we were still in touch – sort of.

'So your mum died recently. Is that why you want to find out more about your birth parents now?'

'I want to know who I am. I was told my mother was a nurse from Switzerland and that my father was an Indian student but is this really true? – I never know what to tell people when they ask me where I'm from.'

'I can relate to that,' said Jenny, playing with her necklace. 'Look at me – my hair, my skin.' I accepted her invitation to look. 'You probably think I'm African but I've got a mixed background too. I'm from Trinidad, of Indian and African parents. It confuses people when I talk about my Indian side so sometimes I just let people assume I'm African.'

Jenny glanced at her papers. My papers. 'So, what might you do with any information?'

'I don't think I want to search for my birth parents. I just want to know more about what happened. I don't resent my mother at all.' I did. I don't now. Do I?

'I know it would have been difficult for her to keep me in those days.'

'That's what most people say, Camilla, but once you find out the basics, you might want to know a little more, then a little bit more, until finally you want to meet them. Have you thought what it might mean for your birth mother and father – and your adoptive father for that matter?'

Again I emphasised, 'It's nothing to do with my adoptive father. It's to do with my...my sense of who I am, or think I am.'

Clearly Jenny just wanted to make sure I knew what I was doing. She didn't seem to be using a prescribed list of interview questions for adopted people: were-you-happy-growing-up-have-you-told-your-parents-what-you're-doing-what-are-your-expectations-what-if-it-all-goes-wrong?

She opened my folder. I tilted my head slightly and tried to read it upside down. 'I can tell you that you were born in New End Hospital, Hampstead.' She paused with her finger on the page. 'If you discover that the circumstances of your birth are…traumatic… what support do you have?'

I was expecting this question – really she was asking what I would do if my mother had been raped. 'I've told my siblings and they'll help me make sense of anything I might find out, I'm sure.' Was I sure?

'OK,' said Jenny, uncrossing her elegant legs. 'I can confirm your mother was Swiss and your father Indian. I've found your basic information from the court records: your name, your mother and father's names, where you were born. Your full adoption file is with the National Children's Home in Highbury.'

'That's where I was adopted from – the nursery there.'

'Well, I've asked them to locate your file. They say that once you've had counselling from me, they'll show it to you.'

Counselling with Jenny! 'So how many sessions would I need?'

'Oh, this is it,' said Jenny.

'So you think I'm sane and I'm OK to find out more information?'

Jenny laughed: 'More than sane, I'd say.' Sane enough to invite her to Women at Reds?

She stood up and smoothed her dress. 'Good luck with your search, and if you have any questions before seeing your file, just give me a ring.'

I left Laurence House dazed by Miss – Jenny, call me Jenny – Coffey. I didn't seem to have learned much from the interview but surely once I saw my file some of the pieces would come together.

Ten days later I got a letter from a Miss Keele asking me to meet her at NCH's Highbury Offices. What was now their office was once the nursery. I haven't been back there since I was carried out in a bundle of blankets forty years ago.

I dressed more carefully for this appointment: a straight black skirt, cropped turquoise jacket over a navy blue M&S ribbed tee shirt and knee-length boots. Because it was cold I put on a bulky wool coat which rather spoiled my look. It was over an hour from Brockley to Highbury by train and Tube. I walked through Highbury Fields arriving at the beautiful two-storey Georgian building my habitual ten minutes early according to the clock set within a copper cupola on the roof. I spent four months of my life in this very building. The children's voices are silent now.

The reception was once the entrance hall to the original house and a grand staircase swept up to the first floor. I asked for Miss Keele and when the receptionist called her, she appeared instantly, tossing back long brown wavy hair. She was unsettlingly young. 'Hello, I'm Miss Keele,' she said walking ahead of me into a large well-proportioned room with mullioned sash windows overlooking the street. Outside it was a cold, clear winter's day.

Miss Keele sat down at the head of the table and indicated that I should sit diagonally opposite. She opened her briefcase, took out a plastic folder with a red cover and laid it carefully on the table in front of her. She then placed her handbag to the left of her. My file was surrounded.

'Miss Coffey told me she enjoyed meeting you,' she said, seeming somewhat surprised. 'I've been reading through your file and, unusually, there's quite a lot of information.'

I leaned forward.

'I see that you and your brother were both adopted from here. You were among some of the first mixed race children to be adopted through us. It's a fascinating story.'

So we were a success for them. How lovely! Everyone likes a happy adoption story.

'Your mother's name was Margareta Zahno and she named you Monica. She was a Swiss au pair working in Paddington in the early 1950s. She was apparently small and slim with long blonde hair.'

This was the next best thing to a photograph. I was slim but obviously took after my father with my black hair and dark eyes. But did I have Margareta's chin, her mouth, her brow? I wondered who I got my terrible eyesight from.

Miss Keele picked up a postcard and slid it across the table to me. 'I suppose I can give you this postcard.' There was no picture, no address. It was a notecard really. But I imagined my mother first making a rough draft and then filling her fountain pen with light blue ink to write in these incredibly straight lines and neat handwriting. Her English was impeccable.

Dear Madam,

It has been suggested to me that I should write to you about the adoption of my baby girl, Monica, who is now six weeks old. She was born on 1st April 1952 at the New End Hospital, NW3 and we are now living in a Mother and Babies Home,

I am Swiss, and came to London in December 1950 to learn English.

My Father is an engineer, and my home is in Fribourg. My baby's Father is an Indian student. As I am not able to make a home for Monica I would like her to be adopted so that she can be brought up in a family, and I hope you are able to help me.

I have to leave this Home in two weeks time, as we are only allowed here until the baby is two months old. As I am feeding my baby, please let me know immediately whether you can take her into one of your nurseries.

Margareta Zahno

I expelled a huge breath. I was suddenly transported to that Mother and Baby Home in Hampstead. A young girl in a foreign country, having a baby on her own and then having that baby wrenched away. I couldn't even begin to understand the enormity of it. She was breast-feeding me and it seemed she'd really wanted to keep me. What pain she must have felt giving me up. I wanted to know more about who she was and why she couldn't make a home for me. I wanted to know everything.

'I suppose I can let you keep this,' said Miss Keele.

'Can't I see my whole file? Can't I take it away? Isn't there something in there that would explain why she couldn't keep me?'

'We can tell you the contents but there's stuff in here – well it shows how adoption was viewed in those days. It's a bit, well you know…the wording they used then. It could upset you.'

Come on, Jane! It's my file and those days were my days. Who are you trying to protect here? I know social workers were racist but what's the difference between then and now? Then, they probably called me coloured and told Margareta there was no way I could be adopted as no one would want me. Now, they might disguise this in modern social worker speech. I'd be described as 'a charming little dual heritage girl for whom a suitable family is sought – must be aware of Indian and Swiss religions and customs'. That will do the trick – no one will apply.

Mildly I said, 'I'd like to know as much as possible, please.'

'Margareta brought you into the nursery here soon after she wrote that letter and you stayed here until you were adopted at six months. The file also mentions that Margareta went back to Switzerland after you were adopted.'

'When was that? Where in Switzerland did she go? Did she go home to her parents?'

I glanced again at my file – it was full of papers. There was more. I thought you were supposed to be able to see the whole file. Frowning, I hunched my shoulders.

'I can give you some information about your father,' she said, by way of compensation. 'This is really unusual as mostly the father is completely out of the picture. Here is a letter he wrote to a Magistrate.'

Dear Madam,

I am very gratified to learn from your letter that an adoption has been arranged for Monica Zahno who is under your care.

I have not so far heard from the court regarding the matter. However, I shall be glad to follow your advice in order to expedite the adoption.

Yours sincerely
Lakhan Raja Rao

I grabbed the note and fell back in my chair. My father! His name hadn't been on my birth certificate but here it was – and he was definitely Indian. And surprisingly he was still in touch with Margareta. Or at least she knew his address. He'd acknowledged my existence. Did he really care about me or was he just signing the forms out of a sense of responsibility? These notes from my parents made me feel connected – more of a whole person.

'You can keep that letter too,' Miss Keele said graciously. In my hands I held the postcard and the letter – the only things I have that have been touched by my parents. Momentarily, I forgot about the rest of the file.

'Now, Ms Coffey said that you just wanted to get hold of your birth certificate and a bit about your biological mother and father. But you might want to find out more once you start to think about it. What I'd advise you to do is to contact the organisation NORCAP – an organisation run by adopted people themselves. They have all sorts of useful information about searching and they offer support for adopted people.' She handed me NORCAP's card. 'We offer a tracing service ourselves if you do want to go further but for now I suggest you take one step at a time and see what NORCAP has to offer.'

I scraped back my chair and stood up to leave.

'We're always here if you want more information,' said Miss Keele, getting up and shaking my hand. 'It's lovely to meet our former children.'

We went back into the lobby and I stumbled down the front steps. The last time I left this place I was six months old and starting my new life.

I made my way back to the Tube, getting out at London Bridge where Southwark Council had temporarily rented an office for the Development Department while it did up some old garages on the Aylesbury Estate to house us. I cut across to Angel Court, our new home, a boring square brick and glass building a few minutes down on the left. Weaving my way through the spaces left by the privacy screens marking our different teams, I got to the policy section where I managed a grand team of two, Anne and Derek, who really didn't need managing. Derek was in, scowling over some plans of the Aylesbury Estate Offices.

'Honestly, there's not enough room for us all here and not enough light. The garages are underground. It's going to be terrible,' he said and then looked up. 'Oh, you're all poshed up! Of course, you went to see your adoption file. What happened? What did you find out?'

'Pretty much nothing!' I said, sitting down in the corner I'd made cosy with a screen behind and to the side of me, and a wall of books on the front of my desk, completing the illusion that I was really in a room of my own. 'It was so frustrating. I couldn't see the file and although she gave me a couple of bits of information to take away I don't think I've got the whole story. But I do now know for certain that my mother was Swiss and my father Indian. And I found out that I was named Monica Zahno.'

'Hey, Monica Zahno is a fabulous name. It really suits you. You could get a new identity by taking your old identity,' Derek said, knowing how I sometimes struggle with who I am. 'Look, let's have lunch and I'll make us some coffee.'

Derek went to our coffee corner where we had a small fridge on top of which was our stash of tea, coffee and mugs. He kept this area obsessively neat – and regularly cleaned out our fridge too.

'There's some bread and cheese in the fridge – shall I make us sandwiches?' I nodded. We kept the fridge stocked with lunch items and took turns to buy food on a Monday. I chatted as he made our coffee and sandwiches.

'She was really unforthcoming. She told me how I could now apply for my full birth certificate and she gave me the contact details for another organisation that deals with adoption. This is my second adoption interview and I don't seem to be much further forward. I did get these letters from my mother, Margareta, and my father, Lakhan, though.'

'That's amazing. Let's see,' said Derek, coming over to my desk brandishing a knife smothered in butter.

'Careful! I don't want any butter on these. You can look at them when we've finished lunch.'

'Is that all she gave you though?'

'She told me a bit about my mother. Apparently she went back to Switzerland after I was adopted. End of story. The adoption worker wouldn't say where in Switzerland but I can't help thinking Margareta would have left an address. I know things were secret then and once you were adopted there was no contact between the birth and adoptive parents but surely she would have said where she was going so she would get news of me from the agency.'

'Perhaps not,' said Derek, handing me my mug and a plate of cheese sandwiches. 'Here, clear your desk if you don't want coffee all over your papers.' He added, 'So did they give you any background about your mother and father?'

'She just gave me this postcard written by my mother asking NCH to take me in. It's so sad. She was breast-feeding me. I'd assumed I went to the adoption agency straight from the hospital, but she looked after me for two months in the Mother and Baby Home. She gives quite a lot of information in this short postcard. I'll read it to you.'

'As long as you're careful with that coffee,' Derek said.

When I'd finished reading Derek asked, 'What next? Do you think you'll try and find them? Where do the Zahnos come from? Are they German, French or Italian?'

'I don't know. I do know that Fribourg is a French speaking canton but Zahno sounds German. I wouldn't have a clue how to trace my mother in Switzerland and perhaps my father also went back home.'

'To get back to you as Monica Zahno, what do you think about changing your name?'

'You know, I think that's a great idea, but I'd want to keep Camilla as I really like that name and it's been part of me for so long. Not bothered about the Wray.'

'So you'd call yourself Camilla Tooth-o,' Derek giggled. He's a German speaker and I know enough German to know *zahn* means tooth.

We finished our lunch, moving on to moaning about our new offices in the underground garages on the Aylesbury Estate.

When I got home I read and re-read my two documents. The letters brought me closer to my birth parents, especially to my mother. I recalled two trips to the Valais region of Switzerland and to nearby Bern, the capital, which is quite near Fribourg. The first was an exciting hitch-hiking holiday where we stayed at some remote mountain hostels; the second a two-week geography field trip taken during the Easter break in our final year at university. They were both a lot of fun but I never really felt connected to Switzerland as my possible homeland.

I prepared a simple dinner of rice and dal – my comfort food. After clearing the dining table in the corner of my kitchen-diner, I settled down to write to NORCAP to see what they could advise. I also wrote to the General Register Office now I'd been cleared to get a copy of my own birth certificate and I knew my original name.

Two days later a white envelope marked GRO came through the post. My birth certificate. It was a long certificate which they had folded to get it into the envelope. And here was the information. I really was an April Fool, born on 1st April 1952 to Margareta Zahno, a mother's help working in the St Pancras district. The certificate also confirmed that Margareta was living at the Mother and Baby Home in Hampstead when she registered me – Monica Zahno – on 17th April 1952. The space for information about my father – his name and occupation – had been left blank. A scrawl at the side of the entry confirmed I was 'adopted'. Although my adoption interviews had given me this basic information I found this birth certificate oddly comforting, validating me as a human being. I could touch it. I could read it. It proved that I was me.

On a Saturday morning in December I was about to leave my flat to go shopping in Lewisham when I saw the post scattered on the floor of our little lobby. There lay a thick A4 envelope franked with NORCAP's initials and addressed to me. I decided I didn't have to go shopping just yet and so I took it back into my flat. I walked through the long narrow hall to my kitchen-diner at the back of the flat.

I placed the envelope on the dining table. Inside I found three pamphlets. I laid them out side by side. The first was a short one giving the background to NORCAP, the National Organisation for Counselling Adoptees and Parents. It was a small voluntary organisation, set up a few years previously and staffed by a couple of paid staff who were assisted by volunteers.

I flicked through the second document, the newsletter. It caught my attention so I started reading it from beginning to end. It had information on 'Search-In Days' at St. Catherine's House where all the registers for Births, Marriages and Deaths were kept. Volunteers would show you how to find records for your birth parents if you knew their name and approximate date of birth. Better still were the stories written by adopted people and their parents: one woman's account of her search which started out as purely academic, a 'finding-out exercise' she called it, but which turned into an emotional journey after writing and calling her mother, and finally meeting her; a woman's story of the hurt that had her grieving for days when she found her mother had died only five years after giving birth to her; a man's account of the rejection from his mother who did not want to know him; and a birth mother's happiness at finding her forty-one-year-old son.

Moved by these stories, and wondering what my own could be, I got up and stared out into the garden. It had started to rain and the garden was mostly colourless on this winter's day but against the back fence I caught a glimpse of the mahonia with its spiny dark green leaves and the first delicate fronds of bright yellow blossoms showing at the top of the shrub.

I turned back to the third pamphlet, *Searching for Family Connections*, a blue photocopied A4 pamphlet stapled together. At thirty pages long it was full of useful information. *You should read this leaflet carefully and proceed as advised*, it told me. So I did.

It began with all the standard advice that Jenny had given me:

Your mother may not have told her family, husband or children of your existence. Can you cope with a rejection? You should discuss your search with your adoptive parents. Don't think your birth mother will solve any arguments with your adoptive parents. And the biggie that everyone loves warning you about: *It is just possible that you could have been born as a result of unpleasant circumstances, e.g. a rape, incest or abandonment.*

There was a wonderful flow chart of the steps to take on your search, reminding me of a game of Snakes and Ladders. Start by finding your mother's name in the electoral register. Mother not in the electoral register? Slither down your snake. But wait a minute, her marriage entry appears in St Catherine's House – mount the ladder with caution. Once you've found your mother's marriage certificate it should be easy to trace her. Ominously the last box warned you: *Consider carefully your position and that of your mother. Proceed with extreme caution after double-checking all details and seeking advice and guidance.*

I mulled over all this. It was rather off-putting. Searching English records was not going to be any good for me as both my parents were born abroad. There would be no birth records and no records of who lived at the family house. And no use looking for a marriage or death certificate for my mother as she had returned to Switzerland. I had no idea how to search in Switzerland, particularly as I only speak French, and not very fluently at that. I put the document to one side and decided to continue on my shopping trip. I had abandoned my search before I'd even started.

However, the idea of changing my name had really taken hold. I rang up Ellen and she said, 'Go for it.' She continued in the style of McCarthy: 'Are you now, or have you ever been, a Wray?'

Patrick's take on my name change was similar. 'I never felt like a Wray, and can understand that you don't either. I don't think Dad would understand at all although Mum would have. But it's your name and you should change it if that's what sounds good to you.'

A couple of weeks later I was walking up the two flights of escalators from the Piccadilly Line at Holborn Station. I was still breathing evenly by the time I reached the ticket barriers so I knew I was in good shape. I made my way to the London Women's Centre. A four-storey Victorian building, owned by the Greater London Council, the Centre was home to twenty or so women's groups: the Lesbian History Group; a computer training group; arts organisations. I was there for the Wednesday evening meeting of the Asian Women Writers' Collective, a small group of South Asian women who met to talk about their work. That evening there were eight of us sitting in a circle taking turns to read out our latest writing. We were a varied bunch which I loved: Indian, Pakistani, Sri Lankan. There were also women of mixed parentage: Italian and Sri Lankan; Pakistani and Scottish; Goan and English.

I read my poem, 'Ethnic Monitoring or a Geography Lesson' which reflected my frustration with recruitment officials wanting to put me in boxes.

Black, Asian, White, FAR EASTERN, Other!
The boxes on the tear-off slip remain blank.
I never thought there'd be a space for Indo-Swiss.
But my mind turns its attention
to the mind behind the confusion
behind those mixed-up boxes…

After I'd finished reading the whole poem, Seema jumped in immediately, 'I didn't know you were Swiss. I knew you're adopted and that part of you is Indian. Did you ever meet your mother?'

'Here's a more interesting story than my poem,' I said, eager to tell my story. 'I've just seen some of my adoption papers and found a couple of letters written by my mother and my father to the adoption agency. It's changed me. I feel I come from both of them and I'm thinking of changing my name from Wray to Zahno to reflect my Swiss side, but what of my Indian side?'

Anita, who was Pakistani and Scottish, and was wearing purple trousers and a fuchsia tunic – her take on a *salwar kameez* – said, 'I'm helping my sister find a South Asian name for my niece and I've got a baby name book. I'll bring it next week.'

Sarbjit, who was rather stern and worked with the computer training group, challenged me: 'Why does your precise mix matter when you define yourself as a black woman at the end of the poem? Why do you need to change your name? Isn't that putting yourself in a box?'

She had a point, but somehow the name Camilla Wray put me in a box I didn't like and the only way I could get out of it was to place myself in another one.

'I really understand,' Anita said. 'Sarbjit, your name reflects exactly who you are. You never have to explain yourself whereas I do all the time. And so does Camilla.'

The following week, Anita and I arranged to meet early at Wesley House so she could show me the name book. She was wearing a long golden sequinned skirt topped with a red silk shirt and a black faux leather jacket. Her curly dark brown hair fell across her face as she said excitedly, 'Look, I've found your new name.' She showed me the book, opened it and together we looked at the names beginning with K. 'See here – "Kamila". It means "perfect" in Arabic. And it's the perfect name for you.'

And so I became Kamila Zahno.

Now, when I'm asked in India 'Your Good Name, please' I'll be able to give them my perfect name. And when that question is followed by 'Your Native Place, please' I will say with certainty, 'London but my father was Indian and my mother Swiss'.

4. SLIGHTLY COLOURED

I was born under a gooseberry bush on Hampstead Heath. Patrick came into being underneath the clock at Waterloo Station. Ellen's first few months were spent on a circular journey travelling, somewhat unnecessarily, from London to Birmingham and back again. And I never got to hear about Tim. This is our story.

In 1952, I crawled out from under a gooseberry bush onto my new father's lap, bouncing and chuckling. I was a lively brown-eyed baby with wisps of blue-black hair, enjoying all the attention from a trio of women sitting opposite on our Tube journey home. My father was a handsome thirty-two-year-old with an unruly cow's lick. It was the longest journey I'd ever made, from north London to Bickley in Kent where my new family waited. At Victoria we changed onto a steam train hissing away which must have been startling for six-month old me. The train left whistling with a high pitched 'wooo', and once it got going the wheels made a repetitive sound as if they were saying, 'You're going home. You're going home'.

Ellen, my sister, recalls how she first heard about me. Although she was only five at the time, she remembers quite a lot.

'There was something in the air at home. The parents were talking about a new baby. Would you be a boy or girl? We went to your nursery in Highbury. I don't think Tim and Patrick came with us. The parents went to the ward to look at you and left me playing with this wonderful metal horse which you could sit on. When they brought me to the ward I didn't want to see you as I was more interested in playing with the horse.

'But the excitement when you eventually turned up! That first day Tim and I fought to take turns to powder your bottom before Mummy pinned your nappy. I can still smell that sweet, soapy talcum powder. And then that first Christmas I thought Father Christmas was pretty smart because no one had told him about you, but he still left a rattle for you in a bootee in the kitchen. I remember asking Mummy, "How did he know?"'

After a few months living with my new family I was officially adopted. It was a family occasion. Ellen remembers the visit to the adoption court. 'All six of us went into a side room with an imposing wooden table and a few chairs. The judge introduced himself and asked us our names.'

Three years before I came along, Patrick's birth mother had travelled up from the south coast to give him to our parents. They met underneath the clock at Waterloo Station – that clock with the four huge faces suspended from the iron roof in the middle of the concourse. Patrick's birth mother held him out to Mummy who took him and – so Patrick recalled her telling him – 'put him over her shoulder and hauled him away like a sack of potatoes'. I can't imagine how Patrick's mother must have felt, handing over her baby. But bringing up a child who took after his African father would have been difficult for a young white single mother.

Talking to Ellen about this book I asked her why she kept moving between London and Birmingham in her early years. 'I was born in London and my mother approached the Children's Society, hoping I'd be adopted. But I found out through my adoption papers the fact I was "slightly coloured" meant that I was "impossible to adopt". They didn't even try. The Society didn't have a baby unit in London so I was transferred to a home in Solihull.'

'So how did our parents find you in Solihull?'

'They lived in Solihull before you and Patrick were born. Dad taught at a school there and I think Mum did some part-time work as a children's doctor in Birmingham. We moved to Bickley in Kent in 1949.'

Three years after Patrick and I were adopted we moved back to Birmingham. Dad really liked the school in London but our parents thought Birmingham might be easier for Mum to get a job, as not only did she know some of the doctors from working there before, but there were quite a few Indians in Birmingham and they thought that there would be less discrimination than in Kent.

For a few months we lived in the upstairs flat of a house that was due for demolition. I remember the boy who lived in the flat downstairs, shaking the drainpipe and releasing a huge spider.

He said, 'This house is going to fall down. We have to move out quickly.'

That night, the spider came to my room. I woke up suddenly and my pillow was bathed in the streetlight coming from the curtains that had been left half-drawn. A massive spider watched me, waiting for me to wake up before pouncing. I could see its legs and arms crossing and uncrossing, flexing for attack. It sat waiting on the pillow. A hum from the streetlight was getting louder and louder. I screamed. Nothing. I screamed again. I began to see other shapes in the room – the cupboard was closing in on me. Surely it held several strangers. I would never get out alive. There was silence except for the streetlight hum. The spider was silently vibrating from the rhythm of the hum. I screamed again. At last the door creaked open and the light from the landing poured in, reaching the cupboard and the spidery pillow. A shadowy figure entered the room.

'What's all the fuss about?' asked Mummy calmly.

'It's the spider,' I sobbed. 'It's going to eat me. And strange men will come out of the cupboard to get me.'

'You silly, that's not a spider, only a piece of fluff.'

I saw now that this was true, but how would such a large piece of fluff arrive on the pillow when it wasn't there before I went to sleep? I continued to sob.

'Why can't you dry my eyes, Mummy?'

'I am, but the tears keep coming. Never mind, darling. Look, I've taken the fluff away and there is no spider.' Mummy rocked me to sleep. I don't remember her holding me so close ever again.

We moved to a new house soon afterwards, the first our parents bought. Built of brick and pebbledash, it was set in a quiet cul-de-sac in suburban Birmingham. On entering the front door we had to remove our shoes in case we scratched the highly polished hall floorboards. Wood panelling concealed cupboards under the stairs. Keen to make their mark on their first house, my parents proceeded to decorate each room with patterned wallpaper and garish floral carpets. The 1930s yellow mottled tiles of the fireplaces couldn't compete with the clashing colours and retreated into the background. The living room was crammed full of six Parker Knoll armchairs arranged along the walls, a wedding present from Daddy's parents, straight from the factory near their house. Two had wing-backs and curved arms while the other four were simple with straight wooden arms and legs. All were covered in a beige material which was scratchy to bare legs. A massive radiogram took pride of place in the corner. In those early days I don't remember it being played. The only radio I ever heard was the portable one we had in the dining room where I would listen to Children's Favourites every Saturday. I liked the story 'Ugly Duckling'.

The others were at school during the day but in the early evening we would all sit on the living room carpet, a red, blue and pink floral affair. My brothers' favourite game was Meccano. We had a small set that they would turn into red and green cars. They could rarely play together without arguing about how to build the cars. My sister, who must have been about eight, would read. I was too young to join them so I would play with Chuffy, my threadbare one-eyed mongrel dog who had been handed down from Patrick. I would get him to lie with Tibby, our cat, when she was curled up in front of the fire. I loved Tibby the best. She never told me what to do or argued with me. She would curl up by my side when I was sitting on the floor and when I stroked her she would purr with contentment. She never bit or scratched me even when I pulled her tail gently. She would just turn and look at me with her big blue eyes.

My parents were proud of their little flock. Daddy used to call us his Heinz 57 varieties which I didn't understand. We weren't baked beans. I thought we all looked pretty normal although Daddy stuck out a bit because he had yellow hair whereas the rest of us were dark-haired. Mind you Patrick had short tight curly hair while Tim had coarse brown waves. Ellen and I had short, straight, silky black hair.

Mummy was short and round. She usually wore baggy dark brown corduroy trousers with long dark-coloured cardigans. Her single black plait, fastened with a rubber band, would snake down her back. Daddy was tall and always dressed in loose grey trousers and a neutral coloured shirt with a soft collar, never a tee shirt. He didn't seem to be as cold as the rest of us so would usually wear a sleeveless woollen pullover in plain green or mustardy yellow.

Before bedtime I would sit on Daddy's knee and he would read me a story. At the end of the day he gave off a light aroma of sweet sweat. I liked it and would sniff him with pleasure while he rocked me on his lap.

'Daddy, pleeese read me *The Little Island* again.'

The island was surrounded by a jade-green sea, topped with foamy waves that shone in the moonlight. Underneath the sea were stripy black fish, curly shells and crabs with fierce-looking claws. Seaweed squeaked on the shore. The fish jumped right out of the water at night. Best of all I loved the grey kitten. I couldn't get enough of this book. Someone called Golden MacDonald wrote it. Her name reminded me of Golden Shred Marmalade. My second favourite book was *Orlando (the Marmalade Cat)*, so perhaps Golden MacDonald also had a marmalade cat and called herself after that.

'You know it off by heart,' said Daddy. 'So why don't we look at it together and you tell me what happens.'

I loved the pictures. They were coloured in lots of different greens: jade-green for the sea, turquoise for the kingfishers, and a curly green for the seaweed. I had never seen these colours anywhere else. Home was mostly yellowy-brown fireplaces and bright swirly carpets. Outside was mostly grey and foggy.

I told the story to Daddy. 'A kitten sails to the island and can't believe it's so small. The kitten says, "This little island is as little as Big is Big." What's Big as Big, Daddy? Is it as big as you?'

'It's bigger. It's as big as the whole wide world – that's more than England and India put together. So do tell me, what happens to the kitten next?'

'The island tells the kitten that he's quite small as well. "Maybe I'm a little island too – a little fur island in the sea," says the kitten, jumping in the air. He has huge blue eyes, like Tibby.'

After reading the story together, I would go to bed. I kissed Mummy but it was Daddy who put me to bed. My room was next to Mummy and Daddy's bedroom and was big. A white carpet covered the floor and much of the room was taken up by an ugly mahogany table with claw-like legs that didn't fit anywhere else in the house. My narrow iron bed was sandwiched between the table and the bay window which looked out over our large back garden. I lay underneath my brown silky eiderdown and Daddy walked two fingers up the bed saying, 'Mr Fox is coming, Mr Fox is coming and he'll tickle you under your chin.' I loved Mr Fox but it took me a while to calm down after the tickling.

'Snuggle down now,' Daddy said, making sure the blankets were tucked right in.

He left the bedroom door slightly ajar so I could see the light from the hall as he knew I didn't like the dark. In the winter it was very cold in my bedroom. I used to wake up in the night freezing as the silky eiderdown had a habit of slipping right off the bed. Pulling it back over me I was soon asleep again. The next morning Jack Frost had dispelled the gloomy shadows and I woke up bathed in the light passing through ferns of ice on the diamond-paned windows.

Around this time, when I was three, Mummy went back to work as a doctor. She was working in various clinics with mums who had just had babies and she couldn't really take me with her. Daddy was teaching English at Sandwell School, so he took me to the nursery there. The other children were slightly older than me. Sandwell was very far from where we lived, in what is known as the Black Country because of all the soot from the dirty industries there. I didn't see any soot and our school was very clean. The children weren't black. In fact they seemed to be quite pale to me. The older children wore a school uniform. There was even a school blazer. I looked really smart in it but didn't like the colours much – maroon with a yellow border. I didn't have to wear a uniform other than the blazer. I was very proud of going to school.

As Sandwell was so far away we had to leave just before eight in the morning. I had to trot after Daddy as he walked really fast. Our bus stop was at a big roundabout about ten minutes away on Chester Road. Daddy told me Chester Road was built by the Romans; it was long and straight so the Roman army could march fast, just like Daddy.

'Daddy, can I sit in the front and give the conductor the money?' I would always ask.

I would pile the coins up by size with bronze pennies and halfpennies on the bottom and twelve-sided golden threepenny pieces in the middle. The pile was topped by a silver sixpenny piece. After about half an hour we had to change buses, this time to a big Midland Red bus which lived up to its name. I used the same ritual on this bus, piling up the coins and giving them to the conductor.

'Well, Camilla, you've got the right change as usual,' he said. 'How do you manage that every day?'

'Daddy has a jam jar at home where he puts all his change at the end of the day.'

'Well you certainly make my life easier. I wish everyone was the same.'

We would get to the school before nine and Daddy would take me to the nursery. I don't remember much about my day but what I especially loved after school was when one of the teachers took me home with her while Daddy finished his day. For about an hour I got to watch television which was thrilling as we didn't have one at home. If the lady on the telly said, 'Close your eyes,' I would close them tightly as I thought she might know if I didn't. I opened them when she said and there would be a surprise, like a dog or a hamster.

I went to Sandwell School for about two years. The first year we didn't learn to read but the teacher told us stories and I played with the other kids. One summer's day we were lying out on the grass and I saw that the sky was moving very fast overhead. I wasn't frightened but wondered what on earth was happening.

I sat up. 'Look, the sky's moving,' I exclaimed to the boy next to me. I think his name was David.

'That's just the clouds moving, silly,' he replied, still lying down.

I lay back down to examine the sky more closely. David was right: there were wispy white clouds moving across the blue sky.

'Why do the clouds move?' I asked.

'It's the wind blowing them,' said David, quite willing to talk about them, even after I'd been silly about the whole sky.

'Oh, is that like the story Miss told us about the fight between the sun and the wind where they try and get a man to take off his coat? The wind tries to blow his coat off but all he does is wrap it more tightly round him. Then the sun shines so much that the man gets hot and takes his coat off.'

'That's sort of right,' said David.

From then on I've always been fascinated by cloud formations – fat curvy white puffs, wispy streaks of tissue, dark rain and even stretches of boring grey curtains.

5. KIDNAPPER OF ORPHANS

I always knew Mum and Dad had met in India during World War Two but didn't know many details. In 2006, the year before he died, I kept asking Dad if I could record some stories from his life but he was reluctant to talk in front of my recorder. I was visiting him in Birmingham when he said unexpectedly:

'I know you wanted to know about my life so I've written two short pieces for you – one about growing up in rural Buckinghamshire in the 1930s and the other about my experience during the War. That piece includes quite a lot about Mum too.'

He handed me several A4 sheets written on both sides. The piece about growing up was rather formal but some of the stories about the Army really came alive.

Mum had been working as a paediatrician in Calcutta for several years before joining the Indian Army Medical Services in 1942. After working for a year she asked to be posted to Kohima in Burma. There she used to sneak off for walks in the jungle alone which was strictly forbidden by the Army. This was typical of Mum, who loved to explore. But she tripped over a tree root in the jungle and broke her leg. I don't know how long she was lying there or who rescued her, but she was transferred to Poona where it was easier for her to recuperate. Once her leg had mended she became a pathologist at the Central Military Hospital.

Dad was called up in 1940. After a spell of officer cadet training in Malvern he set sail for India in December 1941. He didn't see active service and spent his time organising supplies and transport.

In March 1944 he was posted to Poona where he was Station Transport Officer.

They met over breakfast at a boarding house in Poona in March 1944. Unusually in that racially segregated city, where British people rarely mixed with Indians, Mrs Sarafian, an Armenian woman, ran a boarding house that was also home to Mr Doshi, an Indian army officer, and Major Xu, a doctor who had left Japanese-invaded China to join the Indian Army. Two others completed the group: a young Anglo-Burmese woman married to an English officer and the English wife of an army surgeon, both of whose husbands were serving elsewhere in India.

On Tuesdays the residents of the boarding house would eat together at a Chinese restaurant, with Major Xu doing the ordering, and all of them taking it in turn to pay. Dad said they called it the Tuesday Club.

Mum and Dad became very close. They both worked regular daytime hours so had the evenings free to see the latest British and American films at one of several cinemas in the city. They went to weekly concerts of classical music, played on wind-up gramophones with a large horn. But it was books that turned their friendship into love. They belonged to the Poona Club which had a fantastic library. But Mum always preferred Dad's choice of books and hijacked them to read them in her room. It was her booming laugh Dad heard through the wall that made him fall in love. Their romance had only four months to blossom until Dad was posted to an Infantry Brigade Training HQ as a Brigade Supply and Training Officer to Kolar Gold Fields, sixty miles east of Bangalore.

They wrote to each other regularly and Dad told me he had kept letters from Mum. Where were those letters? When Ellen, Patrick and I were clearing the house after Dad died I never came across them. I asked Patrick but he had no recollection of the letters either. I asked Ellen.

'Yes, I've got them,' she said. 'But I haven't read them. Mum was a very private person and I'm sure she wouldn't have wanted us to delve into her life.'

I said, 'May I see them for my book research? I'll be very sensitive in telling Mum's story.'

Ellen couldn't very well refuse so she copied them all for me and sent them through the post in three batches. I received over a hundred letters written between mid-July 1944 and the end of December 1945. Ellen had copied them in black and white so I didn't know what colour ink Mum was using or the texture of the paper. But I recognised her neat no-nonsense handwriting, no fancy loops and very legible. I wished I had the originals actually touched by Mum and Dad, but the thick pile of photocopies was nevertheless a treasure trove. Mum didn't keep Dad's letters. As she said in one of her letters to him, she wanted to leave this life unencumbered by possessions. I understand this. I wouldn't want my own diaries and love letters to be read by anyone. It was only when I read those letters that I was able to visualise her life before she had us. We've lost the art of letter writing. I get numerous trite, safe emails hoping that I'm well and going on to describe detailed renovations to houses I've never visited. But I don't get emails like my mum's letters which were full of wit, humour and love.

I had never known how deeply Mum loved Dad but here on these pages I saw her love story developing over eighteen months. Mum and Dad's relationship wasn't reserved. It was real – desperate even – written against the backdrop of the chaos of the War's finale.

Mum's first letters showed she was fond of my dad and wanted to share their common interest in films and books. I don't think she thought of it as a lovers' relationship. She was, after all, ten years older than Dad with an established career as a doctor. I always knew of this age difference but it had never really registered as unusual when I was growing up. I read with surprise just how much of a difference it made to her.

Dear Young 'Un, she wrote in her first letter, signing it *All the best from Sita Roy*. Left alone in Poona, Mum chatted about all the changes at Mrs Sarafian's boarding house and how she missed the companionship of everyone in the now defunct Tuesday Club. She told Dad *I felt lonely and invested in a Siamese kitten*. This was typical of Mum, who adored cats, but presumably the cat wasn't a substitute for my father!

For the first few months her letters were full of accounts of the books she had bought and read and the films she'd seen. She browsed the shops frequently for books, sending many to Dad in his camp. But sometimes she couldn't find an entertaining one, once settling instead *for a book about glow worms – out of boredom.*

Mum voraciously devoured the classics, something she continued to do when I knew her. Dad had introduced her to Dickens. When I was a young child I remember her talking about a marvellous book *Three Cows*. Or that's what it sounded like to me. I imagined it was set on a farm where the main characters were cows. It was not until my adolescence when I had a broader vocabulary that I realised she had been referring to *Bleak House*. But she drew the line at reading George Eliot.

George Eliot was spoiled for me by having to 'do' Silas Marner with a stupid English teacher when I was fourteen!

Reading this seventy years later, I had to laugh, as the exact same thing happened to me which is a real shame as it was the first book I ever read about adoption.

She continued to see films at the Poona cinemas. I loved reading her accounts of the 1930s black and white classics. We saw some of these together as a family in the 1960s.

I saw Jane Eyre *at the Connaught tonight. Parts of it, the early schoolgirl years were excellent, and again occasionally it caught the spirit very well. Joan Fontaine has lost something since* Rebecca *– she is passionate now but her spirit is different. Orson Wells is good sometimes. I liked the atmosphere of gloom and eeriness, very Brontë, and some of the scenery. The house was ridiculous – American ideas of a house in Yorkshire.*

In November 1944 it was apparent that Dad had taken some leave, returning to stay in a spare room at the boarding house. They seemed to become closer after this. Mum started to write weekly letters and she signed them *With Love*. I liked her humour – in one she signed off as *Love as ever (or never), Sita*. I got the impression that Dad had definitely fallen in love, but Mum was holding off. Dad mentioned he could take some leave again in March but Mum tried to avoid him clashing with a heartthrob.

Leave in March sounds very good but one of my heartthrobs is coming sometime. I would not like him to meet you because it is difficult to explain our fraternal relationship. My heartthrobs are sterile ones, quite unreciprocated, and for all you know you are one. Just someone who is good company…but you see it wouldn't do to have two of you at once.

There was a gap in the weekly letters from mid-March to the end of April, so I guessed Dad did take leave to visit Mum in Poona. Mum started writing affectionate letters every few days from then on. She mentioned a poem:

Is that a recognised poem 'I do not love you – but…?' I remember reading it once. It would do for me – except that I do – a bit!'

I think Mum must have been quoting from the Pablo Neruda poem 'I do not love you except because I love you'.

And then, a week later she wrote:

I would like you to do one thing for me, I would like a picture taken more like yourself. Among the many things I have never done in my life is to have a photo on my table. It would interest me to see one of your profile (like the Rupert Brooke poetic one – all long neck and Adam's apple)!

In May, Mum had some leave but Dad, having taken leave only in March, could not take more. Mum travelled to Coonoor, a hill station in the Nilgiri mountains, to stay with family friends. On the way she arranged to stop in Bangalore for the night, along with her cat, Pfui. Apparently Pfui had been ill and she couldn't take her to Coonoor as the friends had a bull terrier, so she suggested Dad took care of her. I remember Dad telling us the story of how he had to take Pfui in the army truck. Pfui was loose and frightened and apparently scratched him quite badly.

It suddenly seems an awful lark to meet you in Bangalore on Sunday. I do so hope you can manage it. Something to be said for illicit 'love' – more exciting and painful – not that I can really recommend it to you.

But a few days later, she warned him not to be too serious:

At my age it means so much, but you must not feel involved in any way. Don't you see? It must be a pleasant and beautiful interlude. If I allude to the future at any time it is because mortals are weak.

While she was staying in Coonoor it's apparent to me from the letters that she had fallen in love, but still holds off:

I ought to say thank you somehow but I can't. My newest hysterics are – that knowing me better you will find you were cherishing an illusion. The young always go in for ideals.
Your photo is beside my bed on a table behind a vase of larkspurs, geraniums and verbena. It occasioned some comment, but you look so young…

When Mum arrived back in Poona in June she transferred to another hospital which she seemed to enjoy more. She still found time to write to Dad every day.

The 'aunty' preoccupation is because I really so see it as the only role in which I can remain with you mentally. Either of us could fill pads with our 'imaginings' especially the painful and fear-filled ones – but that is what eases me so with you that I know you understand. Purely selfish the world would say. If knowing you've changed the world for me makes you feel arrogant, darling, go ahead. It is not my imagination that – even the general public sees it. How can I be anything but profoundly thankful – apart from any other feeling.

My mother was still uncertain about how much the age difference might influence the relationship. At the end of June she had decided, age difference or not, she was in love.

You will think I'm crazy but I feel as if all my life there had been a pain like a toothache inside, and you with your really absurd and out-of-date kindness and generosity were gradually poulticing it away. It shows too, sweetheart. They have started chaffing me in the Lab for my 'looks' and for the change in my voice. It says something too, that even though I'm half hysterical for lack of sleep, I'm happy inside.

With the War having ended in Europe and Dad most likely be repatriated, marriage was suddenly on the cards. It's hard to piece together when the proposal took place because we didn't have Dad's letters, but on 1st July she wrote:

Sanely or insanely, and I'm afraid, waking or sleeping, I wish with all my heart you could bring yourself to marry me before you go, but it is such crass and utter selfishness that I try to plead against it always. Funnily enough I am sure you will one day, and it would make the machine of the Army easier. Dearest, you must not feel that binds you in any way. You asked me frankly – here is the answer. As you write the Army machine would provide a free passage and probably employ me in England. As officers in the Indian Army we are bound for one year after the cessation of hostilities.

Marriage, for Mum, became urgent when she was given notice that she would be transferred imminently. In mid-July she said:

Fate cannot harm me but she can have a damn good try. I am posted, urgently, to Coimbatore and then after three weeks to BLA [British Liberation Army] in Italy perhaps. I cannot get away before Sunday 15th but could be with you that night. I leave the arrangements to you, where you meet me, how you meet me etc. I had to tell Colonel Browning about us but he has promised not to tell anyone else. Wire me when you get this. I shall stay one day, anywhere you arrange. Our luck seems to have changed – or has it? Perhaps you'll have your answer by the time I arrive. If it is 'no' anyway I can think of being nearer you now than before. Europe is so much smaller than all these oceans between.

So now only to wait till you come. I am really tired of this lift going up and down in my stomach and of feeling sick all the time.

At this point I speculated about why she was keeping her prospective marriage plans a secret. Was it because she was still uncertain? I knew she had mentioned her relationship to her sister Eva but beyond that she didn't mention the rest of her family at all. The trip to Bangalore was postponed till 27th July but this time it wasn't just to meet Dad; Mum was planning a wedding.

My own dearest,

I love you. This is my plan. My reprieve lasts only till the 1st August. I am safe in Poona till then but not for one day more. It might be Greece, Cypress, or Burma. I suggest coming to Bangalore, leaving on Friday night 27th and arriving Saturday. I will stay at Carleston Road and arrange with a padre. You can come for the afternoon for your tooth or any other damn thing – any day after that. The main thing is to get it fixed somehow. It seems difficult to persuade a padre to marry one unless the man asks. Perhaps you can get in for a few hours before I get there. The being together may have to be postponed for a bit, agony as it is. But once we are married you can ask for my release and they won't send me anywhere.

I don't know why this plan falls through but it's evident that, although they did meet in Bangalore on 27th July, they didn't get married, and it seems as though it's off the cards. She wrote in early August:

As time goes on we shall discover that more people will be released from the Army and probably late 1946 will see even me free. That should take the hurry and sting out of the present for you. 14-18 months is a long time but I am ashamed at my blackmail. I take it back – and you must consider yourself free – in every way.

Dad had been sending her letters from his family that made her fear that a life with him in England would not be easy. It was a shame I didn't have those letters, nor did I know what he thought of his family's own uncertainty. I only knew that Mum was increasingly worried and uncertain. On 6th August she wrote:

What does your father mean when he says his mind is fixed but his heart torn all ways? There is so much you must ask him when you go. I am only afraid that when you get back to your normal habitat you will see things with their eyes. It would not be anything extraordinary if you did. Does he think your love for me is due to pity and sympathy or is he wondering for your mother's sake?

And a week later she said:

My interpretation of your mother's letter is that she is sure you will think better of marrying me – so darling, don't expect it to be easy. This is the lull before the storm, I fear. It would be a great help if both your parents would write exactly what they mean. I fear the worst when I read veiled sentences. Be patient, my sweet and brave. If we love each other, surely, surely, they'll come round.

The letters bring home to me how brave Mum actually was, despite her feelings of uncertainty. Here she was, an Indian and ten years older than Dad whose rural working-class background must have felt quite strange to Mum with her upper-class upbringing, reaching across barriers of race and age and class to marry him.

It is the days that are long, not the nights, don't you find? I wake up in the morning, sure of you and me, our ultimate security, our sense of belonging. Then all day, bits begin to ooze away till by night I feel I am ruining your young life. Stupid!

Mum had many relatives and mentioned various visits by them. But she only made reference to telling her sisters about her prospective marriage to an Englishman. They were both supportive, with Eva meeting Dad one day in Bangalore, and Alice helping Mum later to get her discharge from the Army. But Mum had difficulty with the Army. In mid-August Dad wrote to Mum's Colonel to say they intended to marry. The Colonel called Mum into his office. On 14th August she wrote to Dad:

He said to tell you it's OK by him but he doesn't have anything to do with it. He says he doesn't approve but he supposes you know your own mind. I felt like a kidnapper of orphans.

Then there is a gap in the letters until 27th August. I had to rely on what my dad wrote just before he died. The Colonel didn't actually give Mum leave for the wedding and Dad's Brigadier wouldn't give him leave to go to Poona to marry a 'wog' (the Brigadier's words, not Dad's!). It was deadlock until August when Dad was transferred to the Area Headquarters in Bangalore. There, he rented a room in a small boarding house. Mum packed a bag and went absent without leave, staying with friends of her mother's. A few days later, on 26th August, they were married in a Methodist church. Mum had to return to Poona to face the wrath of her Colonel instead of a honeymoon.

My poor mother! She had been racked with doubt about her marriage for many months and now she had to wait and wait for her discharge. On returning from Bangalore she wrote:

I have been to the Indian Army Medical Core HQ. They were very obstructionist – guess why? They asked why an Indian would want to leave India. However I bullied them and though it may take six months it has begun at least.

While Dad got repatriated in October, Mum had still heard nothing and suspected that she was being overlooked since she went AWOL to get married. Meanwhile, life in Poona went on with hospital rounds, knitting endless pairs of socks and reading. At the end of October she kept hearing rumours that her release and passage were being sorted so she enlisted the help of Mrs Sarafian's son to paint her trunks with her name and destination. Buying stencils from the market, they painstakingly inscribed the trunks. From the tailor she hunted down black silk stockings, both as presents for Dad's family and herself. I find it hard to imagine my mother wearing black silk stockings.

Mum had time to speculate what life would be like in England. At thirty-five, she was desperate to start a family, partly because of her age, but mostly because she loved babies. In her letters she speculated what the little Wrays would look like.

I would like one little W to have hair like the tall grass, a lovely goldeny red-brown. My mother had red-brown hair.

I wonder why she said this – did she want us to look white? She certainly wasn't comfortable in her own skin. Talking of Proust she wrote:

Proust is excellent. At least I am very interested. He was half an enemy [referring to his Jewish mother]. *Curiously enough, because I am a mixture and an outcaste I understand them. It has always been them and me against the rest of the world.*

Finally, on 10th November Mum received her release from the Army. She noted:

Curious feeling, being out of the Army and being in bed. My first reaction was one of sheer terror. I have been out of work before and it is the most terrifying sensation. Then too, terrifying but not free. Your letters quietened me a little. It is to me, unbelievable that security and love are just around the corner, like those dreadful nightmares where walls of cotton wool shut one in, then recede before one's touch but remain.

But that's not the end of the story. Mum continued to wait, needing further instruction about her transit to England. She heard nothing for days and asked her sister Alice, whose husband was a colonel in the Army, for help. She toyed with the idea of moving to Calcutta where it would be more comfortable waiting surrounded by family and friends. But on 27th November Alice sent a telegram from Delhi: *Stay there signals flying on your behalf certain success soon keep smiling.* Waiting and more waiting. Mum complained that batches of doctors were being repatriated yet she was not amongst them. On 8th December, Alice sent another telegram: *Congratulations triumphant signal gone your area for proceeding Deolali.* Going to her Area Headquarters she can find no trace of a message about her. For the whole of the next week Mum occupied herself with knitting:

One thing only has progressed, the sleeve of my jumper.

Finally, on 15th December, according to letters posted from the Families Unit, Deolali, Mum had at last arrived in the transit camp to wait for her passage to England. I wondered if Deolali has anything to do with the English slang word *doolally*. I Googled the term and find that it does indeed refer to the madness that many army personnel felt waiting in transit for their journey home.

But Mum, instead of going mad having to wait yet again, was quite upbeat.

The whole business of documentation and medical examination only took ten minutes. It can be very pleasant to laze and read or knit. I suppose after a week or two I shall feel lonely. Just now I feel curiously satisfied and content. The food seems good. It is all one step nearer.

However, frustration set in rapidly:

Isn't it typical of the Army which never knows what its left hand is doing while waving the right about in fine gestures. There was a boat on 17th but no families went at all. I hope I get on the boat of the 27th.

Not one for moping, she spent her time in her usual activities: knitting; reading; and going to the cinema. She described a trip into the town of Deolali where she inevitably found her way into the three bookshops and wandered back by a Hindu temple high on a hill.

Mum's final letter is written on board the ship. She embarked on 28th December 1945 and reached Southampton in January.

But Dad was nearly not there to meet her. Mum's cable announcing her arrival came in mid-December, but on that same day Dad received an order that he was to be posted to the Rhine.

The Ministry of Labour was the body dealing with mobilisation. So Dad played a trick and picked up the phone, saying to the switchboard: 'Get me the House of Commons Ministry of Labour please.'

A few minutes later a voice from the Ministry of Labour came on the line: 'Richard Croft speaking.'

'This is Southern Army HQ, Staff Officer Blake speaking,' said Dad. 'We have a problem – a Captain F C Wray, who was due to be demobilised in a few days, has been ordered to the British Army on the Rhine.'

'Give me his details.'

Dad gave him his own details! A few days later his demobilisation papers came through. He was free.

Mum and Dad moved to Cambridge where Dad studied for his teacher training certificate. He got a job as senior English master in Solihull Grammar School and they moved there in August 1946.

An important part of the jigsaw is still missing. After Mum's misgivings about how Dad's family might receive her, what was that first meeting really like? Recently, I was chatting to Dad's brother, Uncle Harry, who said that when Dad first brought Mum to meet his parents in High Wycombe, dressed in her best sari, she wasn't made to feel welcome.

'They had no idea she was Indian,' he said which I find difficult to believe. Had Dad really never mentioned this in his letters? 'Frank hadn't told Mum and Dad that he had got married and was bringing his wife back from India. He returned home alone and was waiting for his demobilisation. Our parents were expecting their young man home alone and here he was a married man. I didn't know their reaction exactly as I was away, but I gather they were upset. Your mum arrived soon after Frank's demobilisation and I gather that the meeting with the parents didn't go well.'

I was shocked. That Dad hadn't told his parents he was getting married wasn't the impression I got from Mum's letters. But going through them again, I realise that perhaps the relationship was never made clear by Dad and perhaps his parents just hoped it was casual. What a start to married life! I just can't imagine how Mum felt.

Mum's letters indicated that she was desperate to have a family of little Wrays but now married and settled she found she couldn't get pregnant. Living in Solihull with Dad teaching full-time and no prospect of a baby, she took a part-time job as a children's doctor with the post-natal clinics. One of her jobs seems to have been to visit the nurseries of adoption agencies and the idea of adoption must have arisen in my parents' minds. They registered as adoptive parents, but as a mixed race couple how suitable would they have been considered by the agencies?

Piecing together the story from Ellen's adoption records it seems that Mum might have seen Elizabeth, as she was known, on a medical visit and inquired about her adoption. Elizabeth hadn't been seen as adoption material but when Mum told Dad about her, he wrote to the agency asking if they could visit her. According to the file he had pointed out that 'a child of their own might have been slightly coloured'.

Our parents were viewed as ideal because it would mean Elizabeth would be racially 'matched', and the secrecy around adoption could be preserved. A letter in the file states:

We were not considering Elizabeth for adoption because of her mixed blood but it just happens that the prospective 'mother' is a half-Indian half-English doctor and her husband is English. They feel that if they had been able to have a child of their own, she would resemble Elizabeth and they are therefore very attracted to her. They are particularly nice people. The husband is a schoolmaster – they are both young and very fond of children, and will be able to give Elizabeth a splendid home.

And so our family was born.

6. BROWN BUM

My first day at Yenton primary school. Mummy took me to school and all I remember is a lot of five-year-olds crying their eyes out because their mummies were leaving them there. I thought they were stupid. And I didn't like the noise. All we did was play in a sandpit which I thought rather a waste of time because I was used to playing with mud in the garden, putting it into cups, letting it dry out and then upending the dry mud to make a cup of my own. Is this what school life would be like? I thought I would read books and learn to write stories. After about an hour in the sandpit, another teacher came into the room and said to my teacher, 'Camilla can go to the class above because she can read really well. She's already been in nursery at the school where her father teaches.'

So I went into that other class. There were about twenty children there, all bigger than me and they all knew each other. I felt a bit strange, but at least they were reading books. I stayed in that class until junior school and did OK but never really gelled with the other children who all seemed cleverer than me. I don't remember making a special friend at infant school.

One day when I was about seven, a woman came into the classroom asking whether anyone was Jewish and Miss said, 'Yes, Camilla is, aren't you, Camilla?'

'No. I'm not Jewish,' I said.

'Then what are you?' said Miss, just like that.

'I don't know, but I'm not Jewish,' I said. I thought Jewish meant praying in a different way like the Catholics and not having to go to morning assembly, and as far as I knew my parents didn't mind me going to assembly.

Miss was laughing with the woman and said, 'We'd better ask the parents. Camilla's definitely not English, I mean look at her.'

I kept quiet about Mummy being Indian. But it was the first I'd heard about maybe being a different religion and not having to go to assembly.

When I went home I asked Mummy, 'There was a strange lady came to class today asking whether anyone was Jewish and Miss insisted I was, but I'm not, am I?'

'No you're not,' Mummy laughed.

'But then she asked me what I was and I didn't know what she meant. I thought Jewish was a different religion but I don't really know what religion we are.'

'We're not really any religion,' said Mummy. 'But we don't object to you going to the school assembly, if that's what's bothering you. Daddy and I were brought up as Church of England – the English Church – and that's what the school assembly's about.'

'Why were you brought up in the English Church if you're Indian? Why do Indians go to the English Church?'

'Well, India is a huge country with many different religions. Most Indians are Hindu and they worship many gods and goddesses, even in the form of animals like Ganesh, the pottery elephant your uncle gave you. Some are Muslim and they worship one God, just like the Christians.' Noting my frown, she added, 'I know it's very complicated. And to make it even more complicated, my mother, being English, was from the Church of England but my father was what we call a reformed Hindu which takes a bit of the story from the Christians and a bit from Hinduism. They call themselves Brahmos.'

'So am I one of them? I think I'd like to be because it's a mixture, just like me,' I said, eager to at least have an answer that made a bit of sense, even if it all sounded muddled.

'You can be what you like when you're older, Polly.' Polly was my family nick-name, or stable name, as Mummy joked. 'I'll tell the teacher we're both Church of England.'

'But you're not really, are you? I want to be Brahmo.'

I never heard any more about being Jewish or Brahmo from Miss. I just kept my mouth shut. Soon afterwards I transferred to the junior school anyway and Miss stayed teaching the infants. The move wasn't far – just into the next building but it was a big move. There were three classes to each year. I was in Class 1.1 which was the top class in terms of test results. Some of the kids I'd been in class with before were with me and some came from the class below – the sandpit class. I thought maybe I wouldn't feel different in this class but I did.

Maggie and Pamela were two familiar faces from my infants' class and I tried to make friends with them. We were about eight. They took me under their wing but they were like my sister, always giving me tasks to prove myself. I don't think I ever really made the grade. One task was to cross Chester Road. Yenton school bordered this busy road which ran right out of Birmingham. Its four lanes of traffic were divided by a large grassy stretch planted with trees. It was actually easier to cross than a smaller road because you only had to look one way before you reached the grassy bit and then the opposite way to reach the other side. At four o'clock after school there weren't many cars on the road so I found it easy to cross this main road. I think traffic built up an hour afterwards when people like Mummy and Daddy were coming home from work. So I passed that task.

Another question they asked me was to identify various weeds which I couldn't do. They identified chickweed for me and told me to remember it for the next day which I did. To this day, wherever I see this long straggling green weed with small white flowers, I want to pull it up, even out of other people's gardens.

But it was the word 'sex' that stumped me. I didn't know what it meant so Maggie said my task was to find out and tell her the next day. I asked Ellen and she said, 'It means male or female.'

'What do you mean – male or female? Which is it?'

'It means if you ask what sex someone is, the answer must be male or female. I'm female and so are you. So's Tibby the cat. But Patrick and Tim are male.'

I didn't really see the point of this. Why have a word to describe both male and female? It made no sense to me when all you had to ask was 'Is it a he or a she?' The word just passed out of my memory and I couldn't remember it when Maggie asked me what 'sex' meant the next day. All I could remember was that Tibby was a girl just like me.

'My cat is a girl sex,' I said, knowing this wasn't quite right.

'You idiot,' Maggie said. 'Sex is nothing to do with your stupid cat. It means "love". Still, you have two out of three of the tasks right so you've passed and we'll be your friends.'

So the three of us would roam around for about an hour after school. Our favourite place was an old ruin of a house on Poppy Lane. We had discovered a loose panel in the fence at the side of the house and had moved it to see what was beyond. We caught a glimpse of a house through the brambles. The roof had caved in and the brick walls were covered in ivy. There didn't seem to be anyone there so we removed the fence panel, taking care to replace it after we had cautiously climbed through the gap. It was late May the first time we went in and the brambles were frothing with white flowers. I knew these would turn into blackberries at the end of the summer, as I was an expert blackberry-picker. Several fruit trees rose out of the wilderness, already growing tiny, beautifully formed pears and apples. I told the girls we would have to return to pick the fruit. I went first to beat a path to the house, getting really scratched by brambles. I was lucky not to tear my dress because how would I explain that to Mummy? I could hear a blackbird fluting and a chaffinch bowling. Mummy had taught me the blackbird's song and I could make a passable attempt at imitating it. And Daddy had likened the chaffinch's trill to a cricketer running up to the crease and releasing the ball: *trr-trr-trr-keboing*. Even though the house was derelict it felt surprisingly friendly in the sunlight. It had only three walls and the roof was a skeleton exposing wooden rafters. Out of the floor grew nettles which we were careful to pick our way through, although of course we got stung. We made our way to the staircase which lacked a few treads and climbed up to explore the top floor of the cottage. This was quite tricky since many of the floorboards were missing. There were two rooms upstairs, both with tiled fireplaces – I seem to recollect them being green. The glass had fallen out of the windows which gave out onto the wilderness.

'This house must have been bombed,' said Pamela. 'I jolly well hope the bomb isn't still here. Perhaps we ought to look for it downstairs.'

'I don't think any bombs still remain,' I said, confidently. 'We used to play on those old rusty army tanks left up on the hill where the Lyndhurst flats have just been built and never found anything. Mummy used to go with us at first and I'm sure she wouldn't have let us go if there'd been any risk of bombs.'

We made our way downstairs to explore the other two rooms and the kitchen which still had an old cooking range.

'This is really fab,' said Maggie, poking around and opening the oven door. 'Do you think we could get this going again? We could toast marshmallows and pretend we were in an Enid Blyton story.'

'Might be a bit risky, Maggie,' replied Pamela, putting her head right in the oven. 'People would see the smoke and think the place was on fire. We don't want to be discovered by the fire brigade.'

We realised we needed to go back home for tea or our parents would be wondering where we were. 'Let's come tomorrow and explore some more,' I said. We returned two or three times a week to Ivy Cottage, as we called it, and there was never anyone there. Pamela used to sketch while Maggie and I would gossip about school. We didn't play together during the summer holidays. At least I think Maggie and Pamela did, but they didn't invite me and Daddy was funny about having visitors to the house so I never dared invite them. We returned in September to see if the blackberries had ripened. But we found a new fence had been built with barbed wire on top of it and a notice saying DANGER KEEP OUT.

When I was eight I wore round pink wire National Health specs and my hair was cut short with a side parting. The longer part was held back with a kirby grip; I didn't even have a pretty hair-slide. At school I wore pale short-sleeved dresses with a cardigan to keep me warm. My feet were clad either in sensible Clarks or Start-rite lace-up shoes – which our family called clod-hoppers – or sandals.

In the first year of junior school our year teachers organised a fancy dress party. I asked Mummy what I should wear.

'Well, it will have to be something we have already because I haven't got time to make you a costume.' Mummy sounded irritated.

'Perhaps I can wear one of the skirts that Uncle Sanjay gave me, but what would I be?' I had a selection of skirts that he had given me from India. My favourite was a yellow wrap-around skirt with navy blue elephants tramping around the bottom of the material, intertwining their trunks with the tail of the elephant in front. I would wear this at weekends, though not at school. But I thought that perhaps this wouldn't be considered fancy dress. I had a fancier skirt which I loved but it was so dressy I had never actually worn it. It was long and consisted of patterned tiers of intricate embroidery on a pale background. Each tier was separated by a row of tiny mirrors sewn on with red chain stitch. My skirt came with a short sleeveless round-necked top which was closely fitting and had similar, but less intricate, embroidery and mirror work. And to top it all off there was a pillbox hat embroidered with gold metallic thread.

'Yes you could wear the Rajasthani outfit and be a gypsy,' said Mummy, sounding relieved that I'd come up with an answer that wouldn't involve her making anything. 'Did you know that the gypsies came from Rajasthan years ago, so you really would be a genuine gypsy.'

I rushed upstairs and put on all three items. I thought I looked wonderful, although my Clarks sandals didn't really go. They were too clumpy. I especially liked the hat as it covered my hair and showed off my small face. Too bad about the specs. I came downstairs to show myself off to Mummy.

'It's great, although the hat's a little big for you. It shouldn't really be covering your ears, but never mind. It's a beautifully made hat and no one else will have anything like it. So it's worth wearing it.'

When the day of the fancy dress party came, I packed up my costume in an Indian shoulder bag to take it to school. I placed it carefully on my peg in the corridor next to our classroom. I was lucky that I didn't have to be too careful with it as my clothes weren't made out of the sort of material that crushed. Most other people had their costumes on hangers on the pegs. I could see an awful lot of tutus.

We sat on the floor of the hall in a big circle, two rows deep. We went out in groups of five to the classroom next door to change, and then each group was called in one by one to walk round the circle showing off their costume. The first little girl was dressed as a fairy, in a pink ballet tutu dress, green wings and a wand. She was followed by two more fairies, also with tutus, wings and wands. One of the two boys in that first group was dressed as a pirate with a silver sword made out of cardboard; the other as a teddy boy with jeans and an oversized blue jacket, obviously his father's. A few girls were dressed as black cats in black tutus, cat masks and long woolly tails. The boys were pirates, wizards or teddy boys, with a few clowns thrown in. Pamela was the most beautifully dressed girl with a black and white polka dot skirt, cinched in with a wide black belt and silver buckle, topped with a pink satin short-sleeved blouse. To complete the rock and roll look she wore a matching polka dot scarf. With her shoulder length dark hair she really did look glamorous. She also was the best at showing herself off to advantage, twirling around the circle so that her skirt flared out.

As we were grouped alphabetically I was the last child to be called. Mrs Payne announced me: 'Gypsy Girl.' I came running in, trying not to look self-conscious and being careful I didn't trip over my long skirt. I didn't know how my costume would go down with the teachers who were giving prizes for the three best dressed children. My skirt and hat were so different from any other costume and they might not understand what a gypsy was – certainly not a gypsy from Rajasthan. I only had time to do one circuit before we were asked to sit down. I was pretty pleased with my look and asked Pamela and Maggie what they thought.

'It was so boring,' said Maggie. 'Mrs Payne kept calling "Gypsy Girl" but you didn't appear. She had to call you three times. And to be honest, your dress is weird with all those funny mirrors on it. And your hat is far too big. Where on earth did you get it from?'

'It's from India, where the first gypsies came from. My uncle Sanjay brought it last year.' I tried not to get too upset by Maggie; she was always saying something horrible to me.

Now came the judging. The Headmaster, Mr Hodge, and each of the five teachers had three votes and they couldn't vote for the same child more than once so the prizes were given to the three who got the most votes. The six of them each called out three names.

'Camilla, Pamela and George,' the Headmaster called out.

'That's fantastic,' I whispered into Maggie's left ear.

'That's just a bit of joke,' she said, quite loudly. A few of the others around us sniggered.

'Let's just see,' I answered.

Not one of the teachers voted for me, so perhaps it was a joke. Perhaps Mr Hodge felt sorry for me for being rather an ugly and awkward kid, or perhaps he knew I was adopted and felt he should reward me by voting for me. Anyway, as I thought, Pamela, the rock and roller, came first and Gordon – dressed as an amazing clown – got the second prize. I wasn't surprised as his mother was wonderfully creative with clothes, making lovely dresses for his sisters. I knew this because his father was the music master at Daddy's school and I'd been to visit his house a couple of times. Third prize went to one of the tutu fairies wearing a glittery headdress and spotted wings.

After that I decided I didn't really want Maggie and Pamela as best friends. I think they only tolerated me and I'm not really sure why. It was fun playing after school, especially in Ivy Cottage, but I thought I would like to have a best friend of my own. I gravitated towards a girl called Karen Lawson. Karen was a small girl with a thin face and mousy brown hair. She also wore pink National

Health glasses – a point in her favour. We took to hanging around together at break time, mostly playing wild horses which was not really a game but just consisted of charging around the playground tossing our imaginary manes.

George Edwards was the most popular boy in my class. His curly blond hair might have made him look angelic if it weren't for the impish look in his eyes. He had a sidekick, Paul Abbott, also blond but with straight hair, an open look and engaging smile. We didn't wear uniform at our primary school but many of the boys dressed in white shirts and grey shorts and some of them wore a tie. George and Paul were popular. Teachers liked them because they weren't shy and answered questions in class. They always seemed to be surrounded by a group of friends in the playground. I didn't have much to do with any of the boys. Most of them were rather horrid, calling me names – a familiar taunt was 'Four Eyes'. But George and Paul were never part of the rowdy crowd.

I was surprised when they approached me in the morning break one day. It was icy and the previous day someone had made a long slide which had frozen solid overnight. Our playground sloped gently down from the back of the school building towards the bike shed. Once it was fairly smooth you could make it slidier by levelling it with your bum, but that was cold and got your clothes wet. If the day was really cold the best way to make it really slidy was to pour water on it and wait for it to freeze. We would get water from the sinks in the toilet block using our empty milk bottles as containers. The teachers didn't like this so kids had to sneak in to the toilets in ones and twos, hiding the bottles in their pockets. If this was done at the morning break on a cold sunny day, by dinner time that slide would be sparkling like diamonds. Then it was ready for a test run. The ones who made it tried it out first, but usually they were pretty good at letting everyone have a go. Each slide belonged to the class that had made it so sometimes there were rival slides across the playground which made negotiating a normal path back to the classroom treacherous. In winter I had perpetual scabby knees from falling over on ice. I didn't like sliding at all as I knew my balance was hopeless. The only way I would try it would be to crouch down but often I couldn't get any momentum that way and so stopped halfway along the slide to jeers from my classmates.

'Hey, Camilla, Gorilla – you're hopeless,' was one taunt. Or: 'Trust a Four Eyes. She can't even see.'

I was lurking near the back of the queue with my friend, Karen, when George and Paul approached me just as Karen had taken off down the slide. I didn't mind talking to them as it meant I would lose my place in the queue and might not even have to go down the slide as the bell for the end of break was due.

It was Paul who spoke first. 'Even though it's winter, you're still brown.' I wondered whether this was a compliment. I stood up straight.

'Yes, I'm always brown but I'm even browner in the summer.'

'But are you brown all over?' said George.

I thought this was a ridiculous question. 'Of course I am. What do you think?' I had stepped right out of the slide queue by this time and was waiting for the bell.

'Well, is your bottom as brown as your face?' continued George.

'Of course it is,' I said, falling right into their trap.

'How do you know? You can't see it.' I didn't see the point of this conversation and wondered when the bell would ring. I was getting really cold standing around answering silly questions.

'Can we see your bum and then you'll know.'

'How would you do that?'

'We'll meet you in the bike shed after school and you can pull down your knickers and show us.'

Although I didn't like the sound of this, I agreed just to shut them up. I'd got the whole afternoon to think of a way of avoiding them. The more I thought about it that afternoon the more I was determined to outwit them. Most kids didn't have a bike so there were only about twenty or so in the shed at any one time. And on a snowy winter's day I doubted there would be any. There would be no protection from other kids meaning that George and Paul could easily get me in a corner and force me to pull down my knickers.

When the bell went at 3:55 pm I was one of the first to get out of the classroom. I ran down the corridor to the cloakroom, quickly seizing my navy gaberdine mac from its peg. I hated that mac – a hand-me-down from my sister and far too big for me. Not only was it too long but it was so wide that when I tightened the belt, the coat folded into untidy pleats and made me look as if I was dressed in a bundle of rags. It also had a huge hood which I never wore, even if it rained. But I was so glad to be wearing my hideous coat that afternoon. I flung it on hastily, tying the belt and fastening the hood to cover my hair. I would be completely unrecognisable, I hoped. I took care to wait until a bunch of children from the year below left and I mingled with them as we made our way through the playground. They must have thought me odd but didn't say anything.

There were two ways out of the school that we children could use; the main entrance which fronted straight onto Chester Road, was banned for pupils. The first, to the south of the school, was only a five-minute walk from my house, and the second, to the north, was up a long alley leading to Orphanage Road. I used this way out more as I often visited Roger's mother, Mrs Fairchild. Roger was Patrick's friend and his mother took a liking to me and would let me help her bake the cakes she made every day for her family. Other times I would just go home on my own using the back door which we left open. That day I walked up the long alley which was probably a mistake as it meant I had to cross the treacherous playground ice and pass the bike shed. However, I knew I would get a warm welcome from Roger's mother and she lived just round the corner of the alley – if I could get that far.

I passed the bike shed. No one was going in or out. I reached the bottom of the alley. It was narrow with wooden fencing on either side. I was almost running and soon left behind the group of kids I'd mingled with. I didn't know who was behind me. I couldn't hear anything. The snow deadened the sound of footsteps. It took all my nerve not to turn round to see if George and Paul were following. I started to run. I reached the top of the alley, turned the corner and rushed into Roger's mother's house.

'My goodness, you seem to be in a rush today. Did they let you out of school early?' she said.

'No, but it was cold so I ran up the alley.'

'Well, at least you didn't slip,' Mrs Fairchild said, checking my knees. 'I'm making poppy seed cake so come and help me.'

When I got home that evening I didn't tell my parents about the incident. I was ashamed I'd let it happen. The best thing was to try and forget about it. But I was worried sick about what George and Paul would say the next day and whether they would force me to show them my bum. After a terrible night I dreaded school but there was no way Mummy would let me stay at home if I didn't have a cold. She would know if I was lying. George and Paul approached me in the classroom as soon as I entered.

'Hey, what happened yesterday?' said George. I shrank into my chair. 'We saw you walk up the lane with your hood up. As if we wouldn't recognise you. I guess you're too scared to go with us to the bike shed.'

'I'm not scared,' I said bravely. 'But I just don't want to do it. And that's that.'

At that point Mr Evans came in to call the register and the two boys returned to their desk. I felt sick all morning but during the break the boys didn't come up to me and never spoke to me at all about the incident after that. I'd earned their respect by standing up to them. My childhood ended that day. I was all of ten years old.

7. EGGS

At Erdington Girls Grammar School I didn't feel so isolated. At EGGS being 'slightly coloured' wasn't such an issue. At first Maria Bianchi, who was Italian and darker-skinned than me, kept calling me 'coloured girl, ugly girl'. When I told Ellen, who was in the sixth form and a prefect, she had a word with her and Maria never called me names after that.

Our desks were in alphabetic order and I first made friends with Rita Young who sat behind me. Rita broke her leg badly just before Christmas. While she was in hospital for several weeks I didn't have a particular friend to play with. I was sitting on the steps at the back of the school one lunchtime watching a group of girls playing hopscotch. They had all gone to the same primary school further down the road from me at Yenton, so I didn't feel I could join their group. I was freezing from sitting on the cold steps. One of the group, a girl called Helena, saw me sitting there and asked me to join them. She had short mid-brown hair and a long nose and a perpetually puzzled expression. She and I became best friends from that day on. Fifty years later we're still friends.

We had great fun that first year. Our form teacher, Miss Cuffley, had an ancient black and white cocker spaniel called Penny who she brought into school. Penny stayed in the staff room but needed a walk at lunchtime so Miss Cuffley asked if any of us wanted to walk her. Helena and I volunteered. We both loved dogs but only had cats. Our school grounds were extensive. A tarmac playground lay at the back of the school and behind that was the playing field where we played hockey and had a go at athletics. There were tennis courts beside the playing field and at the far end of the grounds was a large garden, known as the New Gardens, tended by the sixth formers. The New Gardens were strictly out of bounds to everyone else but we were allowed to walk Penny there. They were large and divided up into allotments for small groups of sixth formers. The girls used to grow easy things like salads, spinach and potatoes, and also grew candy tuft and marigolds. Much of the garden was a tangle of weeds and brambles with small paths in between, although there was a grassy meadow area which the school gardener mowed sporadically. There was even a small pond full of frogs. Penny loved roaming around the gardens and so did we. We pretended the space was an island and I sketched out a map. We'd been learning about medieval crop rotation in history, so we named the allotments Three Fields; the brambly area was the Wilderness; the meadow became the Savage Heath; and the pond Frog Lake. But we couldn't think of a name to call the island. I took our sketch home and asked Patrick for some ideas.

'We can't think of what to call it – the Island without a Name perhaps?'

Patrick loved Latin, a language we hadn't yet started. 'What about calling it *Sine Nomine* then. That means "Without a Name" but sounds better in Latin.'

Helena and I both liked the name so we agreed to make and colour a proper map of our island. We got a large sheet of cartridge paper from the local stationers and as Helena was the artist she followed my sketch redrawing the map, painting it in shades of green, brown, red and blue. She wrote in the names of places in her beautiful curly handwriting using a dip and scratch pen – pens with nibs that we had to dip into inkwells. I got matches from the mantelpiece in our living room and we burned the edges of the paper to make it look old. That was the first of our ambitious projects.

When we were about fourteen we were learning both French and Latin. We decided to make up a language for ourselves so we could make rude comments about the teachers and other pupils without them understanding. My parents had friends who were learning Esperanto. I was intrigued by this and I found a *Teach Yourself Esperanto* in a second hand shop. We used it as a model for our language: Pricades. It had only three tenses: present, past and future. Nouns weren't gendered and there were no synonyms. Why have extra words when one would do? We soon became quite adept in Pricades, using it on top of the bus to talk about how rude and stupid the boys from Aston Grammar were. We bought two small hardback books and wrote up the grammar in one and the vocabulary in another.

'Why don't we put the books on the language shelves at Hudson's?' said Helena, referring to the big bookshop in central Birmingham.

'Don't be daft,' I replied. 'How would the staff know how much to charge for the books? Anyway, we'd have to make another copy.'

We wrote a novel – in English – as one of our projects, or at least started it. Fans of adventure stories and mysteries, we'd been reading John Buchan novels. We concocted a story about a young man, Stephen, who found his brother dead in his flat in Birmingham. Worried that the police might accuse him of being a murderer, he escaped to Scotland by train. We plotted out the story together but wrote sections alternately. Poor Stephen was left to fester in the woods after Chapter Three, having left the train in the pouring rain somewhere in the Pentland Hills, near Edinburgh. I still have a copy. It's a shame we never got any further.

At school I never made a big thing about being adopted but I did tell Helena when we were about thirteen. We were hanging around in the gym. Maybe it was raining and we'd been sent inside instead of being chucked out into the playground. We were leaning against the floor-to-ceiling bars at the side of the gym, chatting. Helena was talking about her latest visit to her nan who lived in Hastings.

'Have you got another nan?' I asked, dangling from one of the bars with my arms above my head.

'No, because Dad's mum died when I was about eight,' Helena replied, looking up at me.

'Well I've got lots,' I declared proudly, 'But I only know one.'

'What do you mean?' asked Helena with a deep frown on her face.

'Do you know what being adopted is?' I said, lowering myself from the bars.

'Yes, it's when someone's parents can't keep them but they get adopted by other parents. Are you adopted, then?'

'Yes. So I could have eight grandparents – four from my parents and four from my real mother and father. But actually I only know Dad's mum and dad. My other grandparents died before I was born.'

'That's millions!' giggled Helena, completely unperturbed by the adoption story. 'What about Ellen? Is she your real sister or what? And Patrick and Tim – what about them?'

'No, none of us is related. I heard that my real mother was Swiss and my father was Indian but I don't really know any more. I'm not that bothered.'

It had never occurred to Helena that Patrick couldn't have been the child of our parents, since he was obviously African. I guess she'd never met anyone from India or Africa. We were all coloured children to her.

It was not strictly true that I wasn't bothered about my adoption. As a family we must have been told we were adopted when we were really small. I grew up knowing I was adopted, and was told that my mother was Swiss and my father Indian, although I never knew whether this was true. But beyond this snippet Mum and Dad never talked about adoption and what it might mean for us. They were our real parents and we were no different from other families. Except I did wonder from time to time. Was I more like my mother or my father? Black hair from my father? Light coloured skin from my mother? I would sometimes wonder where they were. Did they split up? Did they have other babies? Were they in England, Switzerland or India? Did they think about me ever? I would imagine my mother as a version of myself, oval face, a dimple in her cheek and a sudden grin that would light up her brown eyes. But she would have long blonde hair instead of my black hair. Blonde hair and brown eyes are really striking, I thought. My father remained a complete blank in my imagination.

Helena and I were close all through our school years. With her friends, Debbie and Vicky, we formed a little gang which we named the Bean Brigade. We played together and made up adventures. I can't remember what we played but we stuck around together until the end of the fifth form when Vicky and Debbie left school. Helena and I entered the sixth form.

One day our sixth form teacher, Mrs Oxley, took me aside, 'You and Helena don't take part in form activities. You ought to have more friends. It's not good to go around with one friend.'

I just stared at her. I had no idea what she meant. We didn't really have form activities other than drama and both of us always took part in any plays.

Mrs Oxley looked flustered. 'I mean it's fine having a best friend but you both need to mix more with the other girls.'

'We do. Helena and I go around with Eve a lot. But the other girls go to Mothers Club on Saturday nights and my dad would never let me go there.'

Mrs Oxley didn't know how to reply to that so she just said, 'Oh, I see.' I trotted off to the sixth form common room. I felt as though I'd done something wrong so I never did tell Helena and I don't know whether Mrs Oxley gave her the same talk.

Mothers was a popular club above a furniture store in Erdington High Street, opening the summer we entered the sixth form in 1968. My classmates raved about the music. Fleetwood Mac, Tyrannosaurus Rex, The Who, Steppenwolf and Jethro Tull, as well as the wondrously named Bonzo Dog Doodah Band, all played there. No way would my parents let me go. Apart from the fact that 'it wasn't our sort of music' which was classical, Dad was adamant he didn't want me going anywhere where I might mix with boys. I was puzzled. What was the big deal about boys? It wasn't the lack of boys that I minded – I had two brothers which was enough to be going on with – but it was the restrictions imposed on me that made my life hard.

When I was fifteen my flute teacher said there was a vacancy with the Birmingham Schools' Orchestra so he wanted me to audition. I asked Dad who said, 'No.'

'Why not? Mr Willard said I'm the best flute player he's had in years and I would easily get in.'

'We don't want you going into central Birmingham alone for the rehearsals,' replied Dad.

'But you let me go into town by myself all the time. Besides, Tim played the violin there for a couple of years. I really don't understand.'

'Well he's a boy,' he shouted. 'It's different for you. You just can't and that is that.'

I went crying to my brother Patrick.

He paused and thought for a minute, running his fingers through his curls. 'I think it's something to do with Tim. He used to play in the orchestra and chased one of the girls who didn't think much of him. She went to her mother and her parents approached ours, telling them to get Tim to lay off.'

Mr Willard was disappointed.

'What, does your mummy ask you to help her on a Saturday morning?' he asked sarcastically. I couldn't think of anything to say.

I was desperate to join the orchestra. I knew that it was important to play with other musicians to get a sense of timing and rhythm. As a family we would go to the theatre, films and concerts regularly but Dad seemed to think absorbing these cultural activities was enough. Listening to records and the radio was fine but the graft of practising the piano and flute wasn't appreciated. I wasn't a natural piano player and had to practise hard to get my Grade Eight. I was struggling with a particular phrase in the allegro of a Mozart piano sonata when Dad yelled, 'Why do you have to play that over and over again?'

'Until I get it right,' I said, surprised that he didn't understand. Did he not know that concert pianists did the same thing?

Our parents didn't seem to want us to mix outside our nuclear family. We visited Grandad and Granny in Buckinghamshire three times a year and we usually met our uncle, aunt and cousins there.

I didn't enjoy these visits as it was a long journey in the car and I got travel-sick. And when we got there we were fed a conventional English dinner, complete with overcooked vegetables that you could swallow whole without chewing. Mum never cooked us Indian food but apart from the Sunday roast she would vary our dinners, cooking ratatouille and spaghetti bolognese before these dishes became standard fare in England. And she never overcooked the vegetables.

Mum's relatives only ever came to visit us. We never went to them. As we hardly had anyone else come to the house their visits were memorable. They would stay a few hours – never the night – and we would feed them copious amounts of tea and Mr Kipling's cakes. Mum's sisters, Eva and Alice, both lived in India when we were children and visited us in Birmingham for the day, travelling from London, at least once a year.

Alice and her husband Sameer lived in Kasauli in the foothills of the Himalayas and visited about once a year, sometimes bringing Timin their son who was a few years older than Ellen. Uncle Sameer had been a General in the Indian Army and in 1962 warned that the Chinese were massing their army on the Indian-Chinese border to invade, but he was ignored and sidelined. When the invasion happened, Sameer resigned out of principle. He and Alice turned to training polo ponies, including those for our Royal Family. It all sounded very strange to me and somewhat out of our league. I found it hard to imagine such a life. When I was about ten, Timin came more often as he was studying engineering at a technical college near Birmingham. He would always turn up in grey trousers so we called him 'Grey Tim' to distinguish him from our Tim. He had a sports car he'd fitted with a multi-toned horn. It was a real thrill to be allowed in the seat beside him teasing the neighbourhood dogs with the horn.

Mum also had some distant relatives, Sanjay and Nandita, who came to visit. Sanjay was a jolly character, always laughing. He was tall with a fine moustache above full lips and twinkling eyes. Nandita was a beauty, her hair plaited and coiled behind her head, with a beaming smile. She wore western clothes with flair – a pretty jacket made of black silk, covering a soft cotton top which she wore with loose velvet trousers. They were very fond of Mum, remembering her as a young woman in the 1930s when she was working in Calcutta as a doctor.

Sanjay worked in the tanning industry in Calcutta and it was from him I learned that Indian leather was made from buffalo hide as the cow was sacred and could not be killed. Nandita's family had started the Duckback range of waterproofs, a clever name I thought. That company had invented a waterproofing system in the 1920s and now produced raincoats, hot water bottles and gumboots. I thought it would be great to have some of their gear but for some reason she never brought us any.

They always brought a present for each of us kids. One was an Indian rag doll I called Aisha. The only other doll I had was a 'teenage' doll called Marigold with long curly blonde hair, proper breasts encased in a bra and a variety of dresses. Aisha was dressed in a red and green sari. They made an incongruous pair. Sanjay and Nandita also brought us clothes, including a yellow and blue elephant skirt, as well as the Rajasthani outfit I wore to our school fancy dress party, and a beautiful green short-sleeved shirt patterned with tigers and elephants which I almost wore out one summer.

Mum came alive during these visits. She loved them. Her eyes would sparkle at the talk of what it was like living in India at that time. But there was no contact with her sisters' families other than these visits. We weren't encouraged to know our cousins even though Aunt Eva asked me to stay with them on a holiday in Mallorca one summer. Of course I wasn't allowed to go. Looking back, I wonder whether the concentration on our nuclear family had to do with being adopted. Were our cousins really our cousins if we weren't related by blood?

Our style of family living was very formal in comparison with my classmates. I could drop round to Helena's house and be fed baked beans on toast and watch her TV but I had to book an appointment for her to come round to our house. And, as Dad always wanted to know where I was, I could only drop by Helena's house after school for a short while. Our role in life was to pass exams so why did we need friends or extended family? I sensed we were different all through my teenage years. Love and affection must have been there but it wasn't physical – no hugs or kisses. My dad would say, 'We love you very much,' but it was mostly after he'd just denied us something, as though saying he loved us would somehow compensate for that. Home life wasn't cruel but regimented.

Recently Patrick and Ellen were visiting me at home and we started talking about our upbringing. They agreed that our family life was rather exclusive and isolating. The only thing that mattered to our parents was academic achievement.

'Do you think it was because we were adopted?' I asked.

'The Boss definitely called the shots,' Ellen said, referring to Dad. 'I think that could have applied to any middle-class family in the '50s but I think he over-compensated because we weren't a natural family.'

'Yes,' said Patrick. 'But it could also have been because he came from a rural, working-class family and his efforts got him to university. He wanted to make sure we did too. Also, I think he wanted our adoptions to be successful, and success to him was academic achievement so we were all pushed to achieve high exam marks.'

'I found that hard,' I said, my brow crinkling with the memory. 'I always had high exam marks but never got congratulated. It was as though there was never any doubt I would do well but it would have been nice to be told, "Well done."'

'I think we were treated slightly differently because we were adopted,' Ellen said, ever the analyst. 'I think our family was viewed by our parents and adoption workers as a social experiment. And their experiment had to succeed.'

'Well, I guess it did,' I said. 'We all went to university.'

'But in a way it didn't,' said Ellen. 'None of us could wait to leave home, and when we did we hardly ever came back again. We were never a close family and drifted further and further apart as the years went on.'

This was true. Ellen lost almost all contact with us for a few years after graduation. Patrick went to Madagascar for a couple of years, Tim left to teach in France, and after my undergraduate days in Edinburgh I left to study for a masters in Canada. The only time we came together after that was at the funerals of our parents.

Perhaps Ellen was right and we were part of an experiment. On the outside we were a close family unit, but looking back it seems to me that our parents viewed us as part of their job and that didn't include much affection. Coming on top of six months in a nursery, we may have unconsciously absorbed a sense of emotional dislocation which made it difficult to form close relationships. We just about keep in touch but it's out of obligation rather than love. Of the four of us Tim has been the only one with long-term partners, but most of those relationships broke down because of his refusal to have children. And unlike us, he didn't seem to have any friends other than his current partner. I, like Patrick and Ellen, find it easy to make friends, but have never lived with a partner.

I think there might be something missing in my life that made me want to search for my birth parents. On the other hand I am who I am and meeting my birth parents wasn't really likely to change that.

8. CALENDAR GIRLS

There are New Towns that work and New Towns that don't. Glenrothes is one that doesn't. To start with the nearest train station is Markinch which is several miles from the centre of town. And, in the early '80s, when I worked there, the buses weren't great either. It was an early post-war New Town, built in 1948 with no thought of how to build a community. The atmosphere seemed cold and clinical.

But when I was in my twenties and needed a planning department to sponsor my part-time planning diploma, I couldn't afford to be fussy. I was unemployed because I had finished my contract as research associate working on an experimental geographic information system. Fife Regional Council Planning Department was willing to take me on as an information officer and give me day release to study. It was my first permanent job and I was grateful for that. But it wasn't easy. I was the only woman planner there. Men posted girlie calendars in their offices. I didn't like it but as a young woman and the newest recruit I felt I couldn't object. The women in the admin office had no such qualms. They complained vociferously and often.

Doug seemed puzzled. 'It's not as if we view our wives like that. I can't see what's wrong.'

Tess asked, 'What about us?'

And Cheryl said, 'Yes, how do you view us?'

Doug replied as an afterthought, 'Well of course not you either.' He added, 'You don't understand. We don't know these women in the calendars. They're just very attractive.'

The calendars stayed. Tess and Cheryl retaliated by pinning up the centrefold of *Playgirl*, a hunky blond with all his bits showing – naked except for a gold chain.

Doug objected. 'That's different from our calendars.'

'Yeah, that's offensive,' said Pete.

'Why's that then?' said Cheryl.

'We don't know him but we think he's very attractive,' said Tess.

Doug and Pete couldn't think of an answer. So all the posters came down.

I bonded with the women after that and we used to go to lunch together every day and swimming once a week. It didn't do much for my relationships with the planning boys.

Not something I regretted then and certainly not twenty years later when I got a fuller picture of their predilections. I was visiting La Isla del Sol whilst hiking in Peru. I chatted to one of the young men in our group and asked him what he did at home.

Nicholas said, 'I work as a planner in Scotland.'

'Where?' I said. 'I used to be a planner there for a couple of years.'

'Fife,' said Nicholas and, used to explaining where that was, continued, 'It's a small region just north of Edinburgh.'

'Oh my god. That's where I used to work in the late '70s,' I explained.

'No way!'

'Yes, I used to work with a guy called Danny in the information section. I became the computer expert. We had one of the first desktop computers – an Apple – and I transferred all our data onto that and taught everyone how to use it.'

'I work with Danny now. He's still there.'

'No! After all these years.'

'Yes, you may know some of the others too. I'm the youngest planner.'

'So you have the same job as I had all those years ago.' This coincidence was more extraordinary than the views of the Andes mountain range on the horizon.

'How are Doug and Pete?' I asked. 'Are they still there?'

'Oh,' said Nicholas. 'That was a bit of a scandal. There was talk of employees downloading porn on their computers. Doug left under a cloud. His wife left him soon after that.'

'Bloody hell!'

I remembered the girlie calendars and I wondered what the models would have thought of this incident.

I did my stint in Fife, gaining my planning diploma in 1982. Big cities were the place for me so I applied for jobs in Glasgow and London. After two or three interviews I got a job as a planner for Southwark Council, moving to London in September to work in the Policy and Information Section.

After two years working in the Planning Department, I moved to the newly created Employment Development Division. A number of inner city councils were setting up units to promote local industry and employment, and to help unemployed people into training programmes. Southwark Council was at the forefront of this trend. Three of us moved over from planning after being interviewed for the new jobs and about ten others were newly recruited from elsewhere. It was an exciting time. The Business Section established a new programme to help local people create their own jobs – mostly these were in the restaurant/take away trade, but some were really different. One guy was in the forefront of the computer music industry and wanted to market the programme he'd devised for composing music. I don't think my colleagues understood what he was trying to do and he didn't really have the contacts to market his programme. They didn't give him a grant which I think was a real shame. Another section set up in-house training as well as careers advice. The Women's Carpentry Workshop was a real success, enabling women to train in woodwork skills and get jobs in the construction industry. I was employed as a policy advisor, along with Steve, my colleague from the Planning Department. We developed and evaluated the whole programme and suggested new initiatives. The Division funded voluntary groups and it was our job to monitor them. I had about four projects under my wing, including the Job Share Project. Three local women were promoting the idea of job-sharing, giving practical tips on how to approach employers and how to work with their job-share colleagues. And I monitored the Southwark Trade Union Support Unit which promoted trade unionism across the borough. I enjoyed meeting with these groups and helping them to sort out things like a constitution and other funding applications. I was also invited to events organised by the groups.

The Trade Union Support Unit ran a small event to support the Kent miners during the Miners' Strike and I attended that after work one evening. About fifty people came along. While we were eating snacks and talking, a raffle was held and I bought several tickets. Now I never usually win raffles but this time I won a bottle of whisky which would have gone down very well as I'm partial to a wee dram. But there was a shout from behind me, 'Give it to a miner!' I turned round to greet the group of miners and said, 'Of course.' They cheered and clapped loudly as I handed over the bottle.

The Employment Development Department was a diverse group of about fifteen people, certainly more diverse than the Planning Department in terms of the make-up of its staff. I became more at home with my identity as a black lesbian, and others easily accepted me, particularly as I was well known for supporting equality in the National Association of Local Government Officers (NALGO), the trade union. Being black was to be part of a community fighting racism and being of mixed heritage was accepted, or should have been. It was about how you identified yourself rather than the shade of your skin.

Our boss decided that his staff needed race equality training so he employed a Racism Awareness trainer to give us an in-house three-day course. Racism Awareness Training was known as RAT and was a popular method of training in the public sector. The session was held in our training room in a fine Georgian building converted to offices. It was a rabbit warren of narrow corridors, creaking stairs and oddly sized rooms. We, black and white, congregated around the coffee urn with the sun streaming in through the windows waiting for the trainer. For some reason the boss didn't attend. We wondered why not. Didn't he need to know how to address racism?

Gloria, the trainer, arrived ten minutes late which didn't impress us. She asked us to sit in a circle and to introduce ourselves. As we all knew each other really well we didn't have to do any of the excruciating icebreaker exercises beloved of trainers, such as trying to find people with a birthday in the same month as you. She introduced herself as a qualified RAT trainer and told us the aim of the course was to challenge racist attitudes within ourselves and others. I thought it was the council practices that needed changing as well as individual attitudes, but maybe that was just my trade union background.

She went round the circle saying to each person she identified as white, 'Give me an example of when you've been racist.' The first person she asked was Steve.

'When I get on a bus and there are only a few places, I always try and sit next to a white person,' said Steve, crossing his legs to expose the holes in his fashionably ripped jeans.

'OK,' she said. 'What can you do about that?'

'I could look around and sit next to a black person,' said Steve.

I really didn't want to hear this – if Steve deliberately sat next to a black person on the bus, would that make a difference to racist policing or employment discrimination? I was too timid to challenge either Steve or the trainer.

Then she asked Ron, one of the older men in our group, who always dressed in a three-piece suit and a tie. Ron paused for a good minute, looking uncomfortable. He mumbled, 'I don't have many black friends.'

'And what can you do to make friends?' said Gloria.

'I live in little village in Kent and there are only one or two Indian people in the village. So I don't know. Is it important?'

'I'm not going to answer your questions. But I want to know how it makes you feel only having contact with black people through your work.'

Next she had a go at me. 'But I'm not white,' I said inside my head. I was too afraid to say this aloud to Gloria as I didn't know her position on where mixed race people sat in black politics. So I went along with her.

'I'm a union rep and I was supporting an Asian admin worker who worked in the Social Services department. Asha – as I'll call her – was upset at not being shortlisted for an interview for a promotion in her section and wanted to challenge management. I looked through Asha's application and found she hadn't said how she would address equalities in her job. I told her she must address all the points on the person spec and she turned to me, puzzled and said, "How would I do that in an administrative job? All I do is answer the phone, filing and making sure that the social workers follow up the cases within a certain time limit." I asked Asha whether she used any Asian languages on the phone and she said sometimes she did. "So that might be something you could say," I said.'

'That's not an example of you being racist,' said Gloria.

'No.'

There was a moment of silence. I felt I had to fill it.

'It's just that the new equal opportunities application form doesn't say explicitly that you have to address all points on the person specification. I was thinking of raising it on Staff Side – the group where the trade union reps negotiate with the personnel department. I thought it was a good example of trying to change things.'

Gloria didn't say anything but just moved on, forcing us to listen to more guilt-ridden stories.

After mid-morning coffee, she got us to form two groups – black and white. Although Heather, Jackie, Ed and Parminder, the other black workers, were fine with me identifying myself with them, Gloria hadn't seen me as black and I felt that she would give me a hard time if I put myself in that group.

'Things aren't as simple as black and white. I have a black identity but I'm Indian and European. Where's my space?' I really wanted my black colleagues to say 'Your space is here with us'.

Cold silence. Instead of convincing my colleagues to support me I must have sounded confused. I walked out.

Returning to work on Friday, no one talked about the course so I didn't know what happened after I left. I felt very vulnerable as I couldn't share my feelings with my black colleagues. I wanted to know what they thought of me but was afraid of the answer.

'I sat beside a black person on the bus this morning,' said Steve. 'That's nice for you,' I said.

That evening I went for dinner at Gary and Pat's who lived a couple of streets away. Working closely together with Gary on the Southwark trades union Staffside negotiating team we became friends and the three of us regularly cooked dinner for each other. Gary was a bit of an odd ball with long, very red, straggly hair and a liking for detective fiction. He had a room lined with secondhand crime thrillers that I liked to borrow. I talked about the course and my reaction, reliving it all again. They hadn't experienced a RAT course but said it must have been difficult for me. I can't remember what we had to eat that evening as I kept dwelling on the course.

At around 11 pm I left to walk home. To get to my house I had to walk down a road that ran past an old Victorian cemetery and over a railway bridge with no houses on either side. It was pretty spooky but normally I felt safe as I was a fast walker. That night I was still thinking of all the unresolved issues the course had brought up for me and was walking slowly with my head down. I heard loud footsteps behind me and the clink of a chain.

'It's only someone walking a dog,' I said to myself. 'Nothing to be afraid of.'

I didn't turn around to look or walk any faster. The footsteps rapidly approached and I started to feel afraid. But rather than running I slowed down even further. Surely he would pass me. He didn't. He leaped onto me, forcing me to the ground. My glasses fell off.

'I want to kill you,' said the man, stamping on my glasses.

I froze. I didn't think to scream and I certainly didn't struggle. He hit me several times and I curled up in a ball in the road. A couple of cars passed but no one stopped. Finally I found my voice and screamed. I didn't yell for help but just let out a high-pitched wail. I could hear some people approaching but they weren't hurrying to help me. My attacker saw them coming and ran off. I ran over the bridge, up the pathway of the nearest house, and frantically rang the bell. I remember it having a silly chime like an ice cream bell but it worked because a few moments later a woman came to the door.

'Can you call the police?' I gasped.

'What happened?' the woman said, looking rather frightened.

Before I could answer the couple on the road came up to see what was happening.

'So she wasn't with him,' said the man to the woman, as if it would have made it all right if it had been a lovers' fight.

'I was attacked by a man who has now run off. He broke my glasses and I can't see anything.'

The man at the door turned back into the house and called for the police. A few minutes later the police and an ambulance turned up. I guess I must have looked pretty bad to the man if he had asked for an ambulance.

'Just come into the ambulance for a chat,' said a policewoman as though it was a tea party. I sat on the steps to the ambulance and someone threw a blanket over my shoulders. But the police did take me very seriously.

'Can you tell us what happened?'

'I can't say much at all. I was just walking home from friends round the corner when a man attacked me. I don't understand what he wanted as he didn't take my bag. He just said he wanted to kill me.' I was shaking but not crying.

'You didn't know this man?'

'No, of course not. He was following me over the bridge and then he pounced.'

'Can you describe him? Was he white or black?'

'I really couldn't say. It was such a shock. I could hear a chain jangling behind me but I didn't see it and he didn't hit me with it. I can't remember anything. I think I'm OK now though.'

One of the police officers spoke into a walkie-talkie and described the incident to a colleague. 'We've got a white female around thirty who's just been attacked in St Asaph Road by the bridge. The attacker ran off in the Nunhead direction. Not got a description of the man. See if you can get anyone.'

One of the paramedics said to the police, 'We think she ought to go to hospital. Bruising is beginning around her eyes. If she was kicked on the floor she may have concussion. That needs to be checked.'

So off I went to Lewisham Hospital, my one and only ride in an ambulance. I didn't have to sit in the waiting room at A&E but was shown to a cubicle with a bed. I sat on the bed for ages until a doctor came to check. I was totally disoriented because I didn't have my glasses. The doctor checked me out and said he wanted to admit me for the night as I might have concussion. But I was much more concerned to get my spare glasses which were at home.

'I'm sure I didn't lose consciousness,' I said to the doctor. 'I really want to go home. It's too busy here and it's frightening.'

'Don't be ridiculous,' he said, as if to a child. 'This is a hospital. It's perfectly safe. The police just had a word with me and they said you weren't at all coherent when they spoke to you.'

'I'd just been attacked, for god's sake. Of course I wasn't coherent. I am now. Please, I can take care of myself.'

'Can you get someone to check you every few hours?' the doctor said, pulling on his stethoscope.

'Yes, my flatmate will do that, no problem,' I lied. I was desperate to get home.

'OK. But if you get any headaches in the next two days go to your GP immediately. You're going to get two magnificent black eyes tomorrow but they'll fade. It's a head injury that we have to be really careful about.'

And so he discharged me and I took a taxi back home. It was three in the morning. I was shaken but recovered enough to feel really angry about what had happened. Normally I'm really careful at night, not letting people walk right behind me. I can only think

I was giving off vulnerable vibes to my attacker who must have just had it in for women he saw as weak.

9. WOMEN AT REDS

Not long after I moved to London, in 1982, I bought a flat in Brockley, Lewisham. I joined the Labour Party and started going to the monthly ward meetings, soon getting friendly with Carol, a cheerful character and dedicated Labour supporter. Carol and her partner, Marilyn, lived in a third floor flat in a red-brick block built by the London County Council in the inter-War period. I took to dropping in for tea and socialist chat every few days. Imagine my surprise a few months later when Marilyn rang me up to say she was leaving Carol and would I look out for her and make sure she was OK.

True to my word to Marilyn, I met Carol frequently, going to events at the Albany arts centre in Deptford, films, or just hanging out in the local pub. We'd set aside one Saturday night to spend together when she rang me.

'Do you fancy going to a poetry reading? It's run by this arts organisation Apples and Snakes and showcases new poets. It's in Battersea so it's quite a way but I'll drive us.'

'Not sure whether poetry is my thing but let's give it a go anyway.'

That night only one poet stood out. Halfway through the evening a young black woman of mixed descent came on stage. She had a strong Glaswegian accent and said, 'I'm going to read my poem 'So You Think I'm a Mule'. And off she went.

The poem is about being asked by local people where she comes from. When she answers Glasgow a look of incredulity comes over their faces. 'But you're not pure,' they speculate. At which Jackie Kay retorted:

I'm no mating of a
she-ass and a stallion
no half of this and half of that
to put it plainly purely
I am Black…'

I was bowled over by this poem which exactly reflected my feelings. After the performance I went up to Jackie.

'That's the story of my life too. I'm mixed race and people are always asking me where I'm from. That poem is brilliant. Thanks so much for writing it.'

'I'm flattered,' said Jackie. 'Sometimes it's hard to know what your audience thinks out there and it's really important to me to know that it says something to you.'

Over the next few years, Jackie wrote a number of plays that were produced in London and I always made a point of saying 'hi' to her when I went along. In 1991 she brought out the *The Adoption Papers* – a volume of poems written from the point of view of the child, the birth mother and the adoptive mother. Patrick heard her reading them on the radio and immediately rang me and I told him about 'So You Think I'm a Mule'. We've both been following Jackie's career ever since.

In autumn 1983 Carol and I started going to the Lewisham Deptford Constituency women's section, a bunch of about eight women who wanted to influence the local Labour P arty to be more open to women's issues and to get involved in local and national women's campaigns. We met once a month in a community centre in Deptford. I remember getting involved in the National Abortion Campaign, campaigning to protect abortion rights – I think this particular campaign was to protect the rights of young women under sixteen to access contraception without their parents' knowledge. The group wasn't all about campaigning though, and we became friends. There was something about this small group that made me feel I belonged. We frequently went out for a meal or a drink.

One evening a few of us were sitting in the bar at the Lewisham Labour Club which was situated in Limes Grove, an alleyway off Lewisham High Street. I don't know who raised the fact that there was nowhere for women to socialise in south London. If we wanted a women-only space we would go the women's night at the Drill Hall in Bloomsbury but it got crowded. We thought it would be good to have a space for all women to get together more locally to socialise.

'Why don't we set up a women's night here at the Labour Club?' Carol said. 'It's a decent venue, and the bar is a lovely space. With the hall downstairs we could hold women's events and benefits. I'm sure we'd make a profit for the Labour Club too.'

'What a great idea!' said Cynthia. 'We could hold it on a night when there's not usually many people here – perhaps mid-week.'

'What would we call it?' I queried. 'Women's Night at Lewisham Labour Club isn't very inviting.'

'We ought to think who it's for – who do we want to come? Is there a Labour element to it? Are we just thinking of Labour members?' said Frieda, always the logical thinker.

'I think it ought to be for all women but its name ought to reflect that we want to attract socialists,' Carol said.

We all bought another round of drinks and chucked around a few names: Labour Women, Red Women.

'I've got it,' said Frieda with a broad grin. 'Women at Reds.'

'That's so catchy,' Cynthia said. 'And it assumes the sort of women who come to a "red" venue will be "red" themselves.'

So we had a night, we had a name. All we needed was to persuade the Labour Club Committee to let us organise it. Carol agreed to present our case which was based both on the lack of women's venues in south London and on the profit we might raise for the Labour Club. Cynthia and I went along to give her moral support.

So one Thursday evening, we met the Labour Club Committee, a group of about four or five men, at the Club. We knew most of them so didn't expect to find the meeting intimidating or difficult but thought we'd have to be really convincing as the idea would be strange to them.

Carol started off. 'We think a women-only space would be popular among local women who want a quiet drink without being hassled, to meet other women in a friendly environment and to chat about local issues. We'd advertise through the ward meetings and I'm sure we would attract other Labour members, but it would be open to all women. We plan to open on a Wednesday night when it's quiet here normally and we think we could raise more money for the club in profit from the drinks.'

After listening to this, Fred said, his brow knitted, 'I don't really understand the need or even the attraction of a women-only space. It's not as if this bar isn't welcoming. Women frequently come here. And why do you want to exclude men? Isn't it divisive?'

Cynthia replied, leaning forward, 'Yes, it's a cosy bar but we think the argument for a women-only space is strong. There aren't any other spaces for women to go to in south London. We think it would be a great venue for women to meet like-minded women. I remember when I first came to London I didn't know many people. I joined the Labour Party and I knew about this Club but I wouldn't have come here on my own. I met other women through the women's section and we come here regularly now.'

Fred replied, 'OK I get the rationale and you're right, Wednesdays are normally fairly quiet. But do you really think you'd get more than a few women? Would it be worth it?'

'We think we'd get more than the few who come on Wednesdays,' I said. 'We also plan to hold benefits in the hall and that would raise money for campaigns as well as a decent revenue from the drinks.'

After arguing back and forth for about half an hour, Dave, the committee chair, said, 'OK I think you've made your case and there's no harm in trying it out for a few weeks.'

We trooped out, jubilant. 'That wasn't too bad,' said Cynthia. 'Now the real work starts. We've got to do a constitution and prepare publicity. Also, who's worked behind a bar before? I haven't a clue about measures and stuff.'

'I've done a stint behind the Labour Club bar and I'll show you what to do. It's quite straightforward if it's not too busy,' said Carol.

'But we want it busy!' I said.

Having got our night, we divided up the tasks: drafting a constitution and thinking about how we would advertise the Club. I spent a couple of evenings helping behind the bar so I'd be ready to do it on our opening night.

The evening of the opening, five of us got down to the Club at 6 pm to make sure everything was welcoming. Cynthia brought small posies of flowers to put on the tables. I seem to remember they were chrysanthemums as it was autumn. We knew all the other women from the women's section would be there and some of us had invited women from our workplaces. It was nerve-wracking – like waiting for your own party to start and thinking no one would come. But five or six women from the women's section and the Deptford wards were there on the dot at seven. They all opted for a beer and stood at the bar chatting about how great it was.

By eight there were nearly twenty women; by nine the bar was crammed with about thirty-five women in varied attire: baggy jeans with rolled up bottoms, Indian print tops, stripey jumpers, work-like dresses and skirts, tee shirts printed with *Nicaragua Must Survive*, donkey jackets, quilted jackets, Doc Martens, boots, high heels, perms, short hair, long hair with a small plait down the back. What a success! It was busy behind the bar and sometimes quite difficult.

'A rum and black, please,' ordered a dark-haired woman.

'Sorry, but what's that?' I said with a smile. 'This is our first night and I'm not familiar with all the drinks.'

'It's rum and blackcurrant cordial,' she said. 'And make it with dark rum, please.' I had no idea how much blackcurrant cordial to put in with the one measure of rum so I just said, 'Say when.' Apparently it didn't take much cordial to make the rum and black. I was now an expert!

At 10:30 we called last orders and started clearing up. By 11 pm the last of our visitors had left. When we cashed up we found we'd raised well over £100 which I'm sure was more than the usual Wednesday night takings. Women at Reds was about to take off.

Our next endeavour was to run a benefit for the Kent Miners' Support Group, women who supported miners and their families during the 1984 Miners' Strike. We ran a disco in the hall downstairs, using a woman DJ that Glynis knew. I wasn't much into disco music so I can't remember the records she played but I do remember renting huge speakers for the night and hauling them to Limes Grove in my car. We placed a number of tables, cabaret style, at the back of the hall leaving the front for dancing. We displayed a Kent banner as well as one of our own from the Deptford Women's Section. It was in suffragette colours: purple and green on a white background and, as I knew from carrying it on a Pride march, it was incredibly heavy. By 8 pm the hall was packed with about twenty women from Kent and sixty or seventy women from south London. We'd invited the Kent miners' wives to give a speech. They talked about joining the picket lines, the support they gave to local families, and about organising demonstrations in Leicestershire to support the miners there.

We had to work hard to run Women at Reds and the monthly benefit events. Our committee grew to about eight women. We shared the tasks and had frequent planning meetings. But the way wasn't always smooth. Although we raised enough money to enable us to provide childcare, some women brought their older children. Carol remembers a discussion about the upper age of sons attending the evenings – she thinks we settled on thirteen. She also remembers the arguments we had about whether transgender women were welcome and being shocked when there were some women who didn't think they were. We won that argument though – what on earth was the rationale for not welcoming them?

Relationships were made and broken at Women at Reds as I was to find out. Imani who used to come there said she was attracted to my leggings at first, 'Indian Ocean leggings. Blue with purple and green sea plants. To me you were a sea nymph.'

I loved the way she looked too with her short hair cut close to her head. No straighteners or braids for Imani. I told her that I was a member of the Asian Women Writers' Collective and had written several reviews and poems for magazines such as *Spare Rib* and *Feminist Review*.

'So how about writing a book review for me?' Imani edited a magazine on African current affairs. We settled on Toni Morrison's *Beloved*, meeting several times to discuss and refine my review, though to be honest the draft I submitted the first time was good enough for publication.

Not long after the article was published she asked me to celebrate New Year with her and her flatmate in Hackney. The three of us ended up having a little ceremony involving writing the thing or feeling we most wanted to get rid of on a scrap of paper and letting it fly up the chimney. I don't remember what I wrote. I stayed the night but can't believe I slept on the sofa!

Soon after that we were at a book launch together and I asked her back home. I was laughing about the sofa incident and she said she'd felt uncomfortable because her flatmate didn't like me for some reason. Imani was a warm person, curvy and cuddly. She fitted me perfectly. However, I never liked to go back to her place because of her flatmate. The relationship fizzled out after a few months.

Why did that relationship fail? Was it because of a fear of abandonment? One of my colleagues who had adopted a little girl, Mara, aged two told me about attachment theory. When she sent her to nursery so she could interact with the other children, she discovered that little Mara had started calling her favourite nursery worker 'Mum'. Alarm bells rang in Anna's head. She'd learned about attachment theory in her adoption classes. 'What's that?' I asked.

'It's important that children learn to bond with their main carer as soon as possible,' said Anna, sounding like an adoption counsellor. 'Mara hasn't really had a close relationship with an adult in her life before and it's vital that she identifies me as Mum.'

'So having two mums is a bad thing?' I said. 'What about a father and grandparents?'

'We were told in our adoption classes that children can cope with more than one adult relationship but they should have a primary relationship. If they don't, it can damage their sense of trust forever.'

'That sounds a little dramatic,' I said, not quite believing her. 'Mum is only a name, after all.'

'Well, how do you feel about relationships?' Anna said candidly, almost challenging me. We were great friends and talked a lot about adoption and reunion but this question of trust and relationships hadn't arisen before. It was scary.

'I don't know how I feel. But now you mention it I don't like to rely on people, it's true. It's not that I don't trust them though. I just don't like to ask anyone for help.'

'What about relationships?' Anna was insistent, pushing me.

'Well, you could be right. I don't trust people not to leave me. So it's easier not to have a relationship.'

A light had gone on. I think Anna was right. There were incidents in my early childhood where I can remember my parents showing affection and there was no doubt they cared about me deeply, but was it real parental love? I think I'd never experienced that one-to-one love of a mother for her child. Perhaps I had only ever experienced that special bond with Margareta who had abandoned me. So how could I replicate that bond in adult life?

But Imani did feel right for me unlike my short-term relationships with boyfriends who usually had another girlfriend somewhere in the background. Or actually in the foreground since they always left me for their own true love. I think they sensed I wasn't the committed type and that I held them at arm's length. But I wasn't really sorry about my situation. Those boyfriends just didn't feel right so I was never that bothered when they left.

No truer word was spoken by another friend when I was moaning about my lack of a love life.

'Well, Kamila, you don't try very hard!'

I had to laugh but my friends were right. If only I knew how to.

10. SHAKTI

A plethora of voluntary organisations grew up in the '80s, funded by the London boroughs as well as the GLC before its untimely demise, courtesy of Maggie Thatcher. In Southwark we had the Community Development Unit which funded local self-help groups on Southwark's large council estates, and the Council also set up Women's, Race and Lesbian and Gay Equality Units which funded equality groups. They were an important aspect of my life. Not only was I a funder through my job, I was also on the management committee of Deptford Women's Employment Project. And I was a regular user of Peckham Black Women's Group. Through this group I met Joanna and Diane, both mixed race lesbians. Joanna's mother was Cantonese and Diane's was Taiwanese. Our interaction was mostly through food.

Joanna was a brilliant cook and we were filling our bowls with delicious noodles, tofu, fish and vegetables when she said, 'I saw an ad in the Peckham Women's Centre for something called the International Lesbian and Gay People of Colour Conference – ILGPOCC for short! What a mouthful. It's to be held at the University of London in a few weeks time. I think it's likely to be big. Do you fancy going?'

'Sounds good – a conference for people like us!' I said. 'And I like the American term People of Colour. What's the aim of it?'

'Just getting us all together, I think,' replied Joanna. 'There's lots of workshops. Let's register.'

So on a Saturday in the autumn of 1990 we turned up to Senate House for the sixth ILGPOCC. There were hundreds of us and we filled the imposing Beveridge Hall to capacity. Funnily enough I can remember the atmosphere of excitement and the look of the hall with its wooden panelling halfway up the walls, but I can't remember anything about the speeches and plenaries. Whether this was because I was still numb about my mother who had died two weeks previously I don't know. What I do recollect clearly is going to a workshop with people of mixed parentage. There were about twelve of us, including Joanna, Diane and myself. We talked about being doubly invisible – as lesbians and gay men and as black people, especially if we were, like me, light-skinned.

'It's fantastic being here with all of you,' said Ulrich, who was of Italian and Pakistani origin. 'I feel I've come home. I feel I can be honest. Let's meet again.'

So we circulated a list of phone numbers and addresses. Ulrich took the list and I said I'd help him. A week or so later I rang him to coordinate what we'd do and he said we could meet at Body and Soul, an organisation for people living with HIV, where he was a volunteer. I set up a database and address labels on my Amstrad home computer and sent out invitations. Body and Soul had a comfortable room full of colourful beanbags and a couple of sofas. About eight of us met there one Sunday afternoon to discuss what we wanted to do.

'Will we be a campaigning group and if so what's our campaign?' said Diane.

'I think it's too early to say. At the moment surely we just want to meet others like ourselves and raise our visibility in society,' said Savi.

'So it's really a support group. There's plenty of issues to talk about that I for one have never talked about ever, not to my partner, not to my family,' Terry said. 'I'd welcome a space just to talk about how I feel.'

'What are we going to call ourselves?' Ulrich asked. 'We definitely don't want a name like ILGPOCC.'

Eventually, after trying to think of acronyms for lesbians and gay men of mixed heritage (Leg-Midge?), we agreed on Mosaic which would reflect our mixed origins. Advertising ourselves through the Pink Paper and by word of mouth we rapidly built up a national membership which ran to about one hundred members at its peak. A core group continued to meet monthly at Body and Soul where we would bring articles and discuss issues that came up for us.

Some of the women noticed that magazines such as *Cosmopolitan* had taken to using women of mixed heritage as models and one woman found a *Guardian* article pointing out that the recent prevalence of light-skinned models of fashion magazines, was perhaps a new form of racism: the 'right' blend of exoticism and blackness. The acceptable face of black.

'And we're all supposed to be beautiful aren't we?' I said flicking through the article. 'Which reminds me of a funny story. A few years ago my flatmates invited a couple of friends of theirs for dinner. I don't know what sparked off the conversation but the guy was talking of Anglo-Asians as being stunning. I said that I was of European and Asian mix. "Oh I didn't mean you," the guy said. What was I supposed to say to that!'

Another project we did was to find lesbian and gay and/or mixed race role models: Stephen Twigg, the MP, Merle Oberon, Bob Marley. Terry put together clips of films with a mixed race focus. One film that sticks in my mind is the 1959 film *Imitation of Life*, the story of a daughter, Sarah Jane, who rejects her black mother and passes as white. The end of the film, when Sarah Jane runs after her dead mother's coffin, still moves me to tears. Perhaps because it reminds me of my own situation, although the roles were reversed. It was my adoptive mother who passed as white in her later years while I was desperate to be identified as black.

We talked about being of mixed race but hardly ever about being lesbians and gay men. We were already members of other lesbian and gay groups but for most of us the only people of mixed race that we'd ever met were our brothers and sisters so it was wonderful to talk about our own experiences. The colour of our skin wasn't meant to be important but it was. We spoke of the difficulties of being accepted as black if we had light skin, but that white people saw us as black and we did experience discrimination. Or if at some stage of our lives we passed as white, what did that do to our sense of self? That's why it was important to meet others like ourselves.

Most of the Mosaic members said they'd never talked about being mixed race, not even with their siblings. But I had talked about identity with my brother Patrick. Unlike me he wasn't so hung up on his mixed race heritage. Mum had told him that his birth father had gone back to Sudan and hadn't been willing to support him. Patrick said, 'I knew I had African genes, but I'm comfortable being mixed race British. I look African but I don't feel African. I've been brought up in a British culture.'

'So do you feel Black British then?'

Patrick pondered this question, plucking at his straggly beard. 'Well, it's not really black or white, is it?' I nodded and he continued, 'It's refreshing to see that mixed race is now a recognised category in official statistics.'

'Oh god, yes. Before that we had to tick the Census box saying "Any Other Ethnic Group"'and then fill in what particular mix we were.' I recalled how that made me feel – like an invisible person or an alien.

One of Mosaic's more social activities was to take ourselves off on a Saturday night to Shakti, the Asian club at the Lesbian and Gay Centre in Farringdon. I would wear my most glitzy *churidar kameez* which I'd found while rooting around shops in Southall. The *kameez* was a fuchsia colour, decorated with a leaf pattern in gold which I wore with a gold churidar – tight fitting trousers that were narrow at the ankle – and a gold and fuchsia *dupatta*. We'd get there around 10 pm when it was full, but not too crowded, and we could observe the talent and get ready to dance the night away. We'd enter the hall and there, amongst the dancers, would be a contingent of young – and not so young – men clad in saris, immaculate make-up and nails highly polished. There would be DJ Ritu at the far end with her records and mixers. She would play classic bhangra as well as bhangra-influenced disco music overlaid with other dance rhythms – house, hip hop and reggae. For me Shakti was the

Saturday club I'd never visited as a teenager. If I couldn't dance to Pink Floyd at Mothers Club in the '60s, now I could discover the new British Asian sounds of Bally Sagoo and Apache Indian. Here too was a dance style I could enjoy – arms waving and body moving to the beat. For the boys in saris the movements would have to be quite sedate. Some would wear their six yards of silk with great panache, but others looked distinctly uncomfortable as if they were afraid their sari would unravel on the dance floor, although I never saw this happen.

For me Shakti and the London Lesbian and Gay Centre epitomised the '80s – an era of radical politics in British inner cities which allowed minority groups to flourish and many of us to become visible, even to ourselves. I could push the equalities movement forward in my work as a council officer and political activist, but my real identity was expressed in groups like Mosaic, and at fun nights at Shakti. From the frightened feminist and invisible black lesbian of 1982 I emerged into the '90s with a fighting spirit and new confidence.

11. AN UNEXPLAINED LUMP

In June 2000, I was visiting my friend, Paula, who had moved to Boston with her partner. On my final day we went clothes shopping, but I couldn't squeeze myself into my normal sized clothes – American size 10 – so ended up not buying anything. I wasn't fat, but my stomach seemed distended. I convinced myself that the lump I could feel was muscle gained from my regular morning stomach crunches.

On my first day back at work one of my colleagues was rather rude. 'You've been eating too many burgers over there.'

'Not likely – Paula and Neil are vegan and the only "meat" we ate was in a Chinese restaurant where they make all the vegetables look like chicken or pork.'

'Well your stomach's sticking out.' She got up and came to my desk, saying in a whisper, 'You can't be pregnant surely?'

I changed the subject. It was a Thursday so I said, 'Doing anything nice at the weekend?'

I can't remember what I did that weekend other than worry. If my colleague could see that my stomach was fatter and I was finding it difficult to fasten the zip on my jeans, then this thing in my stomach must be real. First thing on Monday I called my GP to get an urgent appointment and was given one for 11 am. I didn't see my regular doctor, but this one, Dr Kasper Zoldak, was very kind.

'I've got a lump on one side of my stomach,' I said. It doesn't hurt but what can it be?'

'Let's get you up on the table. Now, I'm warning you that my hands may be cold.'

He felt all over my abdomen, pressing down with firm fingers. I winced at the shock of his cold hands, although the actual examination didn't hurt. After a few minutes of prodding he said, 'Well, you're right. You have got a lump there, somewhere in the area of your left ovary. I can't tell what it is so I'm going to get you an appointment with a consultant gynaecologist. Let's look at consultants who have the shortest waiting list.'

'Ah, here we are: Professor Murray at the Royal Free. He seems to have a waiting list of only a week. I'll get you the earliest appointment possible. I'll also arrange for an ultrasound scan at the same hospital so that it'll be ready on the system when you go to his clinic.'

'What could it be?' It suddenly dawned on me that I really did have a lump and Dr Zoltan obviously thought it was serious.

'Don't worry, it could be an ovarian cyst – they're quite common and almost always benign, but they do need to be investigated.'

Don't worry! An ovarian cyst that may or may not be benign. That's fucking terrifying.

Fifteen minutes later I was on the W7 bus to Finsbury Park when Dr Zoltan rang my mobile. 'I've got you an ultrasound appointment at the Royal Free for Thursday afternoon. They'll write to you, but just in case you don't get the letter, go to the first floor. An hour before your appointment you should drink 750 ml of water – and don't pee.' You've got to be kidding. After all that water!

Of course, when I got home that evening I looked up ovarian cysts on a health website. And Dr Zoltan was right: ninety-eight per cent of ovarian cysts in pre-menopausal women are benign. I relaxed somewhat as I knew I wasn't in that two per cent. All my life I'd eaten all my fruit and veg, I didn't smoke and I exercised regularly. That's what they tell you, isn't it? Cancer is all about your lifestyle.

My Thursday appointment was at 2 pm so I spent my lunch-hour drinking my 750 ml of water. I don't drink water at the best of times and it took me a while to get through that amount. If my stomach was extended before, now I was positively bloated and uncomfortable. I couldn't think of anything but peeing all the way to the Royal Free, a half-hour journey, but thankfully once there I didn't have to wait long at all. A young woman wearing a plain blue headscarf took me through into one of the ultrasound rooms. I got up on the table.

'Hi, I'm Mirza,' she said. 'I'm going to make rather a mess of your tummy with this gel. I'm afraid it's rather cold.'

But the room was warm and the gel wasn't as cold as Dr Zoltan's hands. There was a monitor by the side of the table which was turned away from me so only Mirza could see it. Strange. I was sure that pregnant women in *Casualty* watch their baby in the womb during the ultrasound.

I was convinced I didn't have cancer so I cracked a joke with Mirza. 'Can I see the baby?' But Mirza was frowning with concentration, wielding her transducer stick and sending sound waves pulsing into my abdomen. I continued, 'You're supposed to say, "Yes you might be pregnant. You look much younger than your age."'

After a moment, she gave a small laugh, but didn't say anything. Minutes passed in silence. Mirza alternated between looking at her weird plastic wand and the monitor, looking more and more worried. Ten minutes passed, twenty minutes, thirty minutes. Was this never going to end? Finally she said, 'That's us done. I can see a cyst on your ovary. I just need to make a phone call. Would you mind waiting outside.'

I didn't know what to think and Mirza was clearly not giving me further information. But it looked bad from my point of view. I rushed to the toilet and then waited on the bench outside. After a few minutes she came out with an envelope.

'Look, rather than wait for your doctor to see the scan I think it's a good idea to get you down to Emergency now so that you can get a fast-track appointment to see a consultant. You may have to wait a while but it will save you time in the end.'

She handed me the unsealed white envelope. She hadn't even tucked in the flap. I started shaking. I walked down the corridor to the stairs, stumbled down a few steps before I clutched the banisters and practically slid down the three flights to the Emergency Department in the basement. I crouched on the final step and removed the letter from the envelope.

I have just completed an ultrasound on this patient, Ms Zahno, and have identified an ovarian cyst on her left ovary which could possibly be malignant. I will send the scan now to the Emergency Department, but please get a gynaecologist on call to conduct preliminary tests and book her into a clinic next week.

I got up from the stairs in a daze, pushed open the door and entered the Emergency Department, thrusting the letter into the hands of the receptionist.

She went through the ritual of checking all my basic information again, 'Name, date of birth, address, GP. Please wait.'

I waited in the small and very crowded room. Fifteen minutes later a triage nurse saw me and said I would have to wait until they could reach a gynaecologist who was on call within the main hospital. I waited. And waited. Although I always carry a book with me for emergencies I couldn't read. I couldn't think. I went to the toilet which was extremely dirty. There was a buzz of indistinguishable conversation round me which I couldn't absorb. After three hours I was called into a cubicle and a gynaecologist introduced himself as Dr Halkias, a registrar to Professor Murray. He examined my abdomen, took my blood and said:

'I've booked you into Professor Murray's clinic on Monday afternoon.'

'What's happening to me?'

'I can't say anything yet but you have got a cyst which needs to be checked out. Professor Murray is very good.'

'My GP already tried to refer me to his clinic.'

'So the system is working well.'

I went home, realising that no one knew that I had even been to the hospital. What should I tell people? My mind went fuzzy again so all I did was go to bed. I didn't have any meetings or pressing work so I was free to worry. I rang the GP surgery the next morning asking to speak to Dr Zoltan. He rang back a few hours later and I told him what had happened.

'Of course the ultrasound technician is being cautious. We still don't know what that cyst is. Even if it is malignant, there are different stages for ovarian cancer and it can be cured.'

I was not consoled. I told no one. All weekend I took my frustration out on my flat: scrubbing the cherry wood floorboards in the kitchen, cleaning the fridge till it sparkled, removing the cobwebs behind the fridge, cleaning the oven, vacuuming all floors, removing all the cat hairs from the sofas.

On Monday afternoon I promptly arrived at the clinic at 2 pm. I didn't have to wait long for this famous Professor. A nurse ushered me into his room where he met me, together with Dr Halkias, the doctor I had seen on Thursday. The Professor was tall, grey-haired and elegant, and wore sharply tailored grey trousers underneath his white coat.

'Good afternoon, Mrs Zahno,' he said in his Australian accent. 'You have a rather large cyst on your left ovary but you're young – only forty-eight – so I wouldn't have thought it was malignant. Ovarian cancer usually occurs in women over menopausal age.'

At this, I happened to glance at Dr Halkias who looked amazed at what the Professor was saying. Clearly he didn't believe him.

'Nevertheless, it will have to be removed and the operation will be a big one I'm afraid because the size of the cyst means I can't remove it by keyhole surgery. I've looked at my diary. How long will you need to get your work in order? If you can come in tomorrow I have a cancellation the following day and could operate on you. Otherwise I have space for you in ten days' time.'

Bearing in mind that he didn't think the cyst was malignant, I thought I would take the later slot. That would allow me to clear my work at the voluntary organisation I worked for. Professor Murray explained what the operation would entail, adding that he might have to do a hysterectomy too, depending on what he found.

I nearly said I would take the earlier slot, but it would be so inconvenient. I would have to phone all my relatives in the evening. And arrange for cat-sitting. My head just wasn't straight enough to do all this. So I went ahead and signed the forms for my operation in ten days' time.

The next ten days went by in a fuzz. I felt constantly sick and didn't eat. I cleared all my work. I didn't really understand why reactions to my plight were very different.

'You shouldn't tell us you might have cancer because you might not,' said Madur at work. Oh, so I was supposed to keep my fears to myself.

'That sounds bad,' said Ellen. 'Keep me informed.'

At least she believed me but didn't seem overly concerned. Neither Ellen nor Patrick volunteered to come to the hospital with me but I didn't find this surprising as we weren't close. But I did mind that they were so nonchalant.

The Saturday before I went into hospital, my neighbour, Claire, went with me over the road to the primary school's summer fair and we bought some bedding plants. I remember having to sit down hastily as I was feeling faint. She asked me if I'd been eating properly and I confessed to having eaten only a banana and yogurt for breakfast and no lunch. She took me home, sat me down at my kitchen table and made me scrambled eggs on toast and afterwards we planted white and pink busy lizzies in two troughs outside my bedroom French windows.

I turned up at the hospital on Monday morning ready for my operation on Tuesday. There was no bed for me so I was put in a day ward but I was completely alone there and started to cry.

A nurse came by and said, 'There's no reason to cry because, whether you have cancer or not, you could be run over by a bus tomorrow.' Which was rather a strange thing to say the day before a major operation.

Staff came by at different times asking me lots of questions about allergies, previous operations, family history, next of kin. More staff came by to do blood tests, blood pressure tests. I was

Sita Roy, 1938. My adoptive mum in Calcutta.

Gopal Roy, 1920s. My adoptive grandfather in his legal garb.

April Roy, 1926. My adoptive grandmother.

*Dad, Frank Wray, British Army, 1944 and
his parents below*

*I must have been 3 in this photo with Mum
and all my adopted siblings*

*Traditional bucket and
spade holiday in Torquay,
aged about 6 or 7*

*Believe it or not, I was wearing
my school summer dress here,
designed by a sixth former*

I'm in Camilla, Fife, 1977, delighted to see my name up 'in lights'

I'm chilling in Greece, 1985

I'm working in my boxed-in space, Southwark Planning department, 1988

*My adopted brother, Tim and his
partner, Gisela, Berlin, 2003*

*My adopted brother Patrick and his birth mother, Irene,
on a trip to Weymouth, 2016*

My birth mother, Margareta
Zahno, Switzerland, 1960s, striking
a glamorous pose below

The only picture I have of my birth
father, Lakhan Raja Rao,
London, 1970s

My half sister, Nora,
Margareta's daughter in
Mallorca, 2016

*Lisa, my half sister,
Lakhan's daughter in her
red floral dress in Oxford,
2016*

*My chicken nugget family: Kamila, Leon, Lisa, Daniel, Nora, Patrick,
Oxford, 2016*

Three sisters: Nora, Kamila, Lisa, Oxford, 2016

And last but not least, my beloved grumpy cat, Raasay

offered a sandwich for lunch which I declined. But most of the time I was left alone. Finally, evening came and I was ushered into the gynaecological ward on the 6th floor. Being placed in a bed by the window which looked straight out over the skyline of London – from the London Eye to Canary Wharf – made me feel better, and I started talking to the three other women in that bay. I can remember now that two of them were adopted.

I had mistakenly been given dinner as they had omitted to put 'nil by mouth' on the board above my bed. This meant I had to take medicine every hour for the next five hours to empty my bowels. Poor Beatrice, the night nurse, had to listen to my fears, which she did with genuine concern. She didn't say it would be all right, nor did she offer the solution of being run over by a bus, but instead said that she would be thinking of me all day when she was off-duty.

My operation was the first one of the morning so Beatrice had to get me up, washed and into a clean hospital gown by 6 am. I was wheeled into the theatre at 8 am and knew no more until I woke in the recovery room several hours later. All they said at that time was that they had removed the cyst successfully and that I had had a full hysterectomy. The Professor would come and see me in the evening.

I was immobile in my bed because I had an epidural fixed to my back which was feeding me morphine. But I was very happy as I wasn't in pain and the operation seemed to have gone well. When the Prof came by that evening I was listening to my headphones.

'I know what you're listening to,' he said in his laconic voice. 'The cricket commentary on the radio – ball by ball.' I actually laughed which didn't do my abdomen any good.

He came with another colleague, Professor Lehrer, an oncologist. They didn't beat about the bush.

'The tumour is cancerous,' said Prof Murray. I've sent it off to be analysed. There were also visible cells on the surface of the ovary which I've removed.'

I burst into tears. 'Ovarian cancer is a death penalty.'

'No it's not, it's OK,' said Prof Lehrer. 'It's a very early stage cancer and curable.'

'Ninety-five per cent of women at stage 1C are cured,' added Prof Murray.

'But we do want to start chemotherapy as soon as possible, and I'll take care of that with you,' said Prof Lehrer.

I was too frightened and overwhelmed to ask any questions. I spent the next ten days in hospital recovering and getting used to my new status of cancer survivor. I hired a television to go at the end of my bed so I could watch Wimbledon – that was the year when the Williams sisters first reached the final. I (or rather my TV) was very popular with other patients and the nurses and there were no fewer than ten people crowded by my bed for the final. After the first couple of days I asked my friends and family to visit and every day someone came to chat and cheer me up. But although a cousin from Arizona who was visiting my aunt in London came to see me, Ellen and Patrick didn't.

By the time I left hospital I was institutionalised and found it difficult to adapt to living at home with no routine. Gradually I got used to the inactivity. As it was a fine summer I used to sit in the garden and read. I even got through the chemotherapy well. I got used to having an infusion of drugs every three weeks at the hospital where they fed it to me through a drip. I was fine the day after and then I was very woozy for the next three days. After two months at home recovering from the operation I started work again. I found I could do anything, but when I had those three days of wooziness everything took me about five times longer than usual. I remember stuffing envelopes for a seminar I'd organised and it taking me a whole evening to stuff one hundred envelopes, instead of the hour it would have normally taken me. Every time I stuff envelopes now I think of that evening.

By November I had finished my chemotherapy and rapidly became stronger. A friend and I went to Budapest just before Christmas to visit all the hot water spas. That was before many Western Europeans travelled extensively in Eastern Europe and most of the spa visitors were locals, many of whom had been referred by their doctors. I had no problems in displaying my scars as some women had even larger ones. My favourite spa was a small Turkish one where we floated in the pool and watched the delicate star patterns cut into the roof overhead. Another unusual pool was the one outside where you could play chess while submerged up to your arms. Snow lay on the ground and the cold made the steam rise. The men playing chess kept appearing and disappearing.

As far as everyone was concerned I was cured but for five years after my diagnosis I was still worried about a possible recurrence. I wondered whether I'd inherited the cancer gene which increases the risk of breast, ovarian and bowel cancer. Was my mother still alive or did she die of one of these cancers? This was at the back of my mind when, in 2004, I emailed the Registrar's Office in Fribourg in my stilted French. Back came an email saying there was no record of Margareta Zahno being born in Fribourg, but that she may have come from a nearby town in the same canton so I would have to contact other towns. Swiss records aren't centralised and they aren't available online. I knew the Swiss were very organised so the records would be there waiting for me, but where? In the canton of Fribourg there are seven districts. I could have written to all seven but I didn't. Instead I Googled aimlessly for both Margareta Zahno and Lakhan Raja Rao and drew blanks.

Why wasn't my mother looking for me? Like Patrick's did. I remember feeling both excited and jealous when Patrick rang me one evening back in 1994.

'You'll never guess what's happened.' I can still hear his voice choking with emotion which was unusual for Patrick.

'I didn't tell you till now, but a couple of weeks back I had a letter from a lady from the National Children's Home.'

'My god,' I interrupted. 'Your adoption?'

'Yes, but the letter didn't say that. It just said something like she'd received a personal inquiry which she'd like to discuss, but it wasn't urgent. She asked me to ring her. I guessed immediately that my mother was searching for me.'

'I didn't think birth mothers were able to do that,' I said. 'I thought it had to be kept a state secret. We can search when we're eighteen but the parents can't.'

'Wait – I'm telling you,' he continued. I remember him sounding irritated. 'I nearly didn't get the letter because she'd written to Dad and asked him for my address. I suppose NCH knew that we were brought up in Birmingham and just looked in the phone book for Frank Wray and they were lucky.'

'Gosh – he'd only just moved back to Birmingham from Edinburgh when Mum died. That was lucky.'

'Anyway Dad didn't want to give the lady my address but said he would forward a letter if she sent it to him.'

'I wonder what he thought because that's quite trusting of him if she didn't say she was from the adoption agency.'

'I actually don't know because he never told me. I just got the forwarded letter. I rang the number and the woman told me that my mother, Irene, was still alive and would like to meet.'

I had been excited for Patrick and interrupted again. 'You'll have to have a counselling interview. Do you want me to come with you?'

'No, I think I'll just go and see what she has to say. I'll be OK on my own and anyway I think you might not be able to sit in on the interview with me.'

'The interview is straightforward. They just want to know whether you're emotionally stable enough to meet your birth parent. It'll be so fantastic. Gosh, I can't wait to hear what happens. Phone me immediately you have news.'

This was great for Patrick but I was surprised at this change in adoption policy, barely two years after I'd had my adoption interview. Contacting your birth relatives must have become more open. I had thought all that sort of initial contact was protected by the law – it was so secretive when we were adopted.

A couple of weeks later, I was eating my dinner and watching the news when Patrick rang me again. I switched the TV to mute and let my dinner get cold. Without so much as a 'How are you?' he launched into the latest news.

'You'll want to hear about this. I went to the NCH offices in Horsham where they keep the records and met the counsellor. My birth mother contacted NCH herself. The counsellor said she wanted to meet me. Apparently she wondered if she had any grandchildren.' He laughed and said, 'Well I disappointed her there. Anyway the lady asked me various questions about our adoptive parents and what they might feel. I explained that Mum had died a few years ago and that I wasn't sure about how Dad would take it. But I did say I was interested in meeting Irene.'

'So could you see your file?' I remembered how Miss Keele had hidden it from me. Things really had opened up since then.

'Yes. She showed me the file and said I could read it but not take it away. So I was faced with reading it really quickly. It was very strange reading about this person, David Carver, and realising it was me. I didn't think of asking if I could copy any of the information.'

I remember feeling very jealous at this. Reading his own file! What riches. 'Gosh, do you remember much about what was in the file?'

'No, I hardly remember anything but two things stuck in my mind. One was a letter from the local authority to Irene saying, "Thank you for your inquiry, but we have to tell you that it's very unlikely that we'll find anybody to adopt a coloured child." That I remember. Also I must have seen some document with my father's name on it – it was Mohammed.'

'Wow,' I said. 'When I had my interview the counsellor wouldn't let me see the file. I thought one of the reasons for that was because the phrases used in those days were a bit racist. I think she thought it might upset me.' I remembered how I felt then. It brought it all back to me – how it was my information but it was being withheld from me. These adoption people seem to hold all the power.

'I think I was in shock really,' Patrick continued. 'I had breezed along to this counselling session thinking that I could cope with this but then it was a very strange feeling to be reading about me as a baby.'

'So did the counsellor put you in touch with Irene then?'

'Yes. I thought I would like to meet her. I can't quite remember what advice the counsellor gave, but I think it was about going gently. They said they would give my address to Irene and she would probably make contact. And that they would always be there for any advice I might need.'

'Well, that's so amazing. I'm really envious. I haven't been able to find any trace of my mum in Switzerland and I wouldn't have a clue how to search for her. Anyway, do keep me posted. I'm so excited for you.'

I put the phone down. It seemed that he was getting all the information from his file and he could be meeting his mother too. And all without going through the emotional effort of actually conducting the search himself. Yes, at that time I was really jealous.

I didn't hear anything from Patrick for a few weeks. I guessed he was absorbing the information and perhaps they were writing and phoning each other before arranging to meet.

Finally, he rang again, and with barely a hello he said, 'I met Irene yesterday. I'm sure you want to hear how we got on.'

'You bet,' I said eagerly.

'Over the past few weeks we've been writing to each other and we exchanged photos. Then we agreed to meet. It was odd. She wanted to meet me underneath the clock at Waterloo station because that's where she handed me over to Mum and Dad.'

'Oh, that's kind of sad – and romantic at the same time.' I'd like to know this Irene. 'Amazing that she left you there and then meets you again forty-five years later. What did you feel? I can't imagine.'

Patrick, who isn't very good at emotions, said, 'We went for a little walk and had a cup of tea. I think we even went to a gallery and looked at a few paintings but I can't even remember what gallery it was. That was the first meeting.'

'But how did you feel?' I pressed him.

'Actually, I felt a sense of anti-climax. I felt that maybe it was going to be difficult to get to know Irene well. She seemed kind enough but I don't think she opened up.'

I recall feeling intrigued by this. I wondered just how much Patrick opened up himself as I found him quite difficult to talk to. He says very little, nor does he ask questions so you're expected to fill all the gaps yourself. He continued, 'I think I was expecting that she would have told me more about my situation, my birth father, her search for me and how she felt about the whole thing.'

'But didn't you ask all those questions?'

'Not really. I wanted her to say things in her own time rather than bombard her with questions. She did mention the fact that she'd been trying very hard to find me and that she'd thought about me every birthday. But I imagined before the meeting that she would be effusive and more openly emotional. She didn't talk about her life. We were only together a couple of hours and when we went round the picture gallery she was commenting on the pictures. I think she felt it was enough to be together.'

'It couldn't have been easy meeting for the first time in a public place and talking about the birth. Are you going to meet her again?'

'Yes, we arranged to meet next month.'

I remember putting down the phone, my mind whirring. Patrick had a real-life mum and he would meet her again soon. I suppose, it would have been difficult for my mum to get in touch because she wouldn't have known how to search in England. Still, the fact that Patrick and Irene were to meet stirred up emotions in me. Were they enough to spur me to continue my search, or at least try to access my adoption papers? A month later I rang Patrick.

'Hi, have you met Irene again?'

'Yes, I met her recently at her house near Guildford. She still didn't say much. I tried to ask more about my birth father and what she was doing at that time of her life but I didn't get much out of her. She'd made a cake for me though.'

I had to laugh. Patrick was not usually interested in how people feel, and here he was wondering why his mother wasn't showing more emotion.

That was in 1994 but here I was in 2004 and I still hadn't applied for my complete file which might have given me more information to begin a serious search for my birth parents. I gave up my search and waited for my five-year cancer all clear. Not wanting to dwell on the past I threw myself into my work like I'd never had cancer. Illness just wasn't on the agenda so it was a shock when my father became sick a year later.

12. DAD WAS NO OGRE

As a kid I always froze in the winters. We had a coal fire in the living room and two oil filled radiators, one in the dining room, one in the hall but no heating upstairs. Dad always told us how lucky we were to have electricity, running water and an inside loo. He was brought up in rural Buckinghamshire in the '30s and had none of those. He described this vividly when he wrote about himself for me the year before he died.

We had a pump in the kitchen which brought us water from a well and our loo was a big bucket in an outhouse. When it was reasonably full your grandad buried the contents in the garden. That was why our vegetables always thrived! We may not have had electricity or running water but we had a long garden at the back. We grew all the vegetables we needed as well as all kinds of fruit – including a huge strawberry bed. Our only light was a large paraffin lamp on the living room table. Upstairs it was candlelight. Cooking was done over the open fire which had a swivel for the kettle. We all had a weekly expedition – 'wooding' – into the local woods to bring back bundles of sticks for kindling.

His dad, our grandad, was a bus conductor, an avid socialist and unionist. He lost his job in the early 30s because he wasn't on the bus when the driver backed into a wall. Management's reasoning was that it crashed because Grandad was not on the back platform to warn the driver but I think it was an excuse to fire someone who was a union organiser. In the Depression there were few job opportunities so Grandad got a job as a farm labourer and had to walk far to and from the farm. That was another thing Dad always told us when we moaned about walking to school. Despite all the hardships, Dad and his brother and sister had fun living in the country.

Although we were poor, living in the country as children could be magical. There was never any traffic. We rolled our iron hoops along the lanes, chased clouds of butterflies, many of them special to the chalk hills of the Chilterns, and rambled in the beech woods which in spring were carpeted with bluebells, celandines and anemones.

The village school was small, with only five teachers, but did its best for its children. My dad and uncle passed the eleven-plus and went to the Royal Grammar School in High Wycombe. Dad told me of the influence of the headmaster there and of one particular teacher who encouraged him in his love of English literature. He won a scholarship to Cambridge, the first in the school's history. That was in 1938. In 1940, at the age of twenty, he was called up to the Army.

When Dad and Mum returned from the War in 1947 they were keen to start a family. I don't know if they planned to adopt so many of us but they were proud of their family. We were made to feel special but I felt we always had to prove ourselves worthy of our adoption. I never knew the bossy older woman or the young romantic lover who emerged from Mum's letters. Dad became ever stricter as we grew up; I had the impression that Mum would have given us more leeway. Dad's strictness may have been partly down to the fact that he'd got where he was through hard work in spite of his working-class background. And so must we. But I felt adoption added further pressure. Because the mixed race adoption had to work it meant Dad limited what we were allowed to do outside the family. It was as though mixing with other people might corrupt our family. It was like living in a bubble.

There was no doubt that Dad was proud of our achievements but the way he told everyone made it sound as though we'd done well against the odds. Perhaps we had. But it made me feel I should be grateful. Perhaps I should. Looking through my adoption file recently I came across a letter from the adoption agency – obviously a reply to a letter Dad had written boasting of Patrick's and my development. It's dated January 1968 when I was in my O level year and Patrick would have been in his gap year between school and university:

The fact that Patrick and Camilla have mixed racial backgrounds has added to the interest in knowing of their progress and development, for at that time, when they came to you, the placing of mixed race children was in its infancy. I am sure I am right in saying they were pretty well the first this Society placed, and as with any adoption, one can only judge success when the children are grown up. No one could certainly have any doubts about the success of this kind of placement if they know or hear about you. So much is said these days about adoption and the wisdom or otherwise of placing children of mixed race. We know a lot depends upon the adopting parents being suitable for the responsibility, but so far, in any of our placements, we have had nothing to regret.

Of course the agency was delighted to know about our success. For sure we wouldn't have done so well had we been brought up in a children's home. But still, when I read this letter, I feel as though I was the subject of a social experiment. It wasn't down to my own love of literature and science that I'd done well. It was because I had been rescued from illegitimacy and miscegenation. And part of the reason behind Dad's strictness was to make sure that I didn't deviate from a path of study. Growing up was regimented as if the four of us were in a clinic or classroom. Educational success was the key to parental approval. We were cared for well but it was as though we were detached from feeling emotions. Emotions were frowned upon in our family. Doing well academically was the key indicator, not emotional wellbeing.

Am I being unfair? Perhaps, but that's how I felt. I didn't have a great relationship with Dad because of the strictness and lack of emotion.

I wondered whether reconnecting with your birth parents might help heal. I wondered whether it had helped Patrick after he met Irene, his birth mother. I went to Nottingham to talk to Patrick about it. His house was slightly ramshackle which surprised me as he's really artistic. His oil paintings of Guadeloupe were jewels on the wall above the mismatched furniture. We were sitting in his kitchen drinking tea and I began talking about adoption and race. I wanted to know more about how he felt about Irene and how that compared to what he felt about our own family relationships. Had knowing Irene completed something missing in him?

'I don't think so. I think the relationship between Irene and me isn't really equal. She's already told me that she would like more out of the relationship. But I wouldn't like to share the details of my life with her and I wouldn't want to get involved too much in her life.'

I was intrigued about Patrick's lack of emotion when he described his relationship with her. But after all he wasn't the one who did the searching so perhaps his birth family isn't important to him. But how would I know? I hadn't found either of my birth parents.

We talked about adult relationships with parents. For Patrick it's about a caring role when parents get elderly.

'But I don't think that really applies to Irene because she's living independently and doesn't want any help.'

I said, 'We never had that sort of relationship with our parents anyway, so your feelings might be influenced by that. I think contact after we left home was done out of a sense of duty rather than out of a genuine wish to be in each other's company.'

'But isn't that normal?' Patrick said. 'I think children and parents grow apart when the kids are in their late teens and maybe they start growing back together in later life through children or because the parents need support.'

'I don't see that at all. I know most of my friends have fully formed adult relationships with their parents from their twenties onwards – go to dinner regularly, go to football matches, stuff like that – even if they don't have children.'

'That's a different generation though. Our generation was much more formal and we were brought up to keep a certain distance.'

I let the matter drop. I still don't agree. I think it is a matter of being able to express affection and that didn't really happen in our family. I do think it's about being adopted, maybe not in all adoption cases.

When Mum died in 1990 Dad became very depressed and never fully recovered from her death. After all they'd been together for forty-five years. Not only that but he had been Mum's carer for a couple of years and now was at a loose end. He didn't know how to live alone. He took anti-depressants as well as medication for rising hypertension. A few months after Mum's funeral he rang me on a Monday night.

'I've been so ill but the doctor's sorted me out.' He was obviously not himself as his voice was shaky.

I felt guilty. I was in London; he was in Edinburgh. I didn't ring him often enough. I had just started a very demanding job in a small cooperative consultancy. It was hard learning the business aspects of the company as well as bringing in hard cash from my work as a consultant. I had no time for Dad and his grieving.

'What happened? What did the doctor say?'

'I became dizzy at the weekend and couldn't raise my head without feeling I was going to collapse. I got out of bed but I've been crawling around the floor between the bed and the toilet.'

'Oh god, how did you get to the doctor? Did Ellen help?'

'No, she would have been at school.' My sister was a language teacher and commuted from Edinburgh to Glasgow every day. 'I saw a locum last week who increased the dose for my heart medicine. But I saw my regular doctor today and he said it was far too high. It was poisoning me.'

'Sounds absolutely awful. Are you feeling better now?' I asked.

'Yes, I didn't take any medicine today so I'm not too bad. Not dizzy anyway.' We chatted about what I'd been doing for a while before we rang off.

I was worried. Dad had never lived on his own and now, at the age of seventy he was going to have to learn how to be alone. It would be difficult. But I didn't really know how to help him, other than phoning and making the occasional visit. As I said we weren't close and I was busy with my new job. It turned out that Dad had his own plans. He went through his address book contacting suitable women from his past: single or widowed, aged sixty-ish. After a few false starts he found Anne who used to be the secretary at the school where he last taught and who was still living in Birmingham. She became a frequent visitor to the Edinburgh flat. After a couple of years they found a house together in a small neighbourhood, right on the edge of Birmingham. The house was, to my mind, a characterless 1970s semi but there was a field with horses at the bottom of the garden, and an unimpeded view of the Staffordshire countryside from the upstairs bedrooms.

Dad and Anne lived together for thirteen years. I was thankful. And heartless I suppose. I reverted to my infrequent visits, perhaps visiting three or four times a year just for a few hours, mainly when working on projects in the Midlands. They seemed happy enough, travelling frequently. Dad was an active member of a local film society although he was rather stuck in the past as far as films were concerned.

When Anne died in 2006, Dad was bereft again. This time I began to feel really sorry for him. Especially when he asked me if you could buy ready meals made just for one in the supermarket. He fell into a depression from which he never recovered. I visited much more frequently. The house was dirty and after a few months I could smell pee as soon as he let me in the house. I tried to clean the bathroom surreptitiously but what the house needed was a deep clean which he wouldn't let me do. Patrick and I tried to get him to hire a cleaner to no avail. Ellen rang his doctor to talk about his care but the doctor said there was nothing he could do if Dad

didn't want an assessment from social services. These things often
sort themselves out, he said. Which sounded ominous.

He was right. A neighbour found Dad at the bottom of his stairs
one morning, only a few weeks after Ellen had spoken to the doctor.
He'd been there all night. He went to hospital but I don't think he
was ever properly diagnosed as he kept being shifted from ward to
ward. After two months it was clear to me that he would never leave
hospital. After all those years of disliking him I was sorry for him.
Although he'd been miserable without Anne over the past year he
just didn't want to let go of life. He was frightened of death.

In the third month Tim came to stay in Dad's house, making
daily visits to hospital. Dad fell into a coma and I wanted to visit
but I couldn't bear to stay in that house. A friend, who lived in one
of the high-rise office conversions right next to New Street Station,
let me stay in his flat while he was in Paris. I could easily do my
work from Birmingham. From there I could see the trains below me
zooming off to London, Crewe and Manchester as well as to more
local destinations. There were only six stops to the hospital which
made it easy for me to hop on the train to visit Dad. It was easier
than travelling from his house which was served poorly by public
transport. I went every day for a week. One night I was called out
at 11 pm by a nurse who said he could go at any time. But by the
time I reached the hospital the crisis had passed and he was stable,
although still in a coma. For the next few days Tim and I took it in
turns to visit. When Friday came Tim relieved me at lunchtime. I
told him I needed to go to a work meeting in Milton Keynes and
would then go back home to London to get fresh clothes, and come
back to Birmingham the following morning. I'd just reached home
when I got the phone call. Dad was dead.

I returned the next day to find both my brothers at the house.
Ellen arrived from Edinburgh at lunchtime. We divided up the
various tasks dispassionately: registering the death; talking to the
funeral director; organising the funeral. It was as if we were made of
stone. When I returned home I dug out the pieces Dad had written
for me about his life. Sitting on the floor in my living room that

night I wrote and rewrote the story of his life, dividing it into two parts so that Patrick and I could share the reading at the funeral. I came alive at that point. I didn't cry but I was no longer a stone. The whole process of writing was cathartic.

The funeral couldn't have been more different from Mum's. Instead of seven people there were over fifty. The ceremony felt good to me because it was a celebration of his life rather than his death. And it was good that all four of us said something about him. Afterwards, at the pub, people came up to us to say something special about how Dad had influenced them: teachers, pupils, neighbours, and people from the film society. One pupil had a long conversation with me about how Dad had changed his life. Not being one of Dad's star pupils I hadn't heard of him but he'd been struggling at school and had turned around his life because of Dad's influence. I was moved.

Only after his death did I realise that Dad was no ogre. He was well regarded by others. He brought us up in the only way he knew how. He had turned all his children into his students but this was only because he was anxious that we had a good start in life.

13. HATCHES, MATCHES, DISPATCHES

The thought of my birth parents dying without knowing me continued to gnaw away at me. They would be in their seventies. But of course it was really more about me than them. I had so many questions. Where were they? Did I look like them? What were their likes and dislikes? Did I have any sisters and brothers? These were the final pieces in the puzzle of my life.

Now that both my adoptive parents had died I became more determined to get access to my complete records. When I first looked for my file NCH actually withheld it from me but only a few years later in 1997 Ellen was given her whole file, despite being prepped by the social workers that she might be shocked at the views of the adoption workers of the 1940s. At the time I helped her with finding her mother's birth certificate to make her search easier. I visited St Catherine's House in London where all the hatches, matches and dispatches records are kept. I remember it was a winter's day and the building was overheated for the physical work required heaving the heavy tomes from shelf to desk. The registers were colour coded – red for births, green for marriages and black for deaths.

From Ellen's adoption file I had three pieces of information: her name, age and the address of her parents. I knew from the adoption papers that Mildred Brooks was twenty-one at the time of Ellen's birth in August 1947, so she could have been born any time between August 1925 and July 1926. Her birth might have been registered a month or so after this so my plan of attack was to examine five registers starting with July-September 1925 and ending with the same quarter a year later. The first volume yielded three Mildred Brookses but none of them were anywhere near Hull. The second, third and fourth volumes had several babies named Mildred Brooks from Harrogate to Hackney, but none in the east of England. Would the fifth and final volume come up with something, or did she lie about her age? I hauled down the fifth volume dated July to September 1926 and there it was, a third of the way through the volume: Brooks, Mildred; mother's maiden name, Pritchard; district, Hull. I'd got it. In spite of the name being fairly common it was relatively easy to find the right entry if you had those three precious pieces of information. I was jubilant. It had taken me barely an hour.

I rang Ellen that night and told her the good news. She now had enough information to send off for her mother's birth certificate. The adoption papers gave her mother's name and her parents' address in Hull. It was time for a visit. Ellen and I had planned to visit Hull together but for some reason I couldn't make the day she wanted to go. I can't remember the details but I do remember it was quite a turning point for Ellen.

A year after Dad died, in 2008, I met Ellen in a café she frequented in Edinburgh to get her thoughts and feelings on her search. I hadn't seen her since Dad's funeral and she was sporting a classic shoulder length bob. Her hair hadn't gone any greyer since I last saw her and it gleamed darkly. She doesn't often wear her glasses so she had a deep frown which made her look anxious.

The light-filled atrium of the café was a recent extension to a church and there were very few people in at 11 am. The sun glinted down through the glass, shining on our table. I asked her what she wanted to drink and she said, an ordinary coffee. I said, there's no such thing any more. You have to choose between Americano, cappuccino, latte, skinny latte, flat white and I don't know what else. I only drink Americano with cold milk on the side. She said, I know you can have ordinary coffee here. They have a machine for all that but they also have a jug of filter coffee sitting there so that's what I'll have with an ordinary amount of milk. Hurrah for ordinary. I ordered the coffees, returned to the table and got my phone out, laying it on the table between us.

'You don't mind me recording this, do you? I'll wipe it out once I've used it in the book.' She didn't.

'Our parents always had a positive attitude towards adoption in that they told us that we were adopted and a bit about our parents. Especially their origins. But basically we were a nuclear family and the emotional side of being adopted wasn't talked about so the question of tracing our birth origins just didn't arise.'

I nodded. 'In any case it wasn't until 1975 that adopted people could search for their records and all of us were long gone from home by then.'

'I did think about my original parents when I was a kid. I remember worrying about whether they were all right. What had happened to them? Had my birth messed up their whole life? I used to wish there was some way of letting them know I was OK. That worry increased with age.'

'So what was the spark that made you want to search?' I said.

'Mum had died a few years ago, so it wasn't actually her death that spurred me on. I'd been taking homeopathic medicine which improved my health. Homeopathy clears things – all that baggage you're carrying around, it clarifies things. So that's why I started looking.'

She continued. 'I knew a social worker who worked for our local adoption service so I asked him to help me. He told me he could get the papers from the Children's Society but that I'd have to have an interview with him before he could hand over the papers.'

'I remember being amazed at that time that you were allowed full access to your file. You took it away! I was only allowed snippets of information at my interview in the early '90s.'

'But it wasn't an easy interview. They didn't just ask me how I felt. I was dumbfounded at the crass ignorance shown by my friend and his boss. They'd read through the papers before they met me. And they hadn't got a grip on the facts of life. They didn't seem to know that with mixed race babies, the pigmentation is only slightly there at first and that we darken with age. That was the reason the records had to state I was slightly coloured. "Oh," they said, "This statement is highly offensive."'

I interrupted, 'God, yes. I had the exact same thing happen to me. That was the reason the adoption worker said she wouldn't let me see the records. It's as if they're shocked on our behalf and think they have to prepare us! It's them that are offended. After all we've had a lifetime of being called "coloured". It might be offensive now, but it was the common phrase when we were kids.'

'I know. They were applying modern day social work ethics to the practice of the 1940s. I told them that even though I would have been light-skinned as a baby you couldn't pretend I was white to white parents. The fact that I was mixed race had to be stated in the documents. But again, they said, "You might find part of these papers so offensive." I just wanted the papers and I remember thinking that the social workers were causing me more stress than reading my adoption papers would've done.'

Ellen paused to take a sip of her coffee, grimacing because it had gone completely cold.

'It wasn't just about colour,' she continued. 'They thought all the papers might upset me. The whole story of my journey from the Mother and Baby Home to a long-term residential home in Birmingham was viewed with dismay by the social workers. The kindness of the adoption workers was immaterial to them. All they could see was the "shock-horror" of all of this. They were trying to prepare me for what I might feel but didn't seem to see the kindness of the Matron and other workers. The fact that the Children's Society agreed to help my mother was good. Not all adoption agencies at that time took coloured children. And when I read the papers I saw that my mother hadn't been able to keep up the weekly payments she'd agreed to give for my upkeep. I remember being far more upset by this than anything like being called coloured. What the hell happened to her? Dreadful!'

I knew what Ellen meant, and I too got annoyed at the NCH social worker for being offended on my behalf. I'm sure the adoption workers were kind as individuals but the agencies didn't even try to place us because of the colour of our skin. Was this any different from the 'same race' adoption policies of the '80s and '90s? Of course the thinking behind that was more progressive as it was about giving children access to their culture, but it often had the same result – black children wouldn't get adopted.

When Ellen eventually escaped the clutches of the do-gooders from social services she went home to read her file. She found that she was the daughter of a young woman, Mildred, from Hull, a copy typist, and a Sinhalese man from Sri Lanka who worked in the RAF. They must have met in London during the War. Mildred approached the adoption agency who, because there was no prospect of Ellen being adopted and there was no foster parent to be found, placed her in a residential nursery in Birmingham. There, she was seen by our adoptive mother who was working as a paediatrician, and after a few months of statutory to-ing and fro-ing was finally adopted by our parents.

I continued our conversation, sitting there in the Morningside café. By now it was raining and water was running off the glass of the atrium. 'Do you remember that visit you made to Hull?' I asked her. 'You had quite an eventful day as I remember.'

'I toyed with the idea of tracing my mother when I found her birth certificate. But just as I don't want to be traced by her, I thought I should respect her privacy. I don't want to be appropriated by others. I have friends who have suddenly been contacted by distant relatives and a relationship has been forced on them. That's horrendous.'

'Then why did you go to Hull?' I asked, thinking that it was a bit of contradiction.

'I don't really know,' Ellen said fiddling with the buttons of her cardigan. 'I wanted to find out a bit more about my mother and her parents, but without contacting her.'

I remembered what Jenny told me at my own adoption counselling interview – that adopted people often say that they just want to find out the basics, but in the end they want to know more and more and finally want to search for them. There's also something impersonal about searching official records. You can delve into them without anyone really asking what you're doing and why. You don't have to make any decisions about actually meeting the people you unearth from the records.

Ellen continued. 'I had names and addresses so a good place to start was the register office. I was looking for marriage and death certificates. Then the young woman in the register office told me that one of the people I was looking for was in a nursing home just up the road and she'd be able to organise a visit if I wanted because coincidentally she was related to her too.'

'God, that's scary,' I interjected.

'Yes, wasn't it!' Ellen's eyes lit up but suddenly her expression changed to a look of uncertainty. 'I was really excited at first and my first instinct was to tell her why I was looking. But then in the end I said to myself, no. It's kind of like Adam and Eve. If you eat the apple you can't put it back together again. If you've been told about something you can't un-know it. And I couldn't disturb this young woman who was just doing her job.'

This reminder of Ellen's inconclusive search whetted my appetite to complete my own.

Why did I take up my search again then, sixteen years after first trying to access my file? My cancer was over, Mum had been dead for some time and Dad had recently died. I felt a sense of renewal which, oddly enough, made me think about my past. Although I had a sense of self, I felt something was missing, that gaining access to my past would round me off. These days no one really questions why adopted people want access to their past, however happy their upbringing has been. It's natural to want to know. There's a bond of biology isn't there? For me, at that time, it was less about a biological bond, and more about completing the pieces of life's puzzle. I had no thought of what might happen afterwards.

Partly as prep and perhaps partly to psych myself up, I visited Irene, Patrick's birth mother who he'd introduced me to a few years ago. I asked Irene if I could talk to her about her reunion with Patrick. She phones me quite often and we get on so I thought she would agree – and she did. She met me off the train at Guildford Station. Irene is active for her eighty-seven years and lives alone in a small village a few miles from Guildford. Several bouncy dogs that she looks after for friends and neighbours usually surround her. As she never accepts money for dog-sitting her friends give her presents, the most exciting one to my mind being a hot air balloon ride over the Surrey countryside. The dogs keep her active and in the present, perhaps preventing her from dwelling on the past.

We arrived at her bungalow, at the end of a long lane. Built in the '60s, most of the original features were still present: electric fire in the living room, kitchen appliances all separate and looking as though they were bought in the '60s. She had updated the original wallpaper though as she loves to decorate. The whole bungalow was painted a neutral cream. She made me a cup of tea and we moved into the conservatory which was really just a lean-to attached to the back of the living room.

Irene's a northern lass from Preston, but her father died when she was four and her mother moved to Cornwall to take up a job as head teacher of a primary school. Irene went to London University to study physics and maths. I knew about this part of her life. We started talking.

'So what did you do when you left university?'

'My first job was doing research with the electrical company, Philips. I was living in London and having fun, going to dances at least once a week. That's when I met Patrick's father. He was from the Gold Coast – Ghana – and was studying at the Institute of Education.'

'Really!' I expressed surprise. 'Our mother always said he was from Sudan.'

'I don't know where that came from,' said Irene. 'But I said to the adoption agency that he was Egyptian.'

'Why did you do that?' I asked.

'Oh I thought that Egypt sounded closer and people would have heard of it.'

This melange of three African countries mystified me. I have no idea what was going through her head at the time, why Egypt sounded 'better' than Ghana, and why Mum had always said Patrick's father was Sudanese.

Irene showed no emotion at all when she talked about her relationship, and it was hard to get anything out of her at all.

'Where did you go dancing?' I asked. 'And what else did you do together?'

'I don't remember much. It was casual. It was so long ago. I can't even remember his name.' She continued, 'I told him I was pregnant and he expressed sympathy.'

It was hard to gauge exactly how Irene felt talking to me, and still harder to know what she really felt and thought at the time. I was really having to probe and didn't feel too good about being so intrusive.

'Did he offer to help or even marry?'

'There was no point pursuing it. He couldn't.' A final goodbye, I thought.

'And did you tell your family?'

'Yes I told my mother and older sister. I also said the father was African. They were horrified. I couldn't have kept him,' declared Irene.

'It must have been so difficult for you,' I said leaning forward.

Just a one-word reply from Irene who looked away from me: 'Awful.'

There was a long pause before she continued. I was feeling bad at continuing the conversation since it must be bringing back so many memories. But I did. 'Then what happened?'

'There wasn't any possibility of keeping him because he was coloured. Even if a child was white there would have been pressure from everyone, from society, to get him adopted.'

Irene had to leave her job at Philips when she became pregnant but became a housekeeper for the owner of the Hampstead house where she rented a bedsit. With a determination born out of desperation she got in touch with Coram, the Foundling Hospital in Bloomsbury. My brother, the foundling.

Irene and Coram tried to sort things out. 'It was all arranged before the birth that he would go to your family.'

In reality I don't know what exactly happened but I remember Mum saying that Patrick was adopted from NCH and that they approached her as she was known amongst adoption workers for adopting 'coloured' babies. I guess Coram and NCH worked together. However, our parents already had a young baby, Tim, to look after and said they wanted more of a gap before they took on another baby.

What now? Again, entirely unsupported, Irene found a foster family for her, as yet, unborn son. 'I can't remember why I had to find the placement myself but I did. I think I might have seen an advertisement.' Was there really so little child protection in those days?

I was distressed when I thought of how it must have been for Irene, giving up a week-old baby, but she was remarkably prosaic about the whole thing.

'I visited Patrick several times at his foster home near Southampton. It was a loving environment. The woman had a teenage daughter who was potty about Patrick.'

But I remembered Dad saying when Patrick first arrived in our family he was quite disturbed and kept banging his head against the wall, the implication being that there was something not quite right in the foster family. However, is it surprising when you are moved about the place that you find it hard to settle?

The handover to my parents happened when Patrick was about a year old.

'How did you feel handing him over?' I asked.

Irene was wistful. 'Well, it was all going to plan. I had dressed him in a nice little blue corded jacket to hand him over.' The image of my one-year-old brother in a blue corded jacket made me want to cry.

'We met your parents underneath the clock at Waterloo Station. I don't remember much but I do remember your dad being really tall.'

Irene got up suddenly as if the conversation was too much for her. 'I've baked some rolls for our lunch and I need to put them in the oven so we should take a little break now.' Irene was clearly finding the conversation difficult. I felt cruel continuing when Irene returned from the kitchen but I really wanted to hear about how she found Patrick.

'So tell me about how you found him? It's always been a puzzle for me because I didn't think the adoption agency would tell you.'

'I was always really determined to find him. Even when he'd been adopted I had this idea that if I could get a good job I might be able to take him back.' I didn't tell Irene that this would have been impossible, that once you're adopted that's it. Irene paused for a moment. 'When he was in his teens I placed an advertisement in *The Times* on his birthday but I never got a reply.'

My dad, who always read *The Times*, would have had a fit if he'd seen that ad. He thought that adoption was a permanent thing and that there should never be any contact from the birth parents. But Patrick didn't know his name at birth so he wouldn't have done anything about it anyway.

'So you contacted the adoption agency at a later date?' I prompted.

'The first time I did that was when Patrick was twenty-one so that would have been in 1970. The woman there was really horrible. She said I had no right to know about him. I had given him up for adoption and had no claims on him. I felt really awful.'

'And then you must have tried again?'

'Well I had hoped that he would contact me as it's much easier that way round. But he didn't. So I tried again with NCH – that's the agency that had the papers – it must have been in the '90s. I got another interview. The lady there was much more accommodating and said she would try and trace Patrick and find out if he wanted to meet.'

I said, 'And that's where I join the story as Patrick told me what happened at the time.'

At this point some pigeons grazing on the lawn flew up in a squawking flurry and we lost the thread of the conversation. I was interested in what Irene made of the relationship now.

'Has knowing Patrick made any difference to your life?' I asked.

'Not really,' said Irene.

I was surprised.

'Why not? You were so persistent. Surely it filled a gap in your life.'

'I don't see Patrick much and he doesn't call often.' I was not sure how often was often as Patrick told me he called her about once every couple of weeks.

'What sort of relationship would you like?' I asked.

Irene raised her voice even though the pigeons were now silent. 'Filial. That's all. Just a mother and son relationship. You adopted people. You don't understand blood ties. They just aren't there. See, my son Don and I...I could spend all day with Don without saying anything.'

So blood ties really do matter. Do they bind people together like ropes? Are they about obligation, love or something altogether more indefinable? It was time to find out.

Soon after seeing Ellen and Irene I went to the NCH website and found a form I could use to request access to my records. This meant that I would have to have yet another counselling session! They made me an appointment with an adoption counsellor in their offices in Horsham where the records were kept. So in May 2008 I took the train to Horsham, an hour's journey from Victoria. It was good to get out of London and see the trees clothed in their light green spring colours. I decided to walk to the NCH records office which was set back in a cul-de-sac in the middle of a 1960s housing estate.

Here I met Elena Cremona. She was older than my previous two adoption workers, a tall, thin lady in her fifties. She had a slight Italian accent and spoke softly. Elena asked me for my ID and

I presented her with my passport, even though the photo looked nothing like me – and a gas bill for my address. Strange, presenting a gas bill in return for information about your parents. She had a file in front of her but didn't look at it.

'I realise that you've had a counselling session and that you had a look at your files in 1992. That's quite a while ago. What brings you here now?' she said, placing her hands on the file in front of her.

I was rather tense. Was this going to be another wasted journey? Would I be deemed suitable to take control of my own file?

'When I first asked to see my files I was only given a couple of documents. I wasn't even allowed to see the file. I gather that I can now see the whole thing and get a copy. When I had that interview all those years ago I felt that there was more information in there about my mother. I'd love to know more about her.'

'Yes, things have changed since then. We realise the importance of adoptees knowing their background. So there's less secrecy, and we're able to give you the file. But is that all you want? Are you thinking of searching for your parents?' She took her hands off the file and put them on her lap.

The tension went out of my neck and I crossed my legs, leaning back in the chair. 'I think I may well start looking. It could be my last chance at finding out what happened to them. I'm getting old and so are they!'

Elena seemed much more open than the other two adoption workers. But she did want to give me advice before handing over the file.

'Tell me a bit more about yourself,' she said, sounding as though she was really interested.

Groan! Not again! I launched into my now well-rehearsed spiel. Blah-blah-blah. This time I added bits about Patrick and Irene finding each other, as well as Ellen's search.

And to pre-empt her commenting on what a fascinating a story it was I said, 'It's a fascinating story, isn't it? You can understand why I want to know more about my circumstances.'

Elena straightened her spine and pulled her shoulders back as though she was about to give me a lecture. She started counselling me with her adoption worker speak.

'You obviously had a stable background and you're not looking for 'replacement parents' but what are your expectations of any search you might do?'

'I don't expect much. To be honest I've tried to find out about my birth mother but the records are difficult to find in Switzerland, and I sort of came to a dead end. As for my father, I've Googled his name and come up with nothing. I presume he went back to India. I wonder whether the file says any more.' Again I tried to pre-empt some of the standard questions Elena might ask me. 'I know that I might have been born in horrible circumstances, although I do have two letters from both my mother and my father that make me think that the two had been friends. She gave the court my father's address so the adoption agency could ask him to sign the adoption papers. When they got in touch, he replied and actually wanted to see me in the nursery.'

Elena laughed, a lovely tinkling laugh. She'd figured out that I was an old hand at these adoption interviews and wanted to get down to the proper business of what was in the file.

'OK so you're aware that a search might not reveal anything and that even if you're reunited with either parent the demands of a new relationship can result in unexpected feelings for both parties. You might have different expectations of each other – as you've described in your brother's case. The relationship might change over time, from being great to start with and then tailing off. You know some of the stories from the NORCAP newsletters.'

And then she added something unexpected. 'There's one thing that you might not have thought of. There's some evidence of sexual attraction amongst birth relatives who meet, and you need to be aware of this as a possibility.'

'You're right – that's something I would never have thought of,' I said raising my eyebrows and widening my eyes.

'Well I wouldn't worry about it, but just be aware of it if you do meet any of your birth relatives. You come across as a well-balanced, thoughtful person.'

'I do? What makes you say that?' I was pleased she thought that but wondered why.

'Oh, I have all sorts of adoptees sitting just where you are, believe me. I find the younger ones have higher expectations. Sometimes they do their own search and make contact themselves. Then it turns into something they can't handle and they come to us again.'

'Do you still offer an intermediary service?'

'In your case I think NORCAP would be best as they now have a worker who does international searches. But you'd better do this as soon as possible as your parents will be getting on a bit!'

'I do need help with this as I couldn't find her birth records in Fribourg when I asked the local registrar. We'll see what happens.'

Elena promised to send me my original file once she had copied it for the records, as well as information and contacts to help me in my search. She showed me to the door and shook my hand. I didn't feel like walking back to town so I looked for the bus stop. As I waited there I felt really optimistic. It had taken me many years, but I was now on track to find out the secret behind my birth.

14. THE FILE

It's 11 am on a Monday morning. I'm sitting at my kitchen table with my customary mid-morning coffee, with a pile of transcripts of focus groups of non-users of Haringey libraries to make sense of: Turkish teenagers; lone parents with toddlers; older Asian men; and a white youth group. My task is to find out why they don't use the libraries and what I can advise the Council to do about it. There's a ring at the doorbell. I hope it's the postman with my adoption file which I've been expecting for several days. I open the door to my flat and walk through the lobby. I can see through the sunset image on the coloured glass of the front door that it is indeed the postman. Opening the door I see he's carrying a bulky package along with other mail for our house. 'Is it for me?'

'Miss Zahno, Flat 2?' he says. 'Would you sign for this, please?' I scrawl my signature and he thrusts all the mail into my eager hands.

My heart is thumping as I take the package into the kitchen. I can scarcely breathe. I've waited so long for this file. What will it contain? Will it change the way I think about myself, and about my mother? Will it tell me about my mother and father's relationship, about how they met? Perhaps there will be a photograph of my mother. I would normally take care opening Jiffy bags so that I can re-use them, but this time I rip it open tearing the flap. And here it is – my adoption file, along with assorted information on the psychological effects on adult adoptees finding birth parents. I glance at these briefly and find them rather alarming, especially the one entitled *Sexual Attraction Following Reunion*. I sit down, abandoning any thought of writing up the focus groups, shoving all the transcripts to one corner of the table. Finding out about my mother, Margareta, is more important than knowing why people don't use Haringey's libraries. My file has been incarcerated in NCH's archives for over fifty years and now it's free. I feel as though I'm releasing Margareta from prison too and she's in front of me. I put all the articles about the psychology of searching in another corner of my large farmhouse table and ceremoniously place my adoption folder in the middle.

My folder is cheap-looking with a red plastic cover. I pick it up and sniff it. Despite sitting in a cabinet for fifty-five years it doesn't smell musty. The flimsy punch-holed papers are inserted into two bendable metal prongs which don't link together, so you can't turn the papers and read the file like a book. Despite its scruffiness this file holds the key to my birth, and I'm hoping that it will reveal what my mother felt. It isn't thick, but because most of the letters are typed on delicate onionskin paper there are more documents than I first thought – as many as fifty. The sun is shining straight through the kitchen windows onto the table and I'm getting so hot I'm sweating. I scrape back the chair, stand up and open the French windows onto my kitchen balcony and step outside for some spring air. After a moment I come back in, get a glass of water, sit down and remove all the adoption papers, laying them in a neat pile on the table. I begin to read.

The first document, dated 12th May 1952, is a blue National Children's Home memorandum noting that a Miss Chatterji, of the Office of the High Commissioner for India, had phoned to discuss Margareta Zahno's case. NCH advised Miss Chatterji to tell Miss Zahno to write to them herself asking for an interview. The next item is a copy of both sides of the postcard I'd already been given when I went for my first adoption interview. It states who she is, who I am and asks whether it was possible for me, whom she named Monica, to be adopted. Although I already have the original postcard and this is only a copy, it still has the power to move me. Already I'm blinking away my tears.

I pick up a one-page report typed in blue ink on white paper from Miss Dean, who was assigned as Margareta's adoption caseworker.

Miss Zahno came to the office this afternoon, not having waited for a reply to her letter...Miss Z is a very nice girl, and I should think she comes from a good family...She is twenty-three years old, small and slight in build, with fair hair and light brown eyes. She seems very disillusioned and realises what a great mistake she has made. She is herself extremely fond of the baby and distressed at the thought of having to part with her, but realises that she cannot provide for her herself, and being a coloured baby, it would be very difficult to bring her up in Switzerland.

Miss Z has to leave the Mother and Baby Home in which she is now staying, in a fortnight's time, and is anxious to make some plans for her child soon. I explained the difficulties regarding adoption, since the father is Indian, and she understood this, but I promised that we would discuss her problem and try to help her if we possibly can.

I realise I've been holding my breath and let it out with a sigh when I finish reading this letter. I read it twice. Miss Keele, the officious adoption worker who had first discussed my file in 1992, had given me snippets of information, including the fact that Margareta was fair with brown eyes. I feel Margareta's distress at having to part with me, and her terrible feelings of the guilt she's made to feel. She's a mother. She loves me. She wants to keep me. I wonder at the term 'disillusionment'. Is she disillusioned because she thinks she ought to be able to keep me but can't get any help from either my father or her family? Does she really think that I, as a 'coloured' baby, couldn't be brought up in Switzerland? No – it's probably Miss Dean's view.

I take a sip of water, making sure I don't spill any of it on my precious file. I read on. Things moved fast at first for both Margareta and baby Monica. Miss Dean's colleague wrote to Margareta four days later, confirming that NCH would help, but alluded again to the 'difficult circumstances' of my birth and prospects for adoption. Apparently it seemed necessary to find out my religion before accepting me into the Nursery because there's a note on the letter saying Margareta rang to say I was C of E. This isn't a Swiss religion, but I guess she hoped this would increase my chances of adoption, despite my foreign background.

By 21st May, nine days later, I'd been processed. I read my medical notes on the sheet of foolscap paper: *date of birth* 1st April 1952; *weight at birth 6 pounds, 13 ounces; entirely breast fed but now weaning; no evidence of paralysis, syphilis or tuberculosis; normal sight, though evidence of very slight conjunctivitis in the right eye, now normal; hears well; nose and throat in healthy condition; no disease of heart or lungs; in v good condition.* I sound like a second-hand car, suitably vetted for sale.

But despite the official nature of the form, I am moved by the fact that my mother had breast-fed me in the Mother and Baby home for two months. And seeing her neat signature brings her close to me. She must have been grief-stricken signing me away to NCH.

Margareta signed the final form to NCH a week later, on 28th May. She had to pay ten shillings a week for my upkeep as long as I was in the care of NCH and agreed that: *If at any time there shall be more than four weeks in arrears, I will, on receiving notice to remove the child, undertake to provide for such removal within the space of fourteen days after receiving notices, the said removal to be at my own expense in all things.*

How could she afford ten shillings? Now, free of me, she could get a job, but she would be unlikely to earn more than £3 a week in an unskilled job, so this ten shillings would be a good chunk of that. It seems like a fine for bad behaviour. The stress she must have been feeling – how did she cope? Giving away a baby is a bereavement and she wouldn't have had emotional support to get over this. However, from the paperwork in the file I know that she was in touch with the Welfare Office for Swiss Girls in Britain. I hope they helped.

Margareta brought me into the Nursery at Highbury, NCH's main office, on Friday 30th May 1952 when I was two months old.

I was placed under the care of a Sister Black. There's a gap of three months in the file. I'm not sure whether Margareta was allowed to visit me in the Nursery during that time. After all, she was paying her ten shillings for my upkeep. Didn't that entitle her to see me? Visits might have broken her heart over and over again, and I might have found them confusing not knowing who this person was.

By 21st August my potential adoptive parents must have been contacted since there's a typed note in the file from Miss Dean to Sister Black saying that she was going to meet Mr and Mrs Wray – my prospective adoptive parents – on 16th September.

During the initial negotiations, Margareta was kept in the dark and offered no hope that I would be adopted. This attitude was maintained even though Miss Dean was negotiating with prospective adoptees. She wrote a letter to her, dated only a week before she was due to visit Mr and Mrs Wray: *Sister said you expressed your wish again that Monica should be adopted, but as you know, the prospects of our being able to arrange an adoption are very remote and it may be necessary for us to review completely the whole position.*

Meanwhile my would-be adoptive parents were very keen to expand their unconventional family. They wrote to Miss Dean just before she visited them:

We fully understand the position about Monica. We must wait for the mother to come to her decision without haste or pressure, of course. Meanwhile we both long very much for a new baby – our present three are growing up so fast.

I'm puzzled by this. Margareta hadn't been informed about prospective adopters so she hadn't yet been asked to make a decision. She wanted me to be adopted; Mr and Mrs Wray were keen to adopt me. So why did this sound like a tug of war? I have to read the letters several times to get a sense of the order of things. Why is there such a gap in the files? Then I remember my sister telling me she'd gone to visit me in the Nursery in Highbury with my parents before my adoption. That must have happened before Miss Dean's home visit

– in July perhaps. They must have been told to wait until my mother decided whether she really wanted me adopted. Everything was so shrouded in secrecy that it's hard to know what really did happen. I was at the centre of all this. I feel like Nancy Drew, Girl Detective, trying to unravel the darkest of secrets.

I turn back to the file and find a blue memo dated 17th September from Miss Dean to Sister Black saying that she *had a very delightful visit to Mr and Mrs Wray yesterday, of which I will send you a full report. It is, however, urgent to let you know at once that they want to come for Monica on Friday this week, 19th instant, about 4:30 to take her home.* I really want to see that full report but it isn't in the file, and may never have been written. Instead there's a note scribbled on the memo from Sister Black saying: *Yes, this is all right, but I may not be here as I have to go to Bart's Hospital with two children.*

I gasp at the casualness of this decision. After three months of inactivity, I'm adopted within a few days of Miss Dean's visit to my adoptive parents. I know that children weren't officially adopted for a few months so the adopters could always hand them back, but still…Margareta had no time to get used to my adoption which must have felt final. After stringing her along, not raising her expectation that I could possibly be adopted, Miss Dean wrote to Margareta on 17th September on the same day as she sent the memo to Sister Black, saying:

There is a prospect of Monica going to adopters at the end of this week. These are people whom we have known for years, who have been deprived of their own family, and mean to provide a happy home life, and other advantages for two or three little ones, who are needing these gifts. The people in question are particularly suited to having little people and family life. The adopting mother is a Doctor and the adopting father a Master at a Grammar school. In addition to this, they are gifted and have the most attractive personalities. Their position, both financially and in every way, is excellent, and they are longing to lavish love and devotion on Monica.

I imagine I was now a gift, wrapped up in coloured paper. A gift as good as new with a past never to be mentioned and soon to be forgotten.

By the time Margareta received this letter, I was gone from the Nursery. Another memo, dated 23rd September, notes that:

Miss Zahno phoned that she had only this morning received our letter and she was at first a little upset to realise that Monica had gone.

A little upset! I should think she was more than a little upset. All these years later I'm trembling with the cruelty of the circumstances. Margareta was led to believe I wouldn't be adopted. Then she was suddenly informed that I was about to be adopted. And to make matters worse she didn't receive that letter until I'd gone.

If Margareta was upset, my adoptive parents were delighted, writing on 29th September:

We've had little Monica Zahno with us for just over a week now, and I should like to say on behalf of us all that we think she is a marvellous little child. Seriously, she seems quite outstanding and is a most promising baby, lively, very intelligent and affectionate. She is, incidentally, a real advertisement for those who have been looking after her these last few months and she fully lives up to all we have heard of her.

I need a breather after sensing the turmoil that Margareta must have been through. It's taken me an hour and a half to read the file so far and to work out what had happened. I've got more information than I'd hoped for. Aside from the gap in the summer of 1952 when I was in the nursery I think I've gained a more or less complete picture of what happened to Margareta and little Monica. Me. I'm not offended by the attitude of Miss Dean. She comes across as kind, if condescending – but that was the attitude towards single mothers at the time. I take a short break, heating up some carrot soup and making toast. I wonder what is in the rest of the file. I'm only halfway through reading it and wonder if the rest describes home visits from Miss Dean to see how I was getting on with my parents.

I am wrong. Most of the file is taken up with correspondence between Margareta and Miss Dean, rather than official reports about my development in my new home. I learn that Margareta wanted help to find a job as a children's nurse and went to see Miss Dean on 10th October. I find that very poignant. Having lost her own child she tries to replace that relationship by looking after other people's children. She had taken a job as domestic staff at the Ear, Nose and Throat Hospital, thinking that a hospital setting might help provide the right environment for her to get into nursing training. Miss Dean wrote to Miss Oakley, the Sisterhood and Nursing Secretary:

Miss Zahno is very anxious to train with us. She has applied to two hospitals without success. Miss Z thinks this is due to her having a baby, and that at the interview the Matrons may consider she is a girl of not good character in view of the unfortunate occurrence. Miss Z is well known to Matron, and to a certain extent to myself, in that her little girl Monica Zahno, who was resident at Highbury from June 3rd to September 19th, has now been adopted. Miss Z is a superior girl, who feels her position keenly, and I am sure she is worthy of help, and would justify any trust placed in her.

Miss Zahno's day off duty is Friday, and she hoped it would be possible for an appointment to be given her in this connection on Friday 24th October.

This feels very unusual. Did adoption workers help single mothers to this extent? I would have thought that once a child was adopted the workers would concentrate on the adopters rather than the mother. Certainly there was nothing like this in my sister's file. Miss Dean had become fond of Margareta and felt sorry for her. A few days after Margareta visited her, she wrote an encouraging letter to say that, although Miss Oakley was often away from the office, she would definitely be in touch with Margareta. Miss Dean also suggested that Margareta and she meet one evening to have a

chat about the future. A week later Margareta wrote back to say that
Miss Oakley had told her that she was over the age to start training
for nursery nursing. She would therefore be pleased to meet Miss
Dean one evening to discuss how she could help her. Understanding
that the relationship between the two of them is now informal
Margareta enclosed a tuppence ha'penny stamp for a reply.

Miss Dean tried once more to help by sending a note to Sister
Black, the Matron of the Nursery:

*With your experience and contacts I think in all probability you may
be able kindly to make some constructive suggestions which I will pass on
to Miss Zahno.*

On a late October evening Miss Dean met Margareta at the
Lyon's Corner House in the Strand. Sitting at my kitchen table in
north London I am transported to that Lyon's Corner House which
was still serving tea and cakes when I was in London in 1977.
Margareta poured out her heart to Miss Dean. She told her that
over the summer before I was adopted she had been very distressed
at the thought of having to give her baby up. As she'd been told that
adoption would be difficult, if not impossible, she wondered whether
her parents would help her look after Monica in Switzerland. She
had travelled back home that July, determined to tell them about
her baby girl and ask for their help to keep her, only to find that her
father had left her mother for another woman. Margareta was upset
that her sisters hadn't told her this. She was devastated since she
thought that her parents had been happily married for twenty-five
years. One of her sisters was married and, in desperation, Margareta
told her about her baby, but they agreed that now was not the right
time to introduce little Monica to the family.

Miss Dean wrote up this conversation for Sister Black in the
file and was obviously moved by Margareta's story as she added: *It
is quite understandable that this home sorrow, together with her own
burden of the grief of parting with Monica, is making life very hard for
Miss Z just now.*

Attached to this report is one of those now familiar blue memos, asking Sister Black for further ideas for helping Margareta to get a training position.

This seems unorthodox. Miss Dean took the trouble to meet Margareta after work in her own time, listen to her problems and to investigate the scope for help from her own organisation. I'm not sure that our modern welfare system would go to such an extent to help lone parents find work.

But Sister Black didn't appear to think this approach unorthodox and was willing to help. From the scribbles at the bottom of the memo she evidently did two things: she spoke again to Miss Oakley who promised to speak to a matron of another children's home; and she gave Miss Dean a list of staff based in NCH's offices in the south of England. Acting on this immediately, Miss Dean wrote to a Miss Cannon at NCH's Woking office, entreating her to pass on any suggestions as to what Margareta could do:

Miss Zahno is now in a Domestic Post at the Ear, Nose and Throat Hospital which is just a stop gap, as she is worthy of a far better one, being superior in every way, and of a family of good standing. There is home unhappiness now in that her father has left her mother, and she does not seem inclined to return to Switzerland, but rather to stay in England and make her own way.

I don't know in what capacity Miss Cannon worked, but possibly she organised the nursery training for the NCH nursery workers. She wrote back the following day but the same story was reiterated – Margareta, at twenty-three, was too old for nursery nursing. *However,* Miss Cannon added, *there seems to be no reason why Miss Zahno should not apply to take up General Nursing and I am enclosing the attached leaflet which I hope will be helpful.*

At the beginning of November, when I was seven months old, my legal adoption process started. Miss Dean sweetened the pill by reassuring Margareta that I was being taken care of and quoted a recent letter from my parents:

Monica is a really delightful child, and we find it impossible to resist this baby's charms. We feel very deeply for Miss Zahno in her troubles; and she may rest assured that her baby will be given all the care and love we can give.

In mid-November my parents had been approved as my adopters. I wonder why my adoption file didn't include reports of the visits Miss Dean made to our home in Bromley. This letter is all there is:

Mr and Mrs Wray have adopted three other children, one of whom, a little boy, was from us in 1950. As Mrs Wray is an Indian lady and Mr Wray English, they are receiving children of mixed parentage. From the personal contacts of myself, our Matron and visits to the home, this is a particularly happy arrangement and the children are surrounded with the best atmosphere and influence, to which they are all responding splendidly.

Margareta had to sign me away for good in December, taking the adoption consent form to be signed in the presence of a magistrate. She must have been heartbroken to make this final decision, confused and alone as she was in a foreign country in a job with no prospects. I'm tearful sitting in my kitchen all these years later, but my Nancy Drew detecting tendency has me wanting to find out what happened next. I plough on.

I imagine the magistrate pressed her for the father's name and details so she felt intimidated. But by identifying his address, NCH was legally obliged to write to my father since he had to agree to the adoption. Had Margareta given his address to NCH before, they could have gained his consent earlier. Miss Dean was not impressed, writing to Margareta on December 22nd:

It is unfortunate that you did not tell us this when you were interviewed here, for the legal side is likely to be held up and unnecessary trouble has been caused all round.

She then proceeded to write to my father care of the International Language Club, Croydon, saying that he must sign a consent form for my adoption before a Magistrate. *Will you please reply at once for the matter is urgent and the splendid adoption which has been arranged for Monica is held up accordingly? Awaiting your immediate reply*

Wow, the kind Miss Dean is showing her annoyance. But she's right to be anxious as it's Christmas and my father did not answer the letter until 29th December.

I am very gratified to learn from your letter of the 22nd instant that an adoption has been arranged for Monica Zahno who is under your care.

I have not so far heard from the Court regarding the matter. However, I shall be glad to follow your advice in order to expedite the adoption.

I have his signature; he signs himself L Raja Rao. I hope I will be in a position to compare this signature if I ever track him down.

There is a hiatus over New Year and I can feel the urgency in Miss Dean's letters. My adoption was to take place on 13th January but by 7th January there was still no letter from my father saying he'd signed the consent form. She reminded him so he wrote back immediately telling her that he had not been able to contact a magistrate over New Year, but that he had now signed the form. He added:

If it is not inconvenient to you I should like to go over to the Children's Home to see Monica this week before she is adopted. Please allow me to thank you sincerely for the trouble you have taken in this case and for the wonderful work done by the National Children's Homes.

This is surely unusual. All this time Margareta hadn't given much information about him to Miss Dean, but here he is, not only acknowledging my existence, but wanting to see me. Suddenly I have an urge to meet him. Is he still living in London or did he move back to India? He would be in his late seventies now. Is he even still alive? I hunt down my A to Z and look up the address in Croydon. It's right in central Croydon. Worth a visit perhaps?

On 9th January Miss Dean replied to thank him but she had to refuse him a visit:

> *We are extremely sorry for the disappointment we cannot but cause you with regard to your request, but the legal formalities do not ensue until the child has been in her adoption home for some months. In fact these formalities are nearly complete, for all the documentary evidence was in order before the approach was made to you. As, therefore, Monica has been with her adopters since September, you will quite understand that they, having assumed the responsibility and all that is involved for Monica, regard the earlier chapter as closed.*

So my father never got to meet me. He never replied to this letter and I wonder what he thought. Did I linger in his mind for long?

On 13th January my adoption went through and I was signed away for the final time. I was now officially Camilla Wray. The adoption may have been the best solution for both of us, but Margareta must have been left with a Monica-sized hole in her heart.

Margareta and Miss Dean now entered into a much more informal and personal relationship. Miss Dean continued to have Margareta's wellbeing in mind. Just before I was adopted she came up with one more tentative suggestion for work:

> *I am just telling you about an application which was made to me on Friday in case you may be interested. A friend of mine has a daughter living in Sussex with a little girl of three and another baby expected. She and her husband are very anxious to secure a good Nanny. It would be a comfortable home, I know, with many advantages, but I think you will wish for a post which would offer prospects, unless of course, you would care to take this for say a matter of months until you could go on to something more satisfying. Perhaps we can arrange to meet one evening for another chat.*

I'm intrigued with this relationship. My adoption is about to go through and yet Miss Dean is still rooting for Margareta. It's gone beyond a professional relationship but their conversations are still written up and filed in the case file.

They met at the Lyons Corner House again at 7:30 pm on 12th January. I know something of the conversation through an account that Miss Dean wrote for Sister Black. Margareta hadn't told Miss Dean this before but in November she had an accident to her thumb so gave up her post at the hospital. Needing to survive she took up a post as a nanny but was not happy there. Now that my adoption was complete she decided to return to Switzerland where she had lined up a job as a shop assistant in Luzern. Entreating Miss Dean to give her photographs of me, Margareta asked her to be careful not to send any letters on headed notepaper as she had never told her mother about me and felt that she never will tell her.

Margareta, depressed and alone in London, must have thought that she had no alternative but to return home and start her life afresh. Reading this, I can understand completely her choice, but I can't help feeling abandoned for the second time.

Next I find a torn scrap of paper with Margareta's address in Switzerland scribbled on it and the words *Photo from Adopters*. I dig out my photo album and find one taken on my first Christmas. I'm sitting on the five-year-old Ellen's knee clutching some wrapping paper. Did my parents pass a copy on to Miss Dean? Did Margareta ever receive it?

I am sure that in most cases the file would now be closed but Margareta and Miss Dean continued to write to each other. This is a personal correspondence so I wonder why it's in the adoption file. But it means I get more news about Margareta. Miss Dean wrote soon after Margareta left for Switzerland, that she is thinking of Margareta a lot and that her mother must be happy to have her back home. She also shares her own story:

You will, I know, be interested to hear that I have now moved to my little flat with my belongings, and I feel sure I shall be very happy. The address is above and I shall look forward to hearing from you.

Yours with love, Molly

Molly is now interested in Margareta for her own sake and it's a more equal relationship with each of them sharing stories about their own lives. Molly's address has a sticker over it but I hold it up to the light and can see it's an address in Palmers Green, Enfield. I look it up – it's not so very far from where I live now – only four stops from my local station, Haringey. I think about seeing if she's still there, but I got the impression from Mum that our adoption workers were middle-aged so there's not much chance of her being alive in 2008.

There's no reply from Margareta but Molly doesn't give up. She wrote another letter in early March:

I do hope you will not think I am a nuisance but I have thought so much about you…I hope you are happy now that you are back at home and possibly you have secured a congenial post. I miss our meetings, but am glad to feel that you are with your friends again.

We have had one or two sunny days here, and it is decidedly spring-like. Switzerland at this time of the year is, I believe, very beautiful, and I hope you will fully enjoy the amenities of spring and summer in the lovely surroundings of your home.

Do please write to me soon.

Yours with love, Molly

Margareta wrote back immediately in her neat writing, using mid-blue ink. It's a really chatty letter saying that she had stayed with friends in Paris before returning to Switzerland. She had picked up the British habit of talking about the weather which had been sunny for a few days. She invited Molly to visit:

Well, Miss Dean when you are coming for Holyday to Switzerland, you must write to me when you like to come so I can arrange everything for you. And I will be glad to see you again.

Signing off *Yours with Love, Margareta*, she added on the back of the letter:

Dear Miss Dean I must ask you about my little Darling Monica, did you ever ask the second Mother and Father about a little picture for me? If they have one I will be so very happy.

I am sad at the thought of my mother so desperate to have a permanent reminder of me.

Molly was clearly busy since she didn't reply until early May, apologising for the delay and hoping that Margareta had settled and was happily placed in a job. She talked about visiting Switzerland the following year in early summer. The scribble I found in the file 'Photo from Adopters' clearly bore no fruit. She was still trying to get a photo of me from my parents:

I hope to be able to send you a photograph soon. I have not forgotten this, and have to write to the friends in question so will send them a reminder.

There was no reply from Margareta. Molly tried one more time in late August. She talked about my progress obliquely, so that if her family read the letter they would not know that she was talking about me:

The matter in which you are particularly interested continues to progress splendidly. If and when I do come to Switzerland, which I fully intend to do, all being well, not next year but the following one, I shall make a point of arranging to be near your home during the holiday and we shall have lots to talk about shall we not?

I place this letter face down on the pile of adoption papers and stare at a knot in one of the stained pine floorboards that make up my upcycled kitchen table. There are no more letters. The first seventeen months of my life have been reduced to this pile of papers. While Margareta's story has come alive for me through my file there's a hard knot in my stomach that I would like to unravel.

15. MAN U, BRECHT AND BOB DYLAN

An urn with a Manchester United logo, Bertolt Brecht's grave and a Bob Dylan song on a ghetto blaster. These were my brother's funeral symbols. He dropped dead from an aneurism while on holiday in Sicily in 2010. Just like that. No warning. He was sixty-two.

Tim had been living in Germany for many years, at least ten of them in Berlin with Gisela, his partner. She's a primary school teacher, ten years younger than him. I found her friendly and attractive with her curly dark brown hair framing a cheerful face. When she first met him, Tim had been working in a travel agency but when it folded he never got another job. I thought it amazing that he rebelled against our family's work ethic but Gisela was happy to support him. She was totally bereft when he died. She had just come out of the shower and there he was on the floor. By the time the emergency services arrived he was dead.

Patrick left me an incoherent message on my answerphone. He said that Tim had fallen and I thought he'd said that he was dead but I couldn't believe it. I rang back and Patrick, still in shock, told me the news. I felt nothing. Like the news of Mum's and Dad's deaths I didn't seem to feel what you're supposed to when someone has died: shock, disbelief, pain, anger. I could say I felt numb, but I'm not sure the numbness was protecting me from accepting death. I simply accepted it and wanted to move on. The numbness was because I wasn't feeling anything. I felt sorry for them and especially for their partners, but in a way their deaths liberated me. I hadn't been close to any of them for a long time and now I didn't have to maintain an imperfect relationship. Shocking. Gisela, however, felt a grief so intense she couldn't accept it.

The funeral was held exactly one month after Tim died. Gisela had to fly his body back to Berlin and get the death certificate translated from Italian into German before the cremation could go ahead. There was a waiting list for the cremation and another wait to book a slot for a ceremony at the cemetery where the urn was buried. You can't chuck ashes any old where in Germany.

The Dorotheenstadt Cemetery in central Berlin is small and pretty. Although there are only about one hundred graves it's stuffed with important Germans, among them Bertolt Brecht whose plays were right up Tim's street. On that bright mid-November day there were still a few leaves clinging to slender branches, shielding the cemetery from the surrounding streets. About twenty of us attended the ceremony in the small chapel. I'm used to half-hour or hour-long ceremonies, but this was a good two hours, mainly because the German speeches were translated into English. But it was enlivened by a slide show of Tim on his various travels. At the end of the ceremony we all walked slowly to the grave, led by Gisela carrying the urn with its Manchester United logo and Werner, Gisela's best friend, bringing up the rear with a ghetto blaster loudly proclaiming 'Like a Rolling Stone'.

I hadn't visited Berlin since but kept in touch with Gisela through Christmas and birthday cards. Researching family history over the summer of 2014 I wondered if she wanted to be involved so emailed her asking if she'd chat to me about Tim's views on adoption and identity. I wanted to know if he too had looked for his birth parents or even expressed an interest. Gisela was on a summer holiday in France at the time but when she returned to Berlin she booked an October flight to London. I quickly realised how keen she was to be involved in any research into Tim's identity. Four years after his death she was still grieving.

Looking through Tim's papers to see if there was anything relevant she found a letter from our dad – obviously a reply to a request from Tim wanting to know if he had any information on his adoption. It was written in 1986, before any of us started looking for our birth family. It seemed that Tim wanted an answer to the question people would ask him: 'Where are you from?' We'd always been told that Tim's father was French Canadian and his mother English, but, looking South Asian as he did, he must have felt that didn't explain his features. Dad wrote to Tim saying:

Your natural mother was a 17-year-old London girl, who lost her parents in the London blitz in 1941, at the age of 10, and was brought up by relatives. Your father was said to be French Canadian, and an electrical engineer. He had left the scene some time before. You were born in Hammersmith Hospital. Your mother came up to the adoption hearing at Birmingham County Court although there was no need for her attendance. So we did meet her and I have a clear recollection of her. She was of medium height, slight build, black hair (longish), and 'sharpish' but attractive features of a slightly Jewish cast. She seemed an intelligent and sensitive girl, though not particularly educated (understandably, given her war-time background)…She had decided to make a fresh start overseas and she had applied for training as a nurse in one of the dominions and had been accepted.

She had come up to Birmingham to see you. She had named you Timothy so we kept that name as we liked it too. She had brought a teddy bear to give you. It was, of course, a sad occasion but she seemed to be reasonably happy about you and us, though naturally very regretful.

I wondered what Tim thought when he read this letter. Did it satisfy his desire to know his background? There were still uncertainties, not least his Jewish identity and the fact that his father was said to be French Canadian. I had always known my Swiss and Indian identity and likewise Ellen and Patrick knew their Asian and African heritage. As children we'd never discussed what we felt about our identity and only as an adult had I broached the topic with Ellen and Patrick.

The last time I had visited Berlin, Tim and I went to the Jewish Museum. It was my suggestion because I'd wanted to see the building designed by Daniel Libeskind. Tim was keen to show it to me. Its stark exterior is constructed of zinc with empty spaces cutting through the building. I remember the concrete-lined Holocaust Tower with its irregular disorienting walls and dark interior lit only by a small slit in the roof. I can still hear the scrunching sound made by my feet walking over iron faces laid higgledy-piggledy on the floor in another of the spaces. But it seemed to me that the exhibits were not displayed to their advantage.

'The building is wonderful,' I said. 'But the exhibits aren't very interesting. Old documents displayed in glass cases like this. They're a bit boring.'

'How can you say that?' Tim retorted. 'I think they're interesting. It's my history. You know my mother was Jewish, don't you?'

So he'd clung to that odd phrase in Dad's letter, that his mother had a 'slightly Jewish cast'. Tim's putative Jewish identity was obviously important to him, in the same way as my Indian identity was important to me. I didn't know what to say at the time, not having seen Dad's letter. I wish now that I'd asked him why he seemed threatened by my negative views of the exhibits.

Dad's letter gave Gisela and me somewhere to start looking for Tim's background. By 2014 the green, red and black registers of births, marriages and deaths were piled up somewhere in the basement in the National Archives in Kew and the records were now online. One day in September, before Gisela came to visit, I accessed the Births, Marriages and Deaths website to look for all Timothys born in the quarter beginning March 1948 in Hammersmith. The website was really easy to use. All you had to do was to type in the few bits of information and press the Find button. But it wasn't working properly. I imagined millions of people accessing the website to find out their family history. I waited until two in the morning and accessed the site in bed on my iPad. The results came back within seconds. There were only four boys named Timothy but only one of these, Timothy Griffiths, had a mother whose maiden name was the same, indicating she wasn't married. I sent off for the birth certificate from the General Register Office. When it arrived it was clear it was the right one as the birth date matched Tim's. It even had the word 'adopted' printed on the right hand side of the form. His mother was a Rose Winnie Griffiths. Easy.

Then it got more difficult. We hadn't really a lot of information to go on and the name isn't uncommon. I wanted to proceed with caution but Gisela was eager to acquire as much information as possible about his possible birth mother. Based on the age Dad had given, she would have been born in 1930 or 1931. Gisela thought we would start with all the Rose W Griffithses born between 1922 and 1932. Gisela obtained four birth certificates, although I said that was rather a long time-span, given that we thought Tim's mother was only seventeen at the time of his birth. One was born in March 1932 in Bedford who might just have fitted the bill. Could this be her? But Gisela was convinced it was another Rose W from Luton who would have been twenty-six when she had Tim.

Why are you so convinced that this is Tim's mother? I asked her. Because I searched the passenger records for that period and found that she had left on a ship bound for New Zealand, she replied. But why is that a reason? I said. Because your father wrote that she'd been accepted for nurse training in one of the dominions. When did she sail? I asked. Some months before Tim was adopted, she said. Then who was the mysterious seventeen-year-old who turned up in court with a teddy bear if the real mother was on a ship? Tim's mother must have given him to another young woman with the same name and that was the woman who attended court, Gisela said. Perhaps they were cousins, she added.

I couldn't believe that anyone would pass herself off as a mother when she wasn't, particularly as she didn't need to attend the court hearing in any case. I kept quiet but couldn't understand Gisela's insistence that this particular Rose W was Tim's mother.

Gisela arrived in London on a weekday evening in late October with a list of addresses she wanted to visit relating to Tim, his birth and the twenty-six-year-old Rose. We sat in my living room with my trusty Citymapper app and worked out an overground route connecting up all three addresses, since I wanted to show Gisela something of London above ground.

It was warm for the time of year so we were wearing light jackets. After a quick journey we crossed Finchley Road to an area of wide tree-lined avenues. Cutting down a small lane we turned into a street of imposing 19th century residences.

'Remind me why we're looking at this house?' I asked Gisela. I'd been so concerned at working out the perfect route the night before that I'd quite forgotten to ask her why we were visiting these places.

'It's where Rose Griffiths was living before she left for New Zealand. I thought it would be interesting to see it.'

We studied the substantial double-fronted red-brick mansion which would be selling now for several million pounds. A low ivy-clad brick wall separated the front garden from the street. I pondered on the young woman living here in the late '40s. Such an environment didn't fit the background of the woman Dad had described in his letter but perhaps it was a hostel for young women waiting to go overseas. Was this really Tim's mother? I didn't think looking at this house took us any further on our journey to Tim's birth story.

Next up was New Barnet. This was where Tim's mother was living while pregnant. This house really was the place where Tim had spent his first few months, verified by an address on his birth certificate.

'Tim would have been horrified if he'd known he lived here until he was adopted,' said Gisela. 'He wouldn't have considered this to be London at all.'

'Indeed not! This is the outer suburbs, hardly London.'

It wasn't even genteel suburbia, but a traffic polluted area between two major A roads lined with office blocks. To sustain us we nipped into what appeared to be a greasy spoon on Station Approach, but actually turned out to serve delicious pasta dishes and tasty salads. Having eaten our fill of lasagne we came out of the café. Turning down Lyonsdown Road we walked past more small office blocks and mid-20th century brick built houses. We were surprised when we came upon the address we were looking for. It was a huge mansion, built I think in the 19th century, now home, not to mothers and babies, but to the Society of African Missions. I had supposed that Gisela would just take a photo and we'd be on our way, but no, she insisted that I ring the bell and ask if the building had ever been a mother and baby home. Rather nervously I rang the bell. A man of African appearance answered.

'I'm looking for connections to my brother, who was adopted from here in 1948.' I said. 'My name's Kamila and this is my sister-in-law, Gisela. I hope you don't mind me asking but can you tell me if this building was ever a mother and baby home?'

'I don't know as I've only been here a short while, but maybe my colleague, Father Manchala can help. Come through and I'll get him for you.'

He took us through into the large oak-panelled entrance hall which had several comfortable sofas placed beside a fire. We waited for a few minutes until a diminutive man came into the hall. But Father Manchala didn't know either. The Society had moved into the building years ago, perhaps as long ago as the '60s.

'I think it used to be some sort of nursery but I'm not sure. We moved here years ago. But Father Fenton may know. He's very old and has been here for ages. He'll certainly talk to you.' Father Manchala dug into his pocket extracting a card and a pen. 'Here's the number. He's away just now but will be back in ten days' time. The best time to talk to him is after 8 pm – but don't call too late in the evening.'

Gisela was delighted that we might get more information, but I was puzzled. I like old buildings but I didn't see how visiting the place where your partner's pregnant mother lived was helpful. I hadn't even looked up the place where my own pregnant mother was living although I know where it is. But then I remembered I did get a little frisson of excitement when I visited NCH's offices to get my records, knowing that I had lived there for a few months. It was just that I felt the connection was lost once the building changed hands.

It was time to move on to our next stop in Camberwell. The house we were looking for was where Tim's mother was living before she got pregnant. At least I think it was a residential address but because it was listed immediately under the mother's occupation (commercial clerk) it could be her place of employment. The building was in an unremarkable south London street of three-storey terraced houses, an unlikely place for an office. Gisela wanted me to ring the bells to all the flats in the house. I couldn't see the point as surely any relatives of Rose's would have long moved on. But I obliged. There was no answer from the first two bells but a man leaned out of the window of the top flat to ask us what we wanted. Gisela asked whether the place had ever been an office. Not as far as he was aware. All the flats were owned by Southwark Council.

'Gisela, let's move on,' I said, finding it embarrassing to be yelling out Tim's history in the middle of the street. 'I think it's much better if we go home, have a nice meal and talk about what to do next.' She agreed.

When Gisela left a day or two later she gave me a couple of tasks: firstly to phone Father Fenton and secondly to look at the electoral register for the address in Camberwell.

I tried Father Fenton a couple of times but there was never an answer. After trying three or four times I left a message but he never rang back. Instead, I used Google to see if there had ever been a mother and baby home in Lyonsdown Road. This immediately produced a result. 33 Lyonsdown Road was indeed a 'home for single mothers in need of care and guidance'. Known as Oakdene, it was a branch of the Foundling Hospital and opened as a home in 1948. So Tim must have been one of the first babies living there. Interesting, but as his adoption agency was the Children's Society his adoption records would be held there.

I turned my attention to the electoral register of 1948, ordering the volume for Camberwell from the British Library. There were eight people registered to vote in that house so it could have been divided into rooms or flats even then. There were no Griffithses listed. Indeed, if the story of Rose's parents being killed in the blitz were true she may have been living with her mother's relatives who wouldn't have been Griffithses.

I told Gisela what I'd found but she was intent on pursuing the twenty-six-year-old Rose W because of the New Zealand connection and didn't need further corroboration. I asked her how she could ever be certain she'd found the right Rose W. That's when she employed the help of spirits.

She went to séances and after a few false starts she found a couple of spiritual mediums who could contact Tim. And Tim's mother. And our adoptive mother. From the other side my brother said he was fine and he was in contact with his birth mother. His birth mother was definitely the twenty-six-year-old Rose who moved to New Zealand. Now totally convinced she had found the right mother, Gisela went onto the ancestry forums and put the word out that she was looking for this Rose W Griffiths. She found a New Zealand cousin, Marlene – the daughter of Rose's brother and they started to message each other on Facebook. Rose was dead. And Rose's brother was dead. But Gisela wouldn't stop her research for Tim's family.

Gisela's contact with the spirits reminded me of my sister's session with a shaman. Ellen had traced her mother to Hull, but we could find no trace of her after that. Thoughts of her mother were still at the back of her mind. It was important for Ellen that her mother knew how she was. So she contacted a shaman to find out about her mother.

Describing her session, Ellen said, 'So a few months after my trip to Hull I contacted a shaman. She said, "I'm getting lots of blanks and barriers. But you didn't set up this meeting – your mother set it up to let you know she did the best she could. She made a decision to offer you a life she couldn't have made for you herself." I asked the shaman whether that meant my mother knew about me and she said that although she was dead she did know that I was OK.'

'So did that resolve things for you then?' I asked sceptically.

Ellen didn't pick up on the scepticism. 'It did. It allowed me to let go. I believe that my mother knows I'm fine. I know that she did the best for me. That's all I need to know.'

Ellen's shaman may have resolved things for her but aren't they clever at saying things they think you want to believe? The experience allowed my sister to stop her search for her mother. She knew enough and could now be at peace with her past. But for Gisela the search hadn't given her peace of mind. She corresponded with Marlene and pursued her family. She constructed a family tree down to the year 1040. She was keeping Tim alive through her search. There was no let-up to her grief.

I remained unconvinced. I wondered at the use of spiritual mediums and shamans and contacting spirits on the other side. As far as I knew neither Gisela nor Ellen had thought to contact spirits from beyond the grave before this whole question of researching birth mothers came up.

I don't believe in spirits so this didn't work for me. I have a curious nature and what would close something for me is hard evidence. I approached the problem from a different angle. I thought the best way to collect my evidence was through Tim's adoption agency, the Children's Society. However, I found that, as his sister, I wasn't allowed to access his file, even though he was dead. Who are these bureaucrats? Don't they think of us as real people with a real need to find out the background of our dead relatives? How dare they lock everything up and take away the key. I looked up the Adoption Search and Reunion website and found a group named the Descendants of Deceased Adopted Persons: DAP. There's a group for everything and this was the group for me. Set up in 2008 by a woman trying to access her dead father's adoption records, it campaigned for a change in the government's adoption legislation so that close relatives could access the records of their dead relatives. It fought a long hard battle for many years.

At the end of October 2014 the government agreed to change the legislation in our favour so I got my oar in early. I rang the Children's Society, Tim's adoption agency, to ask if they would put me on a waiting list to access Tim's file. Hopefully I would be first in the queue. I chatted at length to a sympathetic man, Manish. We discovered that we both knew Kolkata well and exchanged views on favourite Bengali delicacies and Kolkata restaurants. But he said he couldn't help me as the legislation was new and he needed guidelines to go with the legislation. He was consulting with all the big adoption agencies. He promised to let me know when I could access my brother's file.

I didn't hear anything for months. I rang a couple of times. Manish always knew who I was and was very sympathetic, but said he couldn't help yet. In the summer of 2015 I heard through the British Association for Adoption and Fostering that it had eventually produced guidelines for the adoption agencies so that they could check the identity of descendants looking for their relatives and help them access their adoption records.

So back I went to Manish. He recognised my voice and said he would send me the form to access Tim's file. I duly filled out the form and supplied endless information: Tim's birth certificate, his adoption certificate, his Italian death certificate, his death certificate translated into German, my adoption certificate proving I was his sister. Anything else? Oh yes, my change of name deed! A few weeks later Manish rang me to say he'd pulled the file from the archives but…there was not much in it. Tim didn't appear to have been adopted from there. And there was no record of my parents adopting him.

'What do you mean?' I said, thinking that if they've got a file then surely it meant he was adopted from there. 'I think he may be like my sister who was in your care also. They both ended up in a nursery in Birmingham and were adopted from there, but you still had the full file for my sister. I've seen it!'

'In your brother's case it must be that all his records went to that nursery then.'

'But what do you mean when you say you do have a file, even if it's small?' My voice rose and I started to whine. 'What's in that file and when can I come over and see it?'

'It does have some information about his mother, like her age, but you do know that we're not allowed to give it to you.'

'Wait a minute. Then what's this new legislation?' I was almost crying with frustration now.

Manish continued, sensing I was upset. 'You have to go through an intermediary. We don't act as intermediaries ourselves.'

'You mean I have to go through counselling to get this information?' I couldn't believe it. I'd end up having my fourth interview with that all too familiar person – the intermediary or adoption counsellor.

'I'm afraid so. Look, I know it must be frustrating, but what I'd advise you do is either contact your local council's adoption services or if you go onto the British Association of Adoption and Fostering, there's a list of people who are approved intermediaries.'

'OK, OK. I'm going to say goodbye before I blow a fuse, Manish. Thanks for your help. I know it's not your fault but yes, it's more than frustrating. It's actually making me angry.'

Poor Manish. I put the phone down and immediately went on to the DAP Facebook page. It was full of people trying to trace their dead relatives. There seemed to be one intermediary who was being very helpful. I contacted her. I had to furnish her with those same goddam forms – birth certificates, death certificates, change of name certificates. Round and round we go.

Not the end of the story. My intermediary tried to access the same thin file that Manish referred to but with no success. Was Manish inundated with requests, had he misplaced the file or had it been spirited away? Gisela 1 - Kamila 0.

16. SUCCESS AT LAST

If 2012 is the best year of my life (60th birthday cake, London Olympics volunteer, Everest Base Camp), then 2013 is the worst. In June I discover a lump in my abdominal area so the doctor refers me to a colorectal surgeon at the Royal Free Hospital. I see the surgeon exactly two weeks later.

'Yes there is something there,' he says. 'But I haven't a clue what it is. You'll have to have a CT scan.'

Two weeks later I have a CT scan. The surgeon goes on holiday. Two weeks after the scan I see his registrar.

'I'm not sure where this mass is coming from. It doesn't look as though it's coming from the bowel,' he says, looking rather worried. No, that's not right. Doctors aren't supposed to look worried. 'We need to hold a team meeting. After that I guess the next stage will be to get a biopsy of your mass,' he adds, personalising my lump.

'It's not mine,' I say. 'It's an alien. It doesn't belong to me.' The registrar stares at me, not knowing what to say. 'I'll get you a date and get in touch with you.' I'm dismissed.

I'm trying to enjoy the summer exploring the south of England on day trips: a trip to Whitstable, a gorgeous day out in Dungeness. I'm in Frinton-on-Sea wandering on the cliff top taking photos of the art deco houses there when I get a call from the hospital.

'I've got you a date for your Pepsi scan,' the disembodied voice tells me.

'What's a Pepsi scan?' I ask. 'I don't drink Pepsi.' The waves are gently surging on the shore below and I can't hear the woman's voice well. She spells it out. 'A PET CT scan.'

So the statutory two weeks after I saw the registrar I present myself at the Department of Nuclear Medicine in the basement of the Royal Free. Nuclear medicine sounds dangerous to me – are they going to zap me with nuclear rays? The nuclear person, who is very friendly and comes from Spain, is very proud of the brand new PET CT scanner, of which there are only two or three in the whole of London. I try to speak a little Spanish and find out she's from Valencia. My Spanish isn't up to nuclear medicine terminology so we rapidly revert to English.

Two weeks later I get to see the consultant again. He's looking very sun-tanned. He motions for me to sit down on a chair placed in the middle of the room.

'Is anyone with you?' he says.

I shake my head. It's obvious he expects me to have someone there for support. Other patients I meet are usually accompanied by relatives – a partner or a son or daughter. I don't have any. My siblings don't live in London and I'm not sure they would make a special trip for me. Why don't I bring a friend? Isn't it a favour too far to ask someone to attend a frightening health meeting? Or is it my old fear of being rejected?

The consultant draws up a chair beside me instead of sitting at his desk in front of the computer. It's really odd, sitting side by side in the middle of the room.

'We've looked at your scans in detail and I have to tell you that you have a small mass attached to your pelvis, which you knew about, but there's one in your liver too. But don't worry. It's only small and it can probably be operated on. We think it might be connected to your previous episode of ovarian cancer but we can't treat it here at the Royal Free. We've referred you to University College Hospital – the specialist gynaecological cancer department there…'

I interrupt. 'In two weeks' time.'

'No, I've got you an appointment next Thursday.' He smiles at me. 'Look, it really is possible to treat. And UCLH is one of the best hospitals for ovarian cancer.'

It won't take a mathematician to work out that I would have my first appointment at UCLH eleven weeks after my GP referred me. Eleven weeks. Or almost three months. And that's the Royal Free keeping to its two-week targets for each stage. Exactly two weeks. Not a day less and not a day more. They can't be faulted for not keeping to their government targets.

I land up at Ms Adeyemi's colposcopy clinic. This is for women who've had abnormal cervical smears. I wonder why I'm here. I'm sitting in the waiting room with a lot of young women, some at various stages of pregnancy. I think there must be a pre-natal clinic going on too. The chairs are a deep green colour, and the walls a pale green. A calming green, I suppose. This doesn't calm me. I only have to wait fifteen minutes when a nurse calls me in to see Ms Adeyemi. I enter a large room with two consulting beds. There's a knees-up machine above one of them, familiar to women having a smear test – the one with stirrups where you place your legs so the doctor can shove a horrid cold speculum up your vagina.

'Good afternoon, Kamila,' Ms Adeyemi says. She's tiny and very slim, wearing a scarlet shift dress with a matching belt. I can't believe the height of her heels which must be at least fifteen centimetres. And then, as though she really wants to know, she says, 'Kamila Zahno. Where's that name from?' I give her the all too familiar summary of my origins, pre-empting any questions about my family medical history. 'Interesting,' she says. And I believe that she really is interested as she looks me right in the eye and smiles as she says it. 'Let's get you up on the bed and look at you.'

I obligingly lie on the bed and allow her to examine me. The speculum isn't cold at all. Perhaps they don't use metal these days. I don't look. She prods my tummy and my lump – to me it's a lump not a mass.

'We need to get you a biopsy.' In two weeks, I think. And then she surprises me by saying, 'When I saw your notes I thought I would get that sorted for you. So if you come in on Monday at 10 am that will be done and we can get the results for when you next see me. I've made an appointment to see you again next Thursday.'

I'm in the system. My head is in a strange space. I've been living with this lump for months and now they're going to see what it is. It can't be ovarian cancer again. Not after thirteen years. But it is. Ms Adeyemi confirms that when I next see her.

'I've booked you for an operation to remove the abdominal mass at the end of September and then when you've recovered from that we'll send you to the Royal Free for a resection of your liver.' I'm not keen to go back there, but I gather it's one of only two London hospitals that can do that operation, the other being King's College Hospital in south London.

'Can't you schedule your operation any sooner?' I ask, feeling very worried at this continued delay.

'I'm due to go on holiday. That's the first date after I'm back. A few weeks won't make any difference,' she says with conviction. 'Don't worry.'

I'm not convinced. All these two-week intervals make up months of waiting and of course the cancer can spread in this time. But I'm not the doctor, I'm only the patient patient.

The operation, when the time comes, is fine. I'm only in hospital for three days and my recovery is fast. I have an appointment to see the liver surgeon. He keeps me waiting for two hours and doesn't apologise for the wait. I don't like him. He shows me the scans in full technicolour glory. I don't want to see them. He frightens me by saying he's discovered several tumours in different parts of my liver. Don't worry, he says. We can operate. He books me in for an operation in six weeks' time.

Five weeks roll by – I don't get a confirmation so I ring my cancer nurse at the Royal Free. I don't get through to her, but to a colleague. She confirms that the operation has been cancelled and I will hear soon about it being rescheduled. I hear nothing. I ring the cancer nurse at UCLH who says she doesn't have any control over another hospital. But don't worry, she says. They know what they're doing. I ring the cancer nurse at the Royal Free again. Don't worry, she says. Cancer doesn't spread that fast.

I tell her I haven't had a scan since the one in June and it's now mid-November. There is a short silence and then I hear a gasp at the other end of the phone. She books me a scan and I get an operation date soon afterwards. It's cancelled. I ring a person in the appointments section. She says, you need to be scheduled within a few days otherwise they will miss their referral-to-treatment target. Would you consider another surgeon? Anything, I say. And not so I fulfil your damn target but because I might die. I see another surgeon. The cancer nurse is in the room with him. He's looking at my latest scan on the computer. He looks serious. No he doesn't. He looks frightened. He tells me that the tumour has tripled in size and is now inoperable. Fuck, I think, I'm fucked. He says he has referred me to an oncologist at UCLH. He's the first medic who doesn't say don't worry. He's looking almost tearful. As I leave he grasps my right hand with both of his hands and wishes me luck. Luck, I think. I need a bit more than luck.

Finally I get to meet the oncologist, six months after first visiting my GP. She acknowledges I've had poor treatment but she is calm. She says, I'm going to recommend three cycles of chemo to shrink the tumour and then we're going to refer you to King's College Hospital early next year. She's sent my scans to Professor Evans there and he agrees it's all possible. She says, we'll give you another three cycles of chemo after the operation and you might go into remission. OK, I say. But I've got stage 4 ovarian cancer. I know once it's spread to other organs it's incurable. We don't say stage 4 in your case, she says. We call it 'relapsed' cancer. And yes it's incurable, but many women in your situation live for quite a few years.

How many years is quite a few? I'm very frightened. She refers me for counselling. My counsellor is brilliant. I say I'm frightened of my incurable status although I've accepted it. I want some help to 'live in the now'. She helps me to come to an understanding that it's about refocusing my life, deciding what I want to do and doing it. But being realistic about what I might be able to do, rather than denying my shortened life span. My bucket list.

The tumour shrinks by half after chemo and the Prof gets rid of it altogether when he operates. I ask him when he thinks it will return. Don't think like that, he says. Live your life. I'm planning to write my memoir, I say. The Prof laughs. Why is that funny? I say. It's because I want to write mine, he says, but I never have time.

After my liver operation and chemo there is No Evidence of Disease (NED). That doesn't mean to say it isn't lurking in the corners of my body so I agree to go on a drug trial to maintain my NED status. I might have accepted that my cancer is incurable but that doesn't mean I can't take all the drugs available to prolong my life. As long as I'm feeling well.

It's May 2014. For the moment I can forget about the cancer, live in that famous 'now' and decide what my bucket list is to be. I hadn't been working during my operations and, in any case, work had been steadily drying up over the past year or so. I put out the word that I've retired. I recall my conversation in February with Professor Evans about my book. Now is the time. But an adoption story without a search and reunion might be odd.

That's when I seriously take up my previous half-hearted research into my family history. All I'd done previously when I'd recovered from my first bout of cancer was to write to the registrar in Fribourg who couldn't help me to trace Margareta Zahno. Now I enlist the help of my friend Brian, who's a whizz when it comes to family history, including looking at foreign genealogical sites. He's researched his Jewish history, set up a family website and is always trotting off to see distant relatives in Poland, Estonia and the States. I give him the main points of reference – Margareta's birth year and the Luzern address listed in my adoption file.

A few weeks later we meet for lunch at my place. I spread out plates of cheese, hummus, bread and salad on the table. Brian opens his carefully prepared file and shows me what he had come up with. A list of phone numbers for Zahnos in Fribourg and in Luzern. The address for the official archives in Fribourg. An address for the genealogical society of Fribourg and email contacts of people who will conduct genealogical research for you for free. Addresses and emails for genealogists in Luzern. A list of questions and answers on searching for family history from the Swiss Genealogists' website. And, strangely, a list of church bulletins listing memorial Masses run for four women named Margareta Zahno.

'Why on earth have you included these bulletins?' I say, flicking through the pages.

'You could write to the priests conducting the Mass and see if they'll give you a contact for the family. I think it could be a shortcut to finding your family.'

My mind is buzzing. 'Mmm, I think it's a long shot but I guess it's worth a try.'

I write to those four priests who said Mass for women named Margareta Zahno in the Canton of Fribourg. I email them in French, using my old name Camilla Wray, saying I'm looking for family contacts for Margareta Zahno who was a friend of my mother's in England in 1952. I give the year I think Margareta was born as she told the adoption agency she was twenty-three.

Three emails come back within a few days but I never hear from the fourth. I'm surprised at the openness of the priests. They don't query why I'm looking for Margareta's family contacts. One says the Margareta I've inquired about is too young to be the woman I'm looking for as she was born in 1939. Another doesn't have any contacts for the family. But the third writes back giving me the obituary, not of Margareta Zahno, but her husband. He'd gone to all the bother of researching the death of Margareta Zahno's husband.

Find attached the obituary of the husband of the friend of your mother's, Ruedi Zahno, who died in 1998. His wife died in 1982 as can be seen from the obituary.

PS Here are a few addresses of the children.

The addresses and phone numbers of four children are attached. But it's clear from the obituary that Margareta is a Zahno by marriage, so this Margareta is not mine, alas. If it had been my mother, I could have been in contact with my half-brothers and sisters!

The whole priest thing has turned out to be a red herring. I feel it's more productive to get the Swiss archivists and genealogists to help me. I turn to Brian's file of information and email a few of the contacts. This time I use my own name as I don't think officials would query why I was looking for her.

I am searching for information (birth, death, marriage) about a family member, Margareta Zahno, who came from Fribourg. She was aged twenty-three in May, 1952 so must have been born between May 1928 and May 1929. She came to London in December 1950 but returned to Switzerland in January 1953 to her mother's home in Luzern: Flackehof 9, Rothenburg.

A few days later a guy from the Archives for the Canton of Fribourg emails to tell me that he runs a historical archive and all genealogical information is protected for 120 years. I work out I could start my search in 2049. I don't think I'll live that long. But he does say that most of the Zahnos in Switzerland come from Tafers or Dudingen in the district of Sense. He says if I have more information about her home town and the name of her parents the local Registrar should be able to provide me with more details. I don't find much information about these villages on the internet. Small towns; most of the population speak German; religion Catholic. I find this strange as the rest of Fribourg Canton is French speaking and Protestant. I recall how Margareta proclaimed that I was C of E on my adoption form. Odd.

Then it's the turn of the official from the Fribourg City Archives. He is helpful and writes me a long email in French. My French is passable and I can understand it. He has taken some time on my behalf.

We found that Margareta Zahno, daughter of Ferdi and Anneli, originally from the commune of Guin/Dudingen was born on 22nd

November 1929. According to our city records Margareta Zahno lived in Fribourg from 21st September 1946 and 7th June 1947, and again from 5th September 1947 and 23rd November 1948. If you want to find out more information about Margareta Zahno you should contact the Registry Office in the Sense District. They will ask you for a permit which you get from the Service cantonal de l'etat civil.

I'm not sure what he means by a permit. So that's one piece of information that matches up in that many Zahnos come from Dudingen, but that would mean she would have been twenty-two when she had me, not twenty-three. Would she have told the adoption worker she was older than she was? Or perhaps the Swiss count birthdays from the day they were born so her 23rd birthday would be what we would call her 22nd.

I contact the State Archives in the District of Sense to ask if they have any birth, marriage or death records for Margareta Zahno born between May 1928 and 1929. Early the next morning back comes a reply from the Sense archivist. I turn to Mr Google for a translation.

To undertake genealogical research you need a permit from the supervisory authority. We kindly ask you to contact the Cantonal Office for Civil Status and Naturalization in Fribourg to obtain such authorisation.

I am dizzy from this merry-go-round. I don't know what kind of information they want from me. The phone number is given but I can't find an email address so I pluck up the nerve to ring them, hoping my French is good enough.

The recorded message informs me in both German and French that the office is open Monday to Friday between the hours of 8 and 11:30 am and from 2 to 5 pm. It's 11:10 am but no one answers. It seems that Switzerland consists of people living in fortified towns and villages with gates firmly locked against strangers. I want to bash someone over the head – but these are virtual people! I punish some machines at the gym instead. I do rather well. Anger has fuelled my energy.

But by June I'm starting to feel side effects from the trial drug. My red blood cell count dives to 75 g/L, which is really low, and every time I walk up the stairs at home I collapse in a heap at the top. I have no energy to continue my search. Perhaps I really will have to wait till 2049 when the records will be made public.

A Thursday evening in January 2015. I've just been informed that the trial drug isn't working and I've got new liver tumours. I stop the drug and recover my energy, despite the growing tumours. I agree to another course of chemotherapy but it takes a couple of cycles for the debilitating side effects to kick in, so I'm feeling reasonably well. Now is the time to break into my locked chest, whether it is a treasure chest or Pandora's box. I will break in. I'm not going to wait until 2049 until Margareta is 120 years old. These records shall be mine.

I'm chatting by email to my Geneva-based friend, Leanne, about my frustrating search for Margareta's birth certificate and for her current whereabouts. I tell her that one of my searches revealed that the Swiss record keepers seem able to track people when they move around the country. Would it be worth writing to the archivist in Luzern to see if they can find Margareta who moved to Luzern in 1953? Leanne says, yes they might be able to help and gives me the English language version of the Luzern City Archive website.

Later that night in January, in the calm green of my bedroom, I write to the Luzern City Archivist:

I'm trying to trace a Margareta Zahno who moved from England to Flackehof, Rothenburg in January, 1953. Any information on her movements, her marriage or possible death would be welcome.

I whack off the email and, going by my previous experience, I really don't have high expectations of finding Margareta. I sleep well beneath my cosy duvet, Raasay, my cat, curled up in a ball at my feet. I check on my computer at 10 am the next morning and there is an email from a Mr Walter Honegger saying that the actual address is in Rothenburg – a separate municipality from Luzern – so he had forwarded my email to the local residents' registration office there. Mr Honegger is certainly quick on the uptake but he's now passing me to someone else. I've come to expect dead ends so I don't think anything will come of it. If I can't find my birth family I can spend time thinking about my adoptive family. That weekend I sort out my early photo albums, selecting some of Mum and Dad, taken during their time in India, for framing. A bird in hand…

A few days later, I'm just settling down at my computer with my morning pot of tea when I receive an email from an Ursula Koehl, the archivist in Rothenburg:

We found out that Mrs Margareta Zahno got married and her name after her marriage was Jansen. She lived before in Luzern. We got to know the information that she passed away four months ago. But Mrs Margareta Jansen had a daughter. She lives near Zürich. Her name is Nora Fischli-Jansen. If you need more information about Mrs Margareta Jansen-Zahno please get in contact with Mrs Nora Fischli through her website.

Ms Koehl gives me the name of the website. Simple. I'm shaking and my mouth is dry. I sit on the floor in a huddle. My years of searching have come up with a dead mother. And one who only died four months ago – in October last year. Why did I dither for all those years? But it appears I may have a sister – and I can contact her at the click of a button! After all the locked doors encountered on my previous searches, the door is suddenly wide open, and there's somebody at home. I get up from the floor, sit at my computer and gaze at the wall where I've hung a print of Joseph Crawhall's *Drake*, bought at an exhibition of the work of the Glasgow Boys some years ago. The white bird has settled in a meadow of daisies and dandelions, black eye gleaming. Golden sunshine floods the meadow. Perhaps the drake is searching for a mate just as I am now searching for my sister.

I need to find out more about Nora. I look at the website and translate the German through Google. She's a holistic health coach, running personal courses and seminars using spiritual healing, acupuncture and meditation. The combination of badly translated German and unfamiliar jargon makes it difficult for me to understand what she actually does. Far more exciting than this is the picture I manage to find through Google images.

I pore over her photo. She has long greying hair scraped back from her high forehead which makes her face look long. Her head is tilted back and she has a cheery smile. I find a photo of me wrapped in a red tartan scarf taken at a recent Burns Supper and place it next to Nora. No resemblance. I send both photos to a few friends and no one thinks there's much of a likeness except maybe for a high forehead.

So is this my sister? How do I approach her? I can't just tell her who I am. Her mother – our mother – has just died, and now a sister suddenly appears. I remember what the adoption agencies tell you to do if you are tracing a friend, neighbour or relative of your birth parents. You pretend you're the parent's friend's daughter and say that some papers and photos of the parent have recently come to light. But I can't even do this without changing my name. Zahno would give the game away. I use my Gmail account with my adopted name of Camilla Wray.

Forgive me for writing like this but I have been trying to trace Margareta Zahno who was born around 1928/29 and was from the Fribourg area. She was a friend of my mother's when she was living in London in 1950-1953, where she came to learn English. I know that she left London for Luzern in 1953. I wonder whether this is your mother, Margareta Zahno? Sadly my mother passed away a while ago and I'm also sorry for the loss of your mother, Margareta. I have some old papers about Margareta when she was here and wonder whether you would like to know more.

I have used Google Translate below but do reply in German as I can get that translated.

I wonder about the translation – I hope she can understand! But she doesn't have to read the German. She writes back the very next day:

First of all we can communicate in English because my mother returned from England, met my American father, left for the US, married, got pregnant and came back in 1955 from the US forever. That was short!

Nora's got a sense of humour! She tells me a little about Margareta, who died in October 2014 after struggling with dementia for two years. Nora also tells me that Margareta had chosen a difficult life after England – although she doesn't say why – and adds:

It is joyful to hear that your mother knew her and you may have something to say about her. Because everything is still pretty fresh. I had to do a lot of looking through old papers, photos, etc. and a lot of memories that she told me came to mind. So yes, I would be very interested to hear from you again.

Now I'm getting too near the truth and I'm afraid of what it will bring. What if she doesn't want to know me? Or worse, we might not get on. I've got a new relationship to handle at this stage of my life, but I could be dead in a year. Is it fair to introduce myself as a sister when she might lose me in a couple of years? But I've gone so far now I can't worry about that.

I don't want Nora to have a huge shock about baby Monica so I try to prepare her:

My dear Nora, what did your mother tell you about her life in London? I need to know this as I don't want to give you too much of a surprise. I do have papers and I think (and hope) you will want to know further.

Nora doesn't answer. What have I done? Does she think I'm a fraud? I lie awake at night worrying that I've opened, not a locked door, but a dam. I just wonder why she's taking so long to reply. I ask my closest friends what to do. 'Wait,' they say. 'It's only been a few days. She may not look at her computer every day.'

I take a solitary few days in a friend's flat in Southwold, my favourite seaside town. I distract myself playing with Tim Hunkins hand-crafted, weird and whacky slot machines on the pier – I whack a banker, take a walk round Southwold at dog's-eye level, and make a disastrous journey to a tropical destination. On other days I walk up the lighthouse, have a tour of the Adnam's Brewery, eat fish and chips and walk across the marshes to Walberswick. When I'm back in the flat alone I keep checking my phone for emails. A few days after I arrive, Nora emails me again telling me about her freelance work for the last twenty years as a spiritual healer. Before that she was a human resources manager in a large hotel chain. And she does want to know more:

About England I do not know a lot. My mother liked it that she lived in a household and that is about all I know. So you can imagine I am eager to learn everything about her at that time. I have also found papers in her things that were very interesting for the time when she lived here. So I am ready for every surprise or not. Whatever it is I love her. And everything she did after she got me was done for my sake.

Nora's giving me the cue that she's guessed something is up. It's time to tell her what actually happened. I write a short email about Margareta giving birth to a baby girl, Monica, and about the adoption, adding:

Here's the news that's a surprise but I actually know Monica and she would like you to know all this and to write to you. She would respect any decision of yours to correspond or not. She would like you to know at least that she thinks Margareta would have been proud of her. She would also have loved to have met Margareta but it was not to be.

This is a big surprise for you I know.

Nora seems to be online and emails straight back telling me:

Yes it is a great surprise, but not as much as most people would think. If Monica is my half-sister, I find it very beautiful that we can write and see each other and keep in contact. I have already two half-brothers, so you see it is not something completely new to me. My half-brothers are the boys of my father and his second wife.

Nora is being cautious and not leaping to conclusions. She tells me that the dates Margareta was in England might not match with when she met Nora's father in 1953. Actually they do, although it must have been a whirlwind relationship. Margareta left London in March 1953 and must have met Nora's father pretty much immediately. She left for the States soon after and became pregnant with Nora at the beginning of 1955. That adds up. But some 'facts' I have in my adoption file turn out not to be true. Nora tells me that her grandparents, Margareta's parents, didn't split up which is what Margareta had told her adoption worker. And her grandmother never lived in Luzern, so Nora didn't return to live with her mother, but her eldest sister instead. Nora is a pragmatist and wants to proceed slowly and to verify all the facts, but perhaps Margareta embroidered her story somewhat to gain Miss Dean's sympathy.

You can please tell Monica I welcome her and if she really is the daughter of my mother I will invite her here to show her how she lived and who she was. I am really good at things like that. If this is the truth then it really explains a lot. My mother never wanted to give me away for adoption and even though I did not grow up with her, because she had to work, I saw her once a week. I was given to the family of her sister and grew up with two mothers and fathers. Which at times was not really easy.

Also, if my mother should not be her mother too, then we will find out who is. I doubt a little but it could well be. So let us go about it open minded, for the good of us all.

I'm feeling guilty at my deception. I write back immediately to tell Nora I am Monica. And get this as a reply:

Welcome to my family. I thought it would be yourself. I think, since I am a very practical person, a blood test would give the two of us the truth. Probably. Do you have any pictures of my mother or any handwriting from that time?

Nora tells me she is off on holiday to the Dominican Republic the next day and she won't be checking her email, suggesting that we correspond by Whatsapp instead. This flurry of emails has taken about half an hour. I sign onto Whatsapp and look at Nora's profile photo. A younger me stares back – long dark hair, dark glasses and round cheeks. I send the photo to my old school-friend, Eve, who agrees it's a remarkable likeness. There is now no doubt in my mind that Nora is my sister.

I stand looking out of the window of the top-floor flat in Southwold. The sun is setting across the Town Marshes, catching the bottlebrush heads of the rushes in its glow. Further south towards the coast I can make out the Sizewell B nuclear power station, its white mosque-like dome gleaming in the evening light. I wonder what gleaming dome will suppress the emotions that are threatening to explode inside me.

A couple of days later I return to London. I delve into my adoption file to dig out the postcard written by Margareta to the adoption agency, take a photo on my phone and send it to Nora sitting sunning herself in the Caribbean. I don't get an answer; there's probably no signal. Then a Whatsapp message appears. Nora is sure this is our mother. 'The writing is hers and what's more the way she writes is hers too.'

We don't need a blood test. We don't need any photos. We are sisters.

17. SWITZERLAND

What do you say when you first meet your half-sister in your sixties? Hello? So pleased to meet you? For the past six months Nora and I have been corresponding by Skype and Whatsapp so we know what each of us looks like, what we like to do, and even what we like to eat. But even though we're not total strangers you can't form a real relationship through Skype. What do we have in common aside from a shared mother? Cheese! It may seem counter-intuitive to take cheese to Switzerland but who can resist good Cheddar, crumbly Wensleydale and nettle-wrapped Cornish Yarg. I'd just bought a selection when Nora Skypes to give me last-minute instructions about where to meet – and she asks if I like cheese. We are cheese sisters.

Here I am at Zürich Airport. I walk down the steps from the plane, go through the connecting tunnel, pass through passport control and customs, and there is Nora smiling and waving. I can hear a waterfall roaring in my ears and a wave of fear passes through me. I reach for her, this sister, the first person I have ever met who shares my DNA. Her embrace surrounds me. We say nothing. I gulp back a sob.

We travel home on the train, changing once to a bus, and reach the small town of Richterswil, on the shore of the Zürichsee. I wheel my suitcase up the hill to the Spanish-style housing complex where Nora lives. Entering the house through the hallway, we dutifully remove our shoes and go into the kitchen with its wooden cupboards reaching to the ceiling.

'This calls for a celebration,' Nora says, producing a bottle of non-alcoholic champagne from the fridge. Nora can't drink since her liver's been damaged from the Hepatitis C she acquired through a blood transfusion in the early '80s. 'Here's to my lovely sister.' We toast each other. The champagne tastes like a sweeter version of Appletise.

I gaze at her, thinking she looks less like me now than she did on Skype. Her face is longer than mine, but there is some similarity around the cheeks. 'Do you think we look like each other?' I ask.

She gives me an appraising look. 'I can't see it. Of course we're sisters – we're sure of that – but I take after my father more than our mother.'

I'm disappointed. This is the first blood relative I've ever met. I want us to look alike, be alike, think alike. At least we have cheese in common. I give Rita my gift of cheese.

'Oh thank you. We love cheese – you'll see. And this English cheese is bound to be very different from ours.'

We move into the lounge. Nora must have the complete collection of the gnomes of Zürich. I'm being unfair. There's only one gnome-like figure: a girl in plaits, head topped by a pixie hat and wearing a blue and white checked apron. But in addition there are five Buddhas; a blue-faced Krishna; six dolphins, two of which light up; two ceramic lizards crawling up the wall; six winged angels; seven baby-faced cherubs, some curled up in a basket of their wings; a couple of glittery reindeers which also serve as floor lamps; two seals and a solitary ceramic frog. And in pride of place is a split amethyst rock, displaying its purple plastic crystals, a pottery Mary on a circular pedestal sitting inside.

In contrast to the eclectic collection of ornaments on the walls, the large light lounge is sparsely furnished with a white leather two-piece suite, a flat screen TV and a dining area with a glass table and four green upholstered dining chairs. A green hand-knotted silk rug adorns the solid oak floor. The glass doors at the end of the room give way to a small garden, crammed with ceramic ornaments, as well as what appears to be a wooden lighthouse which seems ill-placed in a landlocked country like Switzerland.

I've brought yet another ornament as a present – a small grey pottery vase adorned by a poppy on one side and feel it will be out of place. I give it to Nora who thanks me while carefully taking out a little paper doily from a cupboard to place underneath the vase.

'I see you have quite a few ornaments already,' I say.

'Oh I know. I don't like most of them but once people see you like dolphins they keep giving them to you. And if they visit, you have to display them. But I do like a certain amount of kitsch and occasionally indulge myself. Don't you just love this blue dolphin lamp?' She switches it on to show the tiny LED bulbs lighting up its body.

We take my luggage downstairs to the basement and she shows me the shower room in the cellar. She's a hoarder: boxes of toilet paper, orange juice, paper tissues, cans of tomatoes – all useful items, but why so many? She takes me on a tour of the house. It's tall and thin: one room wide, two rooms long and four storeys high. We go up to the top floor where there's a hot tub and a beautiful view of Zürichsee over the rooftops of the town. We don't talk about ourselves, but about the house – the leaking hot tub, the neighbour who built a chimney on Nora's part of the roof.

At six Daniel, Nora's husband, comes home. His round rimless glasses combined with a neat trim beard and balding head give him a Steve Jobs look. Indeed, Daniel's a consultant working in the software industry. Nora tells me he's not the hugging kind, and I tell her I'm not either. But she insists Daniel hugs his new sister-in-law. Our glasses clash making us laugh. The awkward atmosphere changes.

Nora's got a plan for me. I remember in one of her first emails that she said she was good at talking about the family. One of the main things she's arranged is a visit to the family home in Schmitten where Margareta grew up, and where David, one of our cousins still lives. But until then, there's lots of talking to do.

Nora is crucial to my understanding of Margareta, this mother who'd been in the background of my life for so long, this mother whose past had been shut out from me. Would Nora's picture of her reveal that she was a mirror of myself: independent, clever, forthright? What connection would I feel to her?

On the second day out come Nora's photo albums along with her feelings. To me places and spaces are often more interesting than people and feelings so my albums are full of mountains, lakes and glaciers. Nora's are all of people. Early photos show Nora with our mum, Margareta, taken on her one-day-a-week visit. Mother and daughter look happy in all the photos and they both wear smart clothes – at least compared to what my family wore in the '60s: a chocolate brown suit for Margareta and, for a six-year-old Nora, a white pleated skirt and a brown jacket. This is really bringing up emotions for Nora. She elaborates on her difficult relationship with her aunt's family and her confusion over the weekly visit by her mum.

'Because Margareta visited once a week I was never really treated as a daughter of my aunt and uncle. Tante Gemma was rather stern and her daughter, Ines, could be quite horrid to me at times. She's much better now – she's mellowed. I remember one time when I really felt left out. Philippe, my cousin was run over and killed when he was ten. I was about eight. I loved Philippe like my own brother. While the rest of the family mourned and Ines got lots of hugs and love, I was left out of the family. I was incredibly upset. This was my first experience of death. No one thought to comfort me. I think the only person who really loved me was Onkel Roger. He cried when I left home to go to boarding school.'

I detect a sense of loss in Nora's voice. You don't have to be adopted to feel you don't belong to your family.

'When I was twelve Mammi sent me to boarding school, a small private Catholic girls' school on the shores of Lake Zürich,' continues Nora. 'I liked it well enough and did well, but I still didn't feel I belonged anywhere. When I left at seventeen, I was on my own and had to make my own way in life, which I think is rather young. The school didn't exactly prepare you for life.'

'So did you go to college after school?' I ask.

'Not at this time – later. I learned to type and got a job as a personal assistant for a government official which was fun.'

Nora starts to talk about her father. 'It was around this time that I met Dad for the first time. I was on tour to the States – I played piccolo in a wind band. We were in New Hampshire, near to where my father was living. So I got in touch and we met. He had never taken an interest in me because he didn't believe that I was his child but when we met he couldn't deny it. Look at this photo.'

Nora shows me a photo of them. They're both wearing white shirts. Her dad is sitting down and Nora is hugging him from behind. They're turning their heads to glance into the camera. There could be no doubt that they are daughter and father: same smile, same nose, same eyes.

She continues, 'He had a wife and two boys, my half-brothers, and we used to spend summer holidays together. Later, he married again and his wife was jealous so we stopped seeing each other.'

Nora doesn't give the impression she was ever close to her father or her two half-brothers and I can understand that. I remember one of the first comments she made to me by email when describing her upbringing: *I grew up with two mothers and fathers which at times was not easy.*

My heart goes out to that forlorn little girl, not knowing her place in the family. And then a few years later being sent off to boarding school. I think it's time to stop looking at the photos and am glad when Daniel dishes up a simple yet scrumptious meal of white fish, polenta (with cheese) and salad.

The next day we spend another couple of hours looking at Margareta's photo albums. I learn a great deal about Margareta from these two hours. Nora points out that Margareta's verve and vitality masks an underlying sadness which comes out occasionally when she's not smiling into the camera. But mostly the pictures are of Margareta and her friends in beautiful locations: snowy mountain regions, sailing on a lake, standing on a bridge in front of a ruined castle.

'She never married but had a number of affairs – she met a lot of men in her job in restaurants. I think she always needed to be with a man. Her greatest love was with the artist Max. You've got two of his pictures in your bedroom.'

'Oh yes, the one of the bridge in Luzern above my bed,' I said, recalling a rather dull picture of the famous Kapellbrücke, a covered wooden footbridge spanning the river just where it emerges into Lake Luzern.

'Max offered to leave his wife and marry Mammi but for some reason she wouldn't. I think she was jealous of his wife and thought she would continue to be jealous even if he left her.'

'I see what you mean about her unhappiness,' I say, pointing to a photo of Margareta and Max taken against the backdrop of the Luzern lakeside promenade. Her eyes are downcast and she wears a tentative smile which looks as though it will vanish.

'They could have been happy together but it wasn't to be,' says Nora as though a higher being had ordained that Margareta should not be happy.

I remember Nora's words when she first wrote to me: *I love her. And everything she did after she got me was done for my sake.* But showing the photos brings out the ambivalence she felt towards her mother. She loved Margareta, but felt abandoned by her. I detect a feeling of resentment that built up throughout her adult life – the fact that Margareta didn't support her financially after she left boarding school, that she didn't keep in contact with Nora's father for her sake, that she seemed to like the high life instead of building an adult relationship with her daughter.

Nora is very generous with her time. Over the next few days she introduces me to a couple of her good friends. Nora thinks this is important so I can correspond with them if anything happens to her because of her advanced liver disease. I particularly like bee-keeping Barbara who lives in the country nearby. She lives alone and works as the manager of a charity which supports people with learning disabilities. I meet Kevin, who is Nora's spiritual healer, though Nora seems bemused when she asks Kevin why she is still so ill despite the healing. 'It's a matter of working on deep breathing and having faith,' Kevin says with confidence. Kevin lays his hands on me and pronounces me well. I wonder how he knows. He tells me deep breathing will help my cancer. I keep quiet. Deep breathing and meditation is very calming and good for the soul, but it doesn't cure cancer.

We talk a lot on our trips out together, but mostly Nora talks about herself and the family. I'm happy with that so I'm taken by surprise when she turns to me on a boat in the middle of Lake Zürich and says, 'You never talk about yourself. What about your family?' It had never occurred to me that she would be interested in my adoptive family or the Indian side of my father's family. I start to tell her but find it strange because there's no real context for her. We don't share anything about my adoptive family and it seems odd to be talking about my own childhood.

Five days after I arrive we visit all our cousins in Schmitten, the family home near Fribourg. We set off in the early morning from the local station. The train winds its way down to the shores of Lake Zürich. Travelling close to the lake we see the Goldcoast on the other side, so-called because it faces the sun most days. In contrast our side is called the *Pfnussel Kuste*, roughly translated as 'runny-nose coast' in honour of its east-facing status. House prices apparently match the hours of sunshine.

An hour later we approach the capital Bern, clustered below us around the deeply cut meander of the River Aare. I have memories of the last time I visited Bern when I flung myself into this fast-flowing river, allowing myself to float down-river through the city – the ultimate urban bathing experience. Changing trains yet again, we are now close to Schmitten. We pass through pine forests, hills and valleys. A river far below is full of children splashing in the water, enjoying the morning sunshine.

On the way Nora fills out some more of the family tree with the names of her uncles – the husbands of Margareta's three sisters. All the sisters have now died but Andris, one of the husbands, is still alive and is expected to come to lunch. Nora also tells me the names of her cousins' partners, all of whom are coming today, except for David's who is divorced.

We arrive at Schmitten station, a tiny station on the line between Bern and Fribourg, and are met by David. He is big and hearty. He hugs me immediately, saying 'Welcome to the family' and it feels like he means it.

He drives us round the small town, showing us the Town Hall, a simple white stone building with a steep, curved roof. We see the small school Margareta went to, high on a hill. After about fifteen minutes we pull into the driveway of the house where Margareta grew up. We enter the hallway and turn right to the kitchen, big enough for a table as well as the kitchen counters and appliances. It leads out into the garden where David has placed a wooden table and two granite-topped tables to accommodate the whole family. At last I was seeing the home where my mother was brought up.

It's mid-morning and all the cousins and their partners begin to arrive. I recognise Ines, the cousin Nora was brought up with, from the photos Nora sent me. At first I don't notice her black and white chihuahua because she's tucked into a bag with only her head peeping out. She's tiny, way smaller than my cat, Raasay.

'This is Steila,' says Ines. 'Romansh for Star.' We speak in hesitant but adequate French.

'I've already seen a photo of you and Steila, a study in black and white,' I say, referring to a photo Nora had sent me showing Ines wearing a black top, sitting on a white leather sofa with Steila perching on the arm. 'She's so cute.'

I go into the house and have a look round the living room. It's in the corner of the house and has two windows, one at the back and one at the side. Despite this the room seems strangely dark, but this is probably because the overhanging roof blocks some of the light. There's a leather sofa, a large TV, a bookcase and little else. David likes photos and pictures on the wall. A corner of the living room is devoted to family pictures. One is a really lovely black and white photo of the four sisters, including of course, Margareta, their mother and grandmother in an oval frame. The girls, all pre-teens, are dressed in identical dark belted dresses with white collars.

I go out into the sunlight and sit down beside Marie-Lise, my cousin Marcus's partner, and we start snacking on some cheese. We all sit down and pass the food around. I'm drinking orange juice but soon the wine is flowing. Nora suddenly taps her glass with her fork and everyone falls silent.

She says in English, 'I'm so glad that you're all here – my six cousins, uncle and your partners. We're a close family and like to meet up. But the occasion is very important to me because I want to introduce you to Kamila, my sister, who I didn't know about until earlier this year. It's so good that you've all turned up to greet Kamila. I can see you've already made her welcome. Kamila, welcome to the family.' She repeats this in German and we toast the occasion.

Then it's my turn. I begin to say 'Thank you', but someone interrupts, laughing and says, 'Say it in German.' So I say, '*Danke schon. Freut mich*,' before switching to English to say, 'I'm so pleased to meet you all. I'm quite overwhelmed that you've all come together on my behalf and welcomed me as a cousin.' I feel awkward now as not everyone speaks English, so I stop speaking and sit down. Marcus says he can see a bit of Margareta in me and a bit of Nora which pleases me.

I remember when Nora first told our cousins of my existence some were shocked, some not. Cousin David, probably the most laid-back of the cousins, had laughed and said, 'So Tante Margareta can still surprise us from beyond the grave.' Will my family and friends think the same of me when they read this memoir when I'm gone?

Everyone carries on eating. The sun moves around putting the table to the right of me fully in the sun so someone moves it round the corner of the house where it's in the shade. I decide to sit there too so I can talk to three more cousins who I've not spoken to yet. They've finished eating and are smoking cigars and drinking beer. We talk in English for a while – pleasantries – but after a few minutes they switch back to German and I leave to find another cousin to talk to. I feel as if I'm at a friend's party mingling with strangers. All this small talk. I enjoy it but would I form a deeper relationship with my cousins?

Then Ines comes to sit beside me. We're both not natural French speakers so struggle a bit, but I feel warm towards her as she seems genuinely interested in me. She starts showing me her bank of photos on her iPhone, including a complimentary one of me that I'd sent Nora. I'm in Queen's Wood in Highgate looking great in my purple Sherpa fleece and jeans, short hair and a big smile. I show her the one Nora had sent me of her and Steila.

'Have you any family photos on your phone?' she asks.

I hadn't thought to bring any specifically to show Nora and my cousins, but suddenly remember I had in fact got some family photos on my iPad. Patrick and I had been sorting out and digitising them. I retrieve my iPad from my bag and load up the photos. We look at photos where Ellen, Tim and Patrick are toddlers and I make my first appearance. I appear either sitting in Mum's lap or, more often, in one of my brothers' laps. I always seem to be in a white shirt with my nappy showing. I don't know if all-in-one Babygros existed then.

I'm not sure whether Nora had told the family before now about our ethnic mix. Ines examines the photos with a curious look. 'They're wonderful,' says Ines. 'What an interesting family.' I normally get irritated when people describe my family as 'interesting', 'fascinating' or 'exotic', but somehow Ines's comment seems genuine. I think it made my own past seem real to her. I had never thought that my newfound family would be interested in my adoptive family for some reason, but both Ines and Nora want to know how I was brought up.

At about five some cousins get up to leave. Everyone kisses me fondly – three kisses on the cheek is the Swiss way. At about 5:30 David gives us a lift to the station and we start our two-hour journey back home.

An important day, meeting all my cousins in one go. But how can you waltz into a family at the age of sixty-three and expect to be part of it?

Although my trip isn't over, Nora hasn't yet told me when we will be visiting our mother's grave. I'm getting impatient but politeness stops me from bringing it up.

18. ANOTHER DEAD END

My father is a ghostly figure even though he gave me my 'slightly coloured' genes. His name first appears on the National Children Homes inquiries form, completed by my mother and dated 21st May 1952.

Full name of father: Raja Rao Lakhan
Whether married: No
Address: Not known
Age: 22
Occupation: Student of engineering
Religion: Hindoo
Nationality: Indian

I know that Rao is a family name occurring most commonly in the south Indian state of Andhra Pradesh. There's Raja Rao, a famous nationalist novelist. And there's Narasimha Rao, the prime minister of India from 1991-1996. But my ghostly Lakhan Raja Rao was unlikely to be so illustrious.

I would have liked to have known more about him, but didn't know where to start searching. When I first got hold of his letter in 1991 there was no Google and no family history internet sites. I assumed he was studying in London in the short-term and would have returned to India where it would be difficult to trace him. I asked my Indian relatives who confirmed the likely Andhra Pradesh origin but who also said that Indian family records would be difficult to find. Many Indians do not have their birth registered.

Surely my father would have had to provide evidence for a passport? Or perhaps passports weren't required for Commonwealth citizens? Who knows?

Anyway, I did nothing until 2004 when I thought I would check whether he ever graduated. I rang the University of London archives that hold records of graduates from 1836 to 1934 which of course was too early for my father. The man on the other end of the line identified himself as Geoff Brownlow and listened to my request. 'I'm trying to find my birth father who was an engineering student in 1952, so he would have graduated then or soon afterwards.'

Mr Brownlow said, 'I'm afraid he's too young for these records as they only go up to 1934. And I think you might be caught between two time periods. If you go to the alumni office I don't think they'll give you the more recent graduate records unless you can prove the person is dead.'

'I can't do that,' I said. I was dissuaded from pursuing this further. It was just so difficult when your path is constantly blocked. I did nothing. Again. For years. It really seems that someone has to die and become a ghost before you can search for them. But then my birth parents have always been ghosts. In some ways it would be frightening to suddenly have them come alive.

Ten years after that conversation with Mr Brownlow, in October 2014, I start searching in earnest for both my birth parents. I Google Lakhan Raja Rao and search for him in the Births, Marriages and Deaths Register but draw a complete blank. My sister-in-law Gisela says, 'Why don't you give me your father's name and I'll check it on Findmypast. I've paid a subscription and I think it's got more information than the free Births, Marriages and Deaths site we've been using which only seems to go up to 1984.'

She returns to Berlin and a few days later emails me to tell me that she'd looked for my father, but like me couldn't find anyone called Lakhan Raja Rao. But she'd then searched just on the name Rao and found three possible records, including a death certificate.

The first two are marriage records for other people called Rao – not Raja Rao. But I get very excited by the third record. In the

Findmypast records Gisela has come across a death of a Lakshan Raja Rao, gender unknown, born 25th October 1930, died in the second quarter of 1998 in Sutton, Surrey. This certainly sounds like my father who, according to my adoption records, was twenty-two in 1952. I'm sure it's my father, even though the spelling is slightly different from the name in my records. I'm sad that it looks like I will never meet him but perhaps I can find out more about him from a son or daughter who may have signed the death certificate. My brother or sister.

I think it's worth a try. I order the death certificate from the General Register Office. Surely a member of the family will have signed the certificate – and their address should be on the certificate too. I'm fired up this time. Could it be true – was my father living in Sutton, an outer London borough, in 1998 when I was also living in London? What a missed opportunity! The sliding doors syndrome which has blighted my search.

A week later a couple of A5 envelopes are carefully laid out on the ledge in our communal hallway by a neighbour distributing the post. One is a bill for my NatWest credit card – and the other is the long-awaited death certificate. It's a cream-coloured certificate folded in half:

Date and place of death: 11th May 1998. 155 Epsom Road, Sutton
Name and surname: Lakshan Raja RAO
Sex: Male
Maiden surname of woman who has married:
Date and place of birth: 25th October 1930. India
Occupation and usual address: Restauranteur (retired). 155 Epsom Road, Sutton, Surrey
Name and surname of informant: Latif MALEK
Qualification: Present at the death
Usual address: 33 Grasmere Avenue, Merton Park, London, SW19
Cause of death: Acute Pancreatitis

Hmmm? I think it's likely to be my father, even though the name is spelled differently. It looks like Lakshan never married. Who was Latif Malek – a fellow restauranteur perhaps? I look up 155 Epsom Road on Google and find that it is the address of an Indian restaurant, Tamarind. So had my father been managing the restaurant before he retired? I look up the restaurant's website and it looks smart with a good north Indian menu. It gets a good rating on TripAdvisor too. I look up 33 Grasmere Avenue, a suburban street in Merton, not far from Tamarind. I'm getting excited now. This is something to go on. I've got two addresses that I can at least go and visit.

I go to the British Library where I've ordered my maximum ten electoral rolls, one for every year from 1998 to 2007, covering the Merton Park ward which is where Latif Malek, the person who was with my father when he died, stayed.

It's a very quick task and it's rewarding too. The Malek family is listed in all the years except for 2004 when the entry to that address is blank. It's a large family with seven family members. I go home and order the electoral rolls for the years from 2008 to 2013. Returning to the library the next day I am really excited to find that the family was still living there in 2013. This bodes well. I can get in touch with them.

I phone my friend Brian and ask for his help. I want to visit the restaurant and the Malek family house – not to ask questions but just to absorb the atmosphere which would help me to imagine how my father lived and died. During the day would be better than the evening so I can see the building but Tamarind isn't open at lunchtime. I meet Brian in Brockley and we have lunch in a local café there. The food is delicious and healthy. Brian chooses a creamy pasta dish while I tuck into a vegetarian pie with salad. Brian drives me to Tamarind. I know this part of south-east London as I used to live here, but once we get to Thornton Heath I'm in unfamiliar territory. The traffic snarls and so I've time to observe the mix of shops and warehousing. This is self-storage country, increasingly popular as people choose to store their accumulated junk rather than move house. However, it's not all miles of suburban grot. We pass by a group of 19th century alms houses, low brick, slate-roofed houses around a square; an old black and white pub; some heathland conserved at the edge of a park.

We reach Tamarind restaurant around 2:30 pm. It's a bright spot at the end of a rather shabby parade of shops by a busy crossroads. Drawing up by the kerb I get out and peer through the sparkling window to see everything set for the evening meal – comfortable padded burgundy coloured chairs surround oval tables of dark wood. Napkins have been shaped into triangles and stand by the place settings. Exposed bricks adorn one wall while the others are painted cream. There are no ornaments. Highly polished oak floorboards complete the modern look of this restaurant. Above the restaurant is a second floor of residential units. I guess this is where my father died. I enter the yard at the side of the building and look up at the two windows and see that there is also a large dormer window in the roof. There are no curtains in the windows and the whole place looks rather ramshackle. I am sad as I think of my father living all alone up there and dying with only his friend or colleague by his bed. Was he an alcoholic? What relationship did he have to Latif Malek? The next step is to get in touch with the Maleks. I get back in the car and we drive to their address.

The Maleks live in a semi-detached house: brick at the bottom but clad with pebbledash on the second storey. A low brick wall encloses the front garden which has been planted with evergreen shrubs. The street is quiet. I get out and take a few photos but feel rather conspicuous. I return to the car and say to Brian:

'There's not much point loitering here any more. I'm not going to knock on the door or anything.'

'That wouldn't be a good idea, I think,' Brian says. 'How do you feel about the day anyway? What do you think you've achieved?'

'Well, it's all part of the exploration. I think I'm building up a picture of my dad and I'm keen to do something now. We could go back to the restaurant one evening and ask the staff there whether they knew my father. But actually what would be better is to write to the Maleks and see if I get a reply.'

Brian drops me off at Morden Tube station. Just seeing the place where my father lived and died makes him less of a ghost. And I might be able to get somewhere in my quest by contacting the Maleks.

I'm not usually a procrastinator except when it comes to my search for my birth parents. I've come to expect dead ends and it's difficult to think of another angle of research. But now that I have an obvious way forward I'm scared at unearthing my ghost. So I don't contact the Maleks for a few weeks. The Thursday before Easter I write a letter to them.

Dear Malek family,

I am trying to find out more about a friend of my mother's, Lakshan Raja Rao, who lived in Croydon in 1953. I believe he was a student at that time. He was born in 1930 and came from India. I found that someone of that name died in April 1998, who was Indian and born in 1930. He died above Tamarind Restaurant at 155 Epsom Road.

His death certificate was signed by Latif Malek, who may have been a friend. Is Latif still alive? Are you able to tell me anything about Latif or Lakshan? Did Latif perhaps work at Tamarind? I would be so grateful if you could contact me.

Best wishes

Kamila Zahno

I think the odds of getting a reply to this aren't very high although I did send them my mobile number. On Easter Saturday I'm in the kitchen getting ready to leave for the Emirates Stadium. A friend of mine has kindly given me his season ticket for the Arsenal v. Liverpool match as a birthday present. A heroic gesture on his part as I know he really wants to go. The match is at 12 noon and I should leave by 11. It's 10:45 and my mobile phone rings.

'Good morning. This is Najma.'

Now I know two Najmas and this doesn't sound like either of them.

'You don't know me. I'm Najma Malek.'

'Oh my god, Najma!' I interrupt. 'You answered my letter. I can't believe it.' My heart is racing and I've already forgotten about the football. This is more important.

'You wanted to know about Rao who was my dad's friend. He lived with our family for many years and we loved him. He was the most marvellous man, so gentle. We called him Uncle Rao and he spent loads of time with me and my brothers and sisters.' Najma sounds excited and very eager to talk to me. In fact, I think she's only just opened the letter. I sent it on Thursday and the next day was Good Friday so the letter would have only just arrived on Saturday.

'Do you know much about his past?' I decide to put all my cards on the table and tell her my story. 'The reason I'm asking is that I think he may be my father from a relationship he had when he was twenty-two and a student living in London. Does that ring any bells?'

'Oh, that's amazing. If you're his daughter you have another half-sister, Lisa, and a half-brother too. What a man!' Another sister and brother. This is really too much to take in.

Najma doesn't seem at all fazed by my mini bombshell. 'I think that's really exciting. It's fantastic that you might be finding birth relatives after such a long time.'

'Do you know much about his background?'

'My father was the one who knew him best, but he has dementia and I don't think you'd get much from him.'

'Oh. So sorry about your father.' Damn. It sounds like I won't be able to find out much about Lakhan and might never be able to 'prove' he's my father. There's a short pause so I fill the gap. 'What about my half-sister and brother? Do you know much about them?

Did Uncle Rao marry?' I'm thinking his marriage must have broken down and that he then went to live with his friend.

'I don't know much. We were really small when Uncle Rao came to live with us and I don't remember him talking about them. But then we met them at his funeral. That was in Oxford and he was buried there. Lisa, your sister, arranged all that.'

I can't let this momentous piece of news slip through my fingers. I've got to make a date to see her family.

'So where do we go from here?' I say.

'Let's meet each other. I'll talk to the rest of the family and perhaps you can come round. I'll give you another ring soon to arrange that.'

'Najma, that sounds marvellous. Thank you so much for ringing me – a stranger.'

'No trouble. We all loved Uncle Rao,' says Najma, sounding upset. 'And I'm sure you are who you say you are. I'll definitely call you again.'

I put the phone down and sit down. After all this time, I may have a sister and brother on my father's side. I walk to the Emirates Stadium in a daze. Once there, I get caught up in the excitement of the match. Arsenal isn't doing badly in the league but this match against Liverpool is important. I introduce myself to my neighbours on either side of me and they ask where my friend, the usual ticket holder, is. I tell them he's given me the ticket as a birthday present and they're impressed at his sacrifice. The seats are high up on the corner by Liverpool's goal which means I'll have a great view of any of Arsenal's goals in the first half. And I see three of them! Tony, to my right, says I must be a lucky influence. In the second half, I see Liverpool score, but Arsenal still have control of the game and they score again about twenty minutes before the finish. Tony hugs me and then confesses he's bet a tenner on a 4-1 score so he doesn't want any more goals! He's in luck. There are no more goals.

After the match a stream of fans leaves the stadium. I think about Najma's phone conversation again. Is Uncle Rao really my father and how will I ever know if it's the right man? What shall I do with this new information? Just wait and see, I guess.

Two weeks elapse and I hear nothing from Najma. I don't want to hassle her but I don't want to let the opportunity to know more slip away either. I phone her.

'Hi, Najma. It's Kamila. We spoke about Uncle Rao. I don't want to bother you but…'

'Oh, Kamila,' she interrupts. 'Thanks for phoning again. I meant to phone but it's been difficult with my dad. We all look after him and he's been ill again. He's got a heart condition as well. I'm going to pass the phone over to my sister, Samiya, as I'm doing most of the caring for Dad and she has a little more time. I know she'll want to meet you.'

After a few moments Samiya comes on the phone. 'Hi, Samiya here. Yes, Najma told me about Uncle Rao and that you might be his daughter. I really want to meet you. I live in Manchester but I come down Fridays and over the weekend to help with Dad. Let's arrange a time to meet.'

I'm excited that she's as open as her sister. 'Fantastic. You suggest a time and place.'

'Best not to meet at the house as it's quite chaotic. Let's meet at Morden Station this Friday at two and go to a café.'

'Fantastic. By the way, you don't have any photos of Uncle Rao do you?'

'I'm not sure we have many family photos but I'll look.'

'Thanks for talking with me and see you next Friday.'

I put the phone down. Again I have this uncertainty gnawing away but at least meeting Samiya would give me an opportunity to ask more questions and maybe his photo would reveal a family likeness.

The following Friday I make the journey to Morden, as usual getting there ten minutes early. There aren't many people around at this time but the concourse is crowded with buses going all over south London. At the side of the station is a flower stall and on a sudden whim I decide to buy a bunch of bright tulips for Samiya. Just as I've paid the flower lady, my phone rings and it's Samiya:

'I'm really sorry but I'm going to be a bit late – I'll be with you around quarter past two.'

'Don't worry. I'm fine here. By the way, you'll recognise me because I'm carrying a bunch of flowers.'

At 2:20 pm I see a small woman in a black coat and leggings come running towards me. Her hair is long and she's wearing it loose so it flows out behind her like a horse's tail.

'Kamila,' she says, hugging me. She is crying. 'You look like him. I can't believe this.'

I hug her too. We stand back, still facing each other and I give her the flowers.

'My mum's going to love these. It's so sweet of you.'

'I saw them and wanted something for you to remember me by.'

'There's a quiet café just nearby. Let's go and have a coffee. And I did find a photo of Uncle Rao. I'm dying to show you that.'

It's a small café with only four or five tables and a counter at the back. The only other people in there are two old ladies having a cup of tea. We both decide to have an Americano and I order the coffees at the counter.

'You do look like him, I think. Look at this photo.' She takes out a photo from her bag and lays it in front of me. It's Lakhan dressed in a gold silk smoking jacket hugging two boys. I can't see myself in his features.

'These are my brothers. Uncle Rao used to spend a lot of time with us and especially my older brother, Asif.' Samiya's eyes water and her voice trembles.

'Wonderful to see a photo of him. Would you lend me this so I can scan it? I'll definitely return it to you.'

'Fine.'

I say rather formally, 'As you don't really know I am who I say I am, I brought the letter my father wrote to the adoption agency. Here's a copy for you,' I say, placing it on the table next to the photo. 'It's in his writing and here's his signature. Do you recognise it?'

'I don't think we would have any written stuff from Uncle Rao. Maybe my dad would recognise the writing. Actually I did tell him I was seeing you. He understood and started to cry. He knew who I was talking about.'

'I'm so sorry about your dad. How's he being looked after?'

'We're all looking after him but we do need an assessment from Social Services and they're being terrible. They don't seem to have access to his health records. The coordination with them and the GP is awful. And I know it shouldn't be that bad as I'm a social worker up in Manchester. But to get back to you and Uncle Rao. It's so wonderful that you thought of writing to us. I told you that if you are his daughter...' Samiya breaks off and looks at my hands which are long and slender but also wrinkled with age.

'Even your hands are like his. I'm sure you're his daughter.' But I want a little more proof than some wrinkled hands.

'I'll see if I can find Lisa's contact details. I'm sure my brother Asif has it. Lisa arranged the funeral in Oxford and Asif helped her. He's abroad just now but I'll remember to ask him when he returns. Be sure to remind me though.'

'So how did he die? He died above Tamarind. I went to see it a couple of weeks ago. Did he own it or did your dad own it?'

'No, neither. Uncle Rao was a bit of a lost soul actually. He just did odd jobs here and there, mostly repair work in restaurants. That's how he met my dad who owned several restaurants. We don't have much to do with the people at Tamarind but Uncle Rao had done some work there.'

So my engineering father ended up living in a family that wasn't his, doing odd jobs in restaurants. Why was he such a lost soul, as Samiya called him? Yet another example of the cuckoo syndrome in my family: Nora brought up by her aunt; and Margareta looking after other people's children in London, while leaving her own to be looked after by someone else.

'Why did he move there from your place?' I query.

Agitated, Samiya winds her hair round her fingers of her right hand. 'Actually, I have to say that he became an alcoholic. I was at uni in Manchester and don't know the ins and outs, but having someone who drank in the house would have been difficult for my parents, who are traditional Muslims. He had worked for Tamarind before and they offered him a flat upstairs.'

I breathe in sharply. 'Yes, difficult for both your father and Uncle Rao I should think.' Who made the first move? Did Uncle Rao think it best he left or was he asked to leave by the Malek family? Somehow I don't think he was just chucked out as the whole family were – and it seems still are – very fond of him.

'Sorry about all these questions,' I continue. 'I'm really quite anxious to find the answers. I hope you don't mind me telling you but I have cancer and I need to find out as much as I can about my adoption as I don't have all that much time left.'

I have no idea how Samiya is going to take this. But we've developed a real rapport over the last half hour or so and I want to be open about my motive for looking for my father. Samiya takes both my hands in hers and says. 'Are you OK? I can understand the urgency. Are you taking any treatment?'

I pause before answering, taking a gulp of coffee. 'I'm doing as well as I can on a regime of drugs and the hospital is great.' I continued, 'Do you know when Uncle Rao met your dad and what he was doing at the time? I was told he was studying engineering when he met my mum.'

'Like I said, Dad met him working in restaurants and they became firm friends. I don't know about the engineering but he was very well educated and he certainly knew a lot about how things worked like electrics and stuff.'

'Do you know anything about his family at all – where he came from perhaps?'

'I know a little, but maybe Asif knows more. You must come and meet our family. We were young kids so it wouldn't have occurred to us to ask much about Uncle Rao. He was just part of the family. I think he came from south India and I believe he had a large family. I know that he was sent here when he was quite young to be educated but that he never went back to India. Looking back I think his life was rather sad.' Samiya's eyes water.

'So you've mentioned Lisa. And your sister mentioned a half-brother. Did my dad marry?'

'No he had a relationship with an English woman and had Lisa but they never married – I don't know why not. I don't think Lisa met Uncle Rao until a few years before he died. That's when we met her anyway. I'm not too sure about Anthony, your half-brother. He comes from yet another relationship. All this happened before Dad and he met so really I don't know much. Both Lisa and Anthony were at the funeral. I think the best thing now would be for me to find Lisa's address.'

Good god! That's three children by three different relationships. What had he been up to? Then he lived in a family that was not his own. And ends up completely on his own. Dying on his own. Just as I might have to.

Samiya and I leave the coffee shop, hug goodbye and go our separate ways, with Samiya promising to get in touch with me when her brother returns to the UK.

When I get home I take a snap of my dad's picture on my phone and send it to Samiya saying that, in case it gets lost or damaged in the scanning process, at least she has a copy. She texts back:

It was lovely to meet u Kamila. Thank u for the flowers – my mum was thrilled and evn my dad took note when I showed him. I've bn sitting with him and he was actually able to ask if u looked like Uncle Rao. I hope u can meet my parents. We all loved Uncle Rao dearly. I hope ur OK. Uv hd a lot to take in. It's bn a real pleasure to meet u. Take care of yourself, hopefully we'll meet again.

Nothing seemed to have worked out for Lakhan Rao – the promise of a career in engineering, a family. He couldn't live with the only family he really knew in later life because of his drinking. What a sad and lonely life. I can't engage completely with his story as I'm still not sure that he is my father. Or am I holding back because it's such a sad story and I don't want my father to have had such a life? Lisa may hold the key to the proof that I need – stories, old photos, his signature. I need to find her.

19. MY BIRTH FAMILY GROWS

I hear nothing from Samiya. I'm disappointed. Had I got so near to finding Lisa, only to be blocked from ever meeting her? She holds the key to my father. Without finding her I'll never be sure whether this Lakshan Raja Rao is really him. Although I was sure she would have asked her brother, Asif, for Lisa's contact details, I wasn't sure what his reaction would be. He'd never met me. He might be much more cautious than Samiya. But she did ask me to remind her if I didn't hear from her. A couple of weeks later I text asking her if she'd had a chance to talk to Asif about Lisa's address. She replies immediately to say that she thinks he will be at the family home at the weekend and she'll find out. The following week she comes back to me unprompted, texting me Lisa's phone number and email.

I immediately compose an email to Lisa telling her everything. I know it's not advisable to lay everything on the line, but I'm so close to finding out whether this is my father, I just have to say what I think. I tell her that her own father, Lakshan Raja Rao, might be my father too and that I've been talking to the Malek family who gave me her address. My email bounces. Horror! I copy it into a text and send that, hoping that I've been given the right mobile number. I wander round the living room in a state of flux wondering what's going to happen. A minute later my phone rings. I know it's Lisa because it's from the number I'd just texted. Her voice sounds excited and youngish.

'Oh my god, Lisa,' I say. 'Thanks for calling back immediately.'

'My sister! I've known about you for ages. Our father had told my mother that he'd had a daughter with a Swiss woman who had returned to Switzerland. I've always wanted to find you but I thought maybe you had been adopted in Switzerland. How would I begin to find you? As soon as you texted I got goosebumps all over me!'

'Then it really is true. We're sisters.' I'm trembling as she says this. I sit down on the sofa. After all this time and the unlikely chance of finding a father just from his name, year and country of birth, I've come up with a definite sister. Another one.

Lisa can't stop talking. She tells me about her family. Is that my family too? Ruby, her mother, became pregnant with Lisa fifty years ago. Lakshan wanted to marry but it was Ruby who didn't. Lisa thinks it was something to do with the 1960s when marriage between a tall blonde and a short Indian man might have been difficult. Lisa puts it down to physical incompatibility. Mmm. Soon afterwards, Ruby met and married Bill who adopted Lisa. They had three other children and adopted three.

Lisa laughs, 'I have many, many siblings. Not only you and the other six but there's also Anthony. Our father had another relationship which didn't work out either, and Anthony is our younger half-brother. I've only met him once. I think he's a bit of a recluse.'

She tells me a little about our father. 'He'd been sent over to England when he was only fifteen and for some reason never went back to India. I first met him when I was twenty-nine and probably met him about ten or so times since. He was a lovely, lovely man. I think it's a shame he could never find the right woman.'

We chit-chat about our lives. I tell her that I'm retired and live near Finsbury Park. I learn that she runs an antiques store in Oxford, The Hive, selling vintage clothes and antique ceramics and china. I ask her about her family and life. She has a son, Leon, who lives with her and a daughter, Indira, living in Madrid. I am Aunty Kamila.

'When can we meet?' Lisa asks me. 'I'm going to Madrid on Thursday this week to visit Indira. Coming back on Monday. What about the following week?'

We agree to meet in two weeks' time. 'You can just take the Oxford Tube, the fast bus, outside Victoria Station and it will drop you off at the High Street near to our shop.'

On a sunny day in late August, I catch the 9:30 am Oxford Tube. I sit right up in front of the bus to the left of the driver. By my side is the carrier bag of saris I've brought for Lisa to give to her daughter, Indira. Lisa had sent me a photo of Indira in a sari on her first trip to India last Christmas so I know she likes to wear them. I wonder what it'll be like to meet Lisa so late in life. What will I have in common with her? Will she be a talker, a listener, or both? The motorway passes through the lovely Chiltern Hills, at one point cutting through a chalk cliff. Lisa texts me telling me she's waiting by the bus stop in a red flowery dress. I'm glad she's told me what she's wearing because I haven't seen her photo.

I text back telling her that we're late and she replies that she's now sitting in the sun outside a café opposite the bus stop drinking tea. Around fifteen minutes later than scheduled we pull up at the High Street close to Lisa's shop. I spot her red flowery dress as soon as I get off the bus. I'm careful crossing the busy road. It wouldn't do to be run over rushing to see my new sister for the first time.

We say it simultaneously: 'At last!' giving each other a huge hug. I sit down, handing her the two saris I've chosen for Indira – a red silk one and another cotton one with a blue paisley pattern.

'Indira will love these,' Lisa says, peeking into the bag. 'I remember telling you that red and blue are her colours.'

I order an Americano with milk, then sit back down opposite Lisa. Although the sun is shining there's quite a cold wind so I put on my jacket. I glance at my sister surreptitiously. She doesn't look at all like me. She looks to be in her forties rather than her fifties. She's pretty with an oval-shaped face, a bright smile and lipstick matching the red flowers on her dress. Her hair, parted to one side, reaches down to her bust and is a rich brown with gold highlights. Her dress is gathered below the bust and falls gently to her knees.

'We don't look like each other,' I say. 'We must both take after our mothers.'

'Maybe the round bit on the end of our noses.' As if to emphasise the point Lisa touches her nose.

She takes out a tube of Neal's Yard Geranium and Orange hand cream and I ask for some. We share stories about our upbringing.

'We've both got huge families of half siblings and adopted siblings!' I say.

'I'm used to that,' Lisa says. 'A sister is a sister – half or full, don't you think. I've wanted to meet you since I was five. I think I said on the phone that Mum told me about our father having another daughter by a Swiss woman.'

Lisa tells me about her many brothers and sisters but I can't take it all in. All I can remember is that there's seventeen years' difference between her and the youngest adopted brother. She's already told me a little bit about her children, Leon and Indira, on the phone when we first spoke. Her phone rings and she glances at it.

'It's Leon,' she says, taking the call. 'My youngest.'

It appears that Leon is at home packing to go to a festival this bank holiday weekend, and we'll soon meet him briefly. I go inside the café to pay for our drinks, then follow Lisa back down the High Street to The Hive. Outside the shop is a jumble of wicker baskets and wooden boxes full of vintage crockery and hats. A stand crammed with umbrellas of various sizes and a couple of Victorian birdcages sit on the pavement. There's a car parked outside, next to which stands a tall young man in his twenties with curly black hair.

Lisa introduces me as Aunty Kamila. We hug but Leon is clearly in a hurry as his car can't sit there for long and he's packing a tent and sleeping bags. I ask him where he's going and he tells me it's a festival in Walesbury Forest near Nottingham – jazz, blues and folk. I tell him that I used to go to the Womad Festival in Reading.

'Oh my god.' interrupts Lisa. 'So did we. I could have bumped into you, even camped right next to you. And we wouldn't have known we were sisters.' Sliding doors again.

We say goodbye to Leon, then Lisa and I enter her house by a side door which gives access to the levels above the shop. A staircase leads to the upper floors of the building. I wait while Lisa clomps up the wooden stairs to the bathroom. A sideboard cluttered with vintage stuff from the shop stands on the left. I note two bare arms, the body parts of shop models. One is straight, the other curves up with the hand held in a beckoning gesture as if to entice me in. Lisa reappears.

'I thought I'd show you my favourite walk and then have a spot of lunch,' she says. 'When we come back I can show you photos.'

We walk along the Cherwell River and along paths into the centre of town where Lisa takes me into the Vaults café, a beautiful 14th century building with simple curved stone vaults soaring high on the ceiling. We both choose goat's cheese soufflé and salad which we take outside to the pretty garden area.

'When did you first meet our father, Lakhan?' I ask.

'It sounds strange saying Lakhan. Everyone just called him Rao. As I told you on the phone I first met him when I was twenty-nine.'

'So how did you find him?' I feel almost resentful that she met our father before he died. My own quest resulted in finding two dead parents. I know I've got two sisters who are very much alive but it's not the same as meeting my own parents.

'Hmm let's think. It was complicated. He searched for me, not the other way round, although I always wanted to meet him. I don't know why he suddenly decided to look for me. Anyway he contacted Uncle Jack, my mum's brother. They'd all worked for Osrams in Surrey in the '60s. My uncle was still living in Surrey and he was in the phone book. Rao rang to find out my phone number but Uncle Jack said he would ask Mum first and asked for his phone number so that I could contact him rather than the other way round. Mum was delighted he wanted to meet me and gave me his number. We arranged to meet at the Lahore restaurant in Surbiton.

My husband, Ian, Indira and my brother Ed came along too. I can't really remember what we talked about, but I do remember that Ed said, "Look, he does that thing that you do – looks away into the middle distance when people are talking."'

I laugh. 'So do I. Not when someone is talking to me, but when other people are chatting amongst themselves I just gaze into the distance.'

'I don't know why he suddenly wanted to contact me, but I think he might have been lonely,' Lisa says.

It suddenly hits me. 'He might have searched for me too but how would he have found me? The only reason I found out about him was because his death records were available. How bizarre that it's easier to search for a dead person than one who's alive.'

'I met him several times but it was quite frustrating. I wanted to know more about where he came from and why he never went back to India. You're lucky you've got an Indian side from your adopted mother. I asked him what his mother tongue was. But all he said was, "I have six languages."' Lisa puts on a fake Indian accent when she says this. 'He would never talk about his childhood and where he was from. I thought he was from Hyderabad, Andhra Pradesh.'

'It's the name Raja Rao,' I say. 'Most of the people with that name are from Andhra Pradesh.'

'But when I visited Hyderabad last year, Asif Malek, the son in the family where Rao lived for so long, rang me to say he actually came from Orissa which wasn't on our journey. I haven't the faintest idea how to search for his family.'

We discuss how difficult it is to find Indian birth records. Lisa, an optimist, thinks it's possible. I tell her I've looked and it seems that they're not online. Maya, my cousin's ex-wife, told me that many people didn't register their births, especially in the pre-War years. I'm not desperate to find out more about Lakhan's family, although I would be interested in knowing. But I can understand that, for Lisa, it would bring the Indian side of her closer.

Lisa tells me more about meeting our father. She met him in restaurants and in the Maleks' house where he rented a room.   He was becoming an alcoholic and moved out of the Maleks' house to the flat above Tamarind in the last few years before he died. Lisa last met him just before he died, in the hospital where he was trying to dry out. She says he was optimistic about beating his alcoholism. He died only seven years after she met him.

'He was a lovely man, so gentle,' is all that Lisa has to offer which is pretty much what Samiya, Latif's daughter had told me.

Lisa and I finish our meal and slowly walk back to her house, diving down some lovely old alleyways and ending up on Oxford High Street. Lisa points out a Neal's Yard shop and I go in to buy the Geranium and Orange hand cream for myself. She chooses another – a Rose one. She produces her money but I insist on buying them both.

We return to The Hive. She takes me through to the large kitchen to get us some water and shows me her balcony, still partly in sunlight. We look at her garden below which has a secret feel to it, bounded on one side by a high wall and on the other by a large shed belonging to the shop next door. There's a clematis in full bloom clambering up the shed. Both the house and garden are extensions of Lisa – largely untamed but arranged with some creative flair. I think it must reflect Lisa's upbringing which seemed to me to be chaotic, creative and loving. We go through into the living room to look at photos. I show her the few I've brought.

'Here's the one of our father that Samiya gave me when she first met me,' I say, producing the photo of Lakhan in a gold silk smoking jacket and hugging two of Samiya's brothers.

'Oh that's so cute. He was always one for wearing those smoking jackets. And look, he's showing the boys some stringed instrument. He knew so much.'

'Here's one of the four of us kids,' I say. 'I think I must have been three. It shows us all sitting on the lawn together.'

Lisa grabs the photo. 'Oh, I'd love it if you could make me a copy.' I give it to her as I've made copies of all the family photos I want.

'These are the photos of Rao's funeral,' she says, taking some photos from a turquoise coloured A4 sized envelope. First we look at a print taken outside the Headington Cemetery Chapel. There's Lisa, her ex, her mum, the kids, and a brother and sister. Anthony, our half-brother, is standing next to her. The Malek family is represented by the mother and four of the children. Latif must have taken the photo as he's not in it. Next we look at a photo of just Lisa and Anthony who she says looks like me. I can't see any likeness. She talks a little about the funeral.

Lisa arranged a simple burial in Oxford. Latif's son, Asif, gave a eulogy. 'It was marvellous. Our dad had mentored Asif through a business course, and he now owns a blue-chip company. I think this was what upset Anthony most as he must have thought that Asif had received the attention and mentoring that he should have got, being his son. After the funeral I promised myself that I would erect a headstone, but I still haven't. My ex-husband's best friend is a stone mason and I asked him if he would make one, but we never got around to it.'

'Perhaps that's something I could help with,' I say. 'It would be something to do together for him. We must go and visit the grave at least.'

'Oh dear,' she says. 'I've never visited it since the burial. I'd have to find out where it is exactly. I did get a double plot.' I'm not quite sure who the second person would be – Lisa herself?

Lisa continues. 'It was non-denominational. We just hired the chapel and the organ. Asif's eulogy was incredibly moving – from the heart.' She hands me a copy. It's only a page long but seems to encapsulate what she and Samiya have already told me about Lakhan.

He possessed many gifted qualities and attributes. His potential was limitless though I knew he always wanted to achieve more. His intellect was profound and his knowledge diverse. He had the marvellous ability to enrich the fertile mind, especially with children. His spontaneity was exciting. His wit was sharp and his anecdotes many.

And then, an acknowledgement of the sorrow in his life:

His existence was nomadic and that was a result of his childhood. He had yearned one day to return to his homeland but tragically he never got there.

This seems to leave more questions than answers. Why did he never 'settle'? Why did he not return to India, even for a visit? What was his childhood like? I promise myself to ask Samiya if she can arrange a meeting with Asif to tell me as much as he knows about Lakhan.

Lisa shows me more photos that Asif had made for her – all of Anthony and our father. Some years after her mum and our father split he had a relationship with a French woman. Anthony was the result. This relationship lasted about five years. I think the family lived in England at the time, but then Anthony's mother left for France, taking Anthony with her. The photos show a young Lakhan with his five-year-old son. One is obviously taken at a safari park where the little boy is petting an elephant's trunk, and the other is a picture of a cliff by the sea. Lakhan is clutching a kid goat who's licking Anthony.

'I only met Anthony that one time – at the funeral,' Lisa tells me. 'We didn't have time to talk. He'd only just got in contact with the Maleks and me a couple of weeks before Rao died. So he never ever met him as an adult. After the funeral we agreed to keep in touch and I had his Facebook and LinkedIn profile, but he never replied. I'll show you.'

Lisa takes me through to her office and we settle down at her computer. But she can't find Anthony on Facebook. She looks at her LinkedIn account and there he is. Anthony Richards, Supply Chain Manager for Amazon. A black and white photo smiles back at us. He looks to be in his fifties. I don't think he looks like me but Lisa says she can see a likeness, though she can't actually pin down any particular feature. He studied Business Studies at South Bank University and is clearly a sporty guy, listing football and golf as his interests. Lisa thinks I should send him a message via LinkedIn but I'm reluctant. I've got more than enough family stuff to sort out, and if he didn't keep up with Lisa, whom he actually met, why would he be interested in me? We shut the computer down and Lisa suggests tea in the café next door.

We enter the spacious Spanish café bar and order mint tea and a chocolate brownie which is deliciously squishy. Lisa picks my brains about where to go in India as she is planning to return in winter. I suggest Simla but it might be cold.

'Will you go to Orissa?' I ask.

'We thought we would, but I don't really know where to start in terms of finding our father's family. We should ask Asif if he has any more information.'

'Bhubaneshwar is the capital of Orissa, but under the British Raj, when Lakhan was born, it was Cuttack. God knows where his birth records would be now. I can write to my friend Ratna, in Kolkata. I've asked her before and she arranged for me to see an aunt of hers in Hyderabad. That's when we thought he came from Andhra Pradesh. But her aunt couldn't really advise either. There's no harm asking Ratna again. You should go to Orissa anyway – there are some very holy temples at Puri on the coast – you'd love it.'

We decide we've talked enough today and return to her shop so I can have a browse. Lisa introduces me to Ginny, who's going to India with her and she's excited at the prospect of Puri. She takes a photo of us together – Lisa in her red floral dress and me in my blue floral top. The shop is a real treasure trove – dresses, tops, jackets and shirts, beautifully arranged by colour take up half the shop, with the other half full of ceramics and china. The more random bric-a-brac clutters the pavement outside. The shop is busy. A young man asks for a shirt to be altered, and an older man asks if the jacket he left for alteration is ready. A woman admires a Susie Cooper tea set.

Leaving the shop I admire the Victorian birdcages outside and Lisa, catching my eye, says I can have one as a present asking me which size I would prefer. I choose the smallest one and she goes back into the shop for a paper carrier bag. We return to the bus stop where the Oxford Tube has just drawn up. Kissing her quickly I mount the steps, waving madly and promising to send the photo of us together. The bus is full and I go onto the upper deck, its glass roof making it light and spacious. I place the birdcage by my feet, take out the Geranium and Orange hand cream, which will always remind me of Lisa, and smooth it on my hands. She texts me:

I think we have the philosophical Indian gene in common don't you?

I'm not sure what she means and I don't know if there's such a gene but I'm glad Lisa is my sister.

My father left his short life with many questions unanswered. Why was he sent alone to England when he was only fifteen and never went back? Why did he have three children with three different women but was unable to sustain a relationship with any of them? Very similar to Margareta in that way. Why did he turn to alcohol? But from what Lisa and Samiya told me he had something warm and attractive about him. After all, he'd wanted to see me at the nursery in Highbury which not all fathers in his situation would have done. I would like to have met him but, as with my mother, I was too late.

20. ONE DAY IN LUZERN

I've a strong feeling for place so perhaps I can find my mother through the place she inhabited. I'm hoping that a day in Luzern, where Margareta spent her adult life, will resolve something for me about my adoption. If Darjeeling didn't conjure up my adoptive mother's spirit, why would Luzern conjure up my mother, Margareta? But I am your eternal optimist.

It's with excitement that Nora and I get ready for our day in Luzern. It's a really sunny day and Nora is wearing calf-length white trousers and a white top. I'm in my usual jeans and a blue and white long-sleeved cotton top. I wasn't sure what was on the agenda and was surprised when it started off as a sightseeing trip. When Ines met us at the train station we immediately leaped on a tram to visit a stone carving of a wounded lion, symbolising Swiss mercenaries who were massacred during the storming of the Tuileries Palace in Paris during the French Revolution.

I discover that Nora is full of phobias and anxieties. She tells an Australian tourist who we bump into that she would be worried about visiting Australia because of the scorpions. The tourist is bemused and says that great white sharks are more of a danger.

Later, when I'm back in London and we're Skyping each other she reveals more unfounded fears, like going out and being afraid that a dog will bite her. I think it's related to her feelings of abandonment and she agrees. But knowing that doesn't make it any easier for her.

We make our way downtown. We pass the Hofkirche and decide to have a quick look, despite Nora saying the cathedral is plain inside and not worth seeing. Knowing her taste for the Baroque, I think Nora's plain might be Renaissance. And so it is. We stay for about twenty minutes – me admiring the magnificence of the soaring stone vaulted ceiling, and Nora admiring the Baroque additions.

We walk down to the lake lined with grandiose hotels constructed in the Beaux Arts style. Awaiting us in front of the Hotel Schweizerhof is the Luzern City Train, a blue and white striped miniature train that goes around the old part of Luzern. It sounds as though it will be a bit of a whistle stop tour. The day is flying past without my learning about Margareta through visiting her haunts and her grave.

We sit on the train. I snap at Nora. 'I can't get this audio commentary to work in English.'

'That's because you're half blind,' she snaps back, leaning over and switching the dial to the number which is supposed to give you the English language commentary. 'Oh, sorry,' she says. 'It's because the trip hasn't started yet. Wait till the train starts. This is the right place on the dial for the English.'

I don't say anything. After all she has been incredibly good to me, arranging for me to meet all our relatives as well as taking me up Mount Pilatus, a trip round Zürichsee and this day in Luzern.

The tour finished, we alight from the train and wander round the old town. We enter Ledergasse, a narrow cobbled street with five-storey buildings on either side. A few shops and small cafés are housed on the ground floor but above are clearly apartments.

'This was where our mother lived in the '60s and '70s,' says Nora pointing up to the third floor of one of the buildings. The façade is neat with six-paned windows set off by plain wooden shutters. 'She loved living there.' Nora sounds nostalgic on Margareta's behalf. 'Our mother loved being in the centre of things and one of the restaurants she worked in is on the corner. Look.' She points to a low yellow building named the Zeughauskeller. 'It was only one room with a small kitchen and bathroom, so no room for me.' Nora now sounds regretful. 'I used to visit her there every week. There were young women working in restaurants in the whole building so it had quite a friendly atmosphere. Mammi was allowed to use the roof.' She points up to the projecting balcony with railings covered in a trailing vine. 'In the late '70s the landlord wanted to renovate the apartments so he chucked all the girls out. Mammi found a new apartment on the hill overlooking the city and lived there for forty years.'

Seeing where Margareta lived and worked brings home to me the real woman. But there was no room for either of her daughters in her busy nightlife amongst the bars and restaurants of central Luzern. Was this from choice? I don't think so. In 1950s Switzerland what alternative did a lone mother have with only secondary education and no training? I'm not surprised or resentful she gave me up for adoption, and when I look at Nora's early life, I'm actually glad. There's an insight I couldn't have foreseen at the beginning of my journey.

We amble down narrow pedestrianised streets to wider boulevards lined with a mix of international high end shops: here you can buy your Gucci shoes, your Marco Polo jackets and your Rolex watches. We enter a department store where Nora is entranced by the hosiery department on the ground floor. Ines and I take the lift to the top floor, home to a Mövenpick restaurant. I recall the Mövenpick Marche in the basement of the Swiss Centre in Leicester Square – long since gone – with its self-service food bars piled high with colourful salads, Swiss cheeses, charcuterie and even Bircher muesli. Ines ignores the food counters, continuing up a short flight of stairs to the roof terrace. We choose a seat with a panoramic view of Luzern. The dazzling white towers of the fairy-tale Chateau Gütsch, now a five-star hotel, look down on us from the wooded hill opposite. I give Ines a present I brought for her: a silk scarf with a leaf design in soft purples and greens. She unwraps it, exclaims, '*Sehr hübsch*,' and drapes it around her neck. It goes beautifully with her white shirt. We wait for Nora, who appears to be lost amongst the socks. Ines tells me of an odd phone call she got in February.

'It was from an official in Rothenburg asking me if I knew Margareta Zahno. "Yes," I replied, "She was my aunt, but she died last November. Why do you want to know?" The woman told me that someone was looking for her. So I gave her Nora's contact without thinking. I mean you could have been anyone!'

'Well I'm so glad you did,' I say. 'The official must have tried to find someone who had lived at that address in Rothenburg and come up with you.'

Nora appears bearing a Greek yogurt but no socks. Ines and I go down to choose something to eat: a salad for Ines and a carrot soup for me.

Eating fairly quickly we leave the store and continue sightseeing. Ines and Nora show me Luzern's most famous landmark, the Kapellbrücke, the covered wooden bridge depicted in the picture above my bed. It's now mid-afternoon and I'm still wondering whether I'll learn more of Margareta. But no, at the station we hop on a tram and mount the hill, getting off ten minutes later on the street where Ines and, her husband, Gion live. Their apartment is located within a white modern block, although it still retains the traditional Swiss chalet style with a high-pitched roof and windows on all sides. Inside we are greeted by the lovely Steila whose whole body trembles as she wags her tail to say she is very pleased to see Ines. I lean down to pet Steila but she backs away. The apartment is minimalistic: furniture with clean lines and everything in its rightful place. The open-plan dining and sitting room gives way to a conservatory and balcony where there is a view of mature trees in the neighbouring gardens.

Making tea for Nora and herself, and coffee for Gion and me, Ines then produces a cake, similar to a cheesecake, but made of yogurt with a pink cherry-flavoured topping. Delicious and light. After devouring most of the cake Ines, Nora and I leave, taking Ines's car.

'Would we have time to visit the house in Rothenburg where you lived?' I ask tentatively as I open the car door.

'Ines and I discussed that,' says Nora. She's already in the car and turns round to talk to me as I get in. 'It's all changed. So, what's the point? It's only a house. But we're now going to visit the cemetery where Mammi's ashes are laid.'

I suspect the house in Rothenburg brings back too many sad memories for Nora, but it's good news that we're going to the cemetery. Surely I would feel some sort of connection to Margareta there.

The car climbs a hill. On the horizon is a tall blocky high-rise building – a major hospital. The Friedental cemetery is high above Luzern and it's good to think of Margareta's spirit looking down on her beloved city. We pass between the two neoclassical porticos that mark the entrance. According to her wishes, our mother's ashes have been placed within a community monument very near the entrance to the cemetery. It's a triangular concrete structure placed on a circle of stone, patterned in grey and white blocks. Three stone tiers sit on the circle underneath the triangle and a box has been placed on top of the highest tier.

'Where are the ashes?' I ask Nora.

'A few weeks after Mammi had been cremated we had a small ash-scattering ceremony here,' she says with no emotion. 'It was just Ines and Gion, Daniel and me that came. The ashes are placed in that box and they go into the ground beneath the monument. It's what she wanted.'

Bouquets of flowers wrapped in cellophane lean against the wall surrounding the monument, flowers from the mourners of the recently dead. A light breeze rustles the packaging. I expected there to be a list of people engraved in the wall. But there is nothing. All that is left of our mother are her invisible ashes laid to rest in a communal grave.

After twenty-five years of searching I have missed my mother by a few months. I can't see her, hear her, touch her. I take Nora's word that she is here.

Who was she really, this mother of mine? Who was I to her? I will never know. Nora told me that Margareta had said to her when she was dying, 'I'm taking a secret to the grave with me.' I was that secret but now I am visible.

We stand staring at the communal grave, the hard granite lines of the monument reflecting my feelings. I have lost a mother before I ever knew her. But my quest was never to replace my own adoptive mother. My quest was never a search for a mother's love. How can it be? All I ever wished for was to put the last few pieces of my puzzle together. Over the past ten days Nora has given me a picture of her life with Margareta. That's what my life would have been like with Margareta, it would have been like Nora's – a life with a mother who was never really there.

I'm at the end of my journey. I've pieced together my puzzle and satisfied my curiosity. I have two new sisters, a niece and nephew and many cousins who have enriched my life. But do I feel a special biological bond? Not really. Why should I? At the beginning of my journey I was excited to have some proof of my Indian and Swiss heritage. Here I am. This is my identity. I changed my name to reflect that. I went on a quest for my birth family. But at the end of the journey I have to ask myself whose legacy can I claim: my adoptive Bengali family, my dad's rural working-class background, my Swiss mother or my South Indian father? All or none? My adoptive mum was ambivalent about her own mixed heritage. And so am I. But she, not my birth father, gave me my Indian side. She and her relatives. I'm proud of being part of them. Despite her shadowy presence, she was more present than Margareta would have been. And that knowledge allows me to bridge the distance that had grown between me and Mum.

EPILOGUE

I had been thinking of writing a book on adoption and identity for some time. It would be a social history of the adoption of mixed race babies born in the immediate years after World War Two. Full of examples of my family and other adopted people, it would be my retirement project. The book would be analytical, using my research skills.

My diagnosis of incurable cancer hastened my plans. I retired and the book became an important legacy for me. With aggressive treatment and periods of feeling unwell I decided to concentrate on documenting the experiences of my family rather than travelling round the country to interview other people. I interviewed Ellen, Patrick and Tim's partner to gain insight into their feelings of adoption, search and reunion using an adapted questionnaire from a British Association of Adoption and Fostering study of Chinese adoptees, born post-War, who arrived in the UK in the '60s. Using the questionnaire elicited some interesting views from my siblings but it was too analytical. Their feelings and stories didn't quite emerge. And when I started writing my own story I found feelings difficult to write about. How could I unlock our stories?

I joined two creative non-fiction courses, one of which focused on memoir writing. I enjoyed these, wrote little pieces and improved my creative writing skills, a difficult thing to do for a researcher. But I still thought I would focus on social policy around adoption in the '50s, using my family as an example. This didn't work. I lacked an authentic voice.

My tutor on the memoir course, Damian Barr, asked me why the memoir was important to me. I mentioned my cancer and the desire to record something for posterity. Damian was amazed that I hadn't mentioned this before. Of course I'm not defined by my cancer, but it's an integral part of my life now.

I went home and wrote what is now my Preface. The words flowed. I revised my chapter on coming home to Bromley, expanding the stories of my early childhood. I had found my voice and transformed my writing.

I was influenced by several authors writing about adoption as well as those writing about cancer, although I found only one like me who wrote about both! Jackie Kay's *Red Dust Road* was an early inspiration – her memoir of her reunion with her Nigerian father and her Scottish mother, written in her own inimitable style. It was the first book I read that had me thinking I too had stories like hers. Could I write them down? Then followed Jeanette Winterson's *Why Be Happy When You Could Be Normal*, a memoir of her bleak adoption experience and reunion with her mother. What I like about Winterson's writing is her uncompromising style. Like me, she acknowledges her difficulty in knowing how to love. I came across Nicky Campbell's *Blue-Eyed Son*. Campbell is one of the presenters on the popular TV programme *Lost Long Family* – stories of search and reunion. I don't watch the programme often – they are mostly successful and happy reunions. That's what makes good TV. But I was interested in Campbell's memoir. He reflects constantly on his feelings for his adoptive and birth family and raises the question of whose legacy you can claim from those family's histories – a question I also struggle with. Recently I met Katharine Norbury at my memoir-writing course and devoured her memoir *The Fish Ladder* in which she talks about the search for her birth family as well as her experience with cancer.

Then there were the writers inspired by a cancer experience. A Canadian friend sent me a series of articles in the *New York Times* by the late Oliver Sacks, who was dying of liver metastases from his previous ocular melanoma. In the first of his articles, written just when he is diagnosed, he wrote, 'I have to live in the richest, deepest, most productive way I can…I feel a sudden clear focus and perspective. There is not time for anything inessential. I must focus on myself, my work and my friends.' Yes! This need for those of us who know we are dying to be productive is acknowledged in Atul Gawande's *Being Mortal: Illness, Medicine and What Matters in the End*. He talks about people whose time is winding down becoming less interested in the rewards of achieving and accumulating and more concerned about their legacy; to focus on an external goal to make life worthwhile. 'We have a deep need to identify purposes outside ourselves that make living feel meaningful and worthwhile,' he writes. That's one reason I wrote my memoir.

We also want to focus on the small and wonderful. The most moving piece I read was Clive James's poem 'Japanese Maple' in which he describes the maple tree his daughter gave him which marks the passage of time with its leaves turning to flame each autumn. James, dying from leukaemia, wanted to live long enough to see the maple tree change colour. In fact he has lived to see two autumns of flaming leaves. Those of us who know that our lifespan is limited often wish to focus on something beautiful outside of ourselves – the blackbird's first spring song, the scent of sweet box in the depth of winter – but the whole experience can also open up new opportunities for creativity.

These writers' stories weren't mine, but the themes were. They inspired me to find my own voice and to improve my writing.

I started writing the book in January 2015. At the same time I was researching my own birth family. I wrote quickly. My search was successful. I finished my first draft a year later. Damian critiqued some of my chapters, teaching me the skill of micro-editing and attention to detail. We discussed the themes in my book and the emergence of my voice. My editor, Rahila Gupta, read the whole draft, advising on the writing style and identifying gaps – including the stories I didn't want to write! Members of my memoir-writing group commented on the structure within each chapter. Above all these writers identified my difficulties in writing about my feelings.

Why couldn't I identify my feelings for my adoptive mother, or what I really felt meeting my two half-sisters for the first time? Why was I looking? Who was I really? They identified that there was something of me bubbling like a hot spring beneath the surface, but my feelings never quite emerged. I rewrote. The chapters I didn't want to write got written, revealing a greater understanding of what was important to me. The hot springs started to erupt throughout the book.

It was hard to concentrate, given the toxic treatments I was having. My search for my birth family yielded results and I was sustaining new relationships with two sisters as well as writing about them. But in spite of this I completed my memoir.

Writing my book certainly gave me a focus and my consultant is convinced that it's helped me stay alive. Like Clive James I never expected to see my own Japanese maple turn to flame in 2016, but I did. I had arrived too early for my own death and too late for my parents' death. Life's endless contradictions, no longer to be teased out in writing my memoir, but to be pondered over in the waiting room.

My book describes a journey that hasn't finished. To quote Winterson's ending to her memoir, 'I have no idea what happens next.'

REFERENCES

The author and publisher acknowledge the following sources of quotations reproduced in this book on the pages listed.

p 103 Jackie Kay, 'So You Think I'm a Mule', *Feminist Review*, November 1984, Vol 17, Issue 1, p 80, © Jackie Kay, 1984, used by permission of The Wylie Agency (UK) Limited.

p 248 Oliver Sacks, 'My Own Life', *The New York Times*, 15th February, 2015.

p 249 Atul Gawande, *Being Mortal: Illness, Medicine and What Matters in the End*, Profile Books Ltd, 2014, p 127.

p 250 Jeanette Winterson, *Why Be Happy When You Could Be Normal*, Vintage, 2012, p 230.